D1270127

DUBIOUS VICTORY

DUBIOUS VICTORY

The Reconstruction Debate in Ohio

ROBERT D. SAWREY

THE UNIVERSITY PRESS OF KENTUCKY

Scholarly publisher for the Commonwealth,
serving Bellarmine College, Berea College, Centre
College of Kentucky, Eastern Kentucky University,
The Filson Club, Georgetown College, Kentucky
Historical Society, Kentucky State University,
Morehead State University, Murray State University,
Northern Kentucky University, Transylvania University,
University of Kentucky, University of Louisville,
and Western Kentucky University.

Editorial and Sales Offices: Lexington, Kentucky 40508-4008

Library of Congress Cataloging-in-Publication Data

Sawrey, Robert D. (Robert Dixon).
Dubious victory : the Reconstruction debate in Ohio / Robert D.
Sawrey.
p. cm.
Includes bibliographical references (p.) and index.
ISBN 0-8131-1776-3
1. Reconstruction—Public opinion. 2. Reconstruction—Ohio.
3. Public opinion—Ohio—History—19th century. I. Title.
E668.S28 1992
973.8—dc20 91-40414

This book is printed on recycled acid-free paper meeting
the requirements of the American National Standard
for Permanence of Paper for Printed Library Materials. ♾

To my Mother, who taught her son that he could accomplish anything he was willing to try. Thanks for the boost to my self-esteem and for your confidence in me. I hope you appreciated what your faith in me has meant. I wish you could be here to read this book.

To Dad, who has never quite seen the merit of studying history but has usually kept it to himself. More importantly, I have never doubted your support or willingness to help me in any way you could. You have been a rock and a refuge.

To Ger, who helped me rediscover myself and whose boundless love is matched by her commitment to my work. I truly doubt that I would have accomplished much with my life without your love and help. I hope you know how much I appreciate them.

CONTENTS

TABLES & MAP

ACKNOWLEDGMENTS

While working on this project I have experienced and benefited from the knowledge, advice, and support of many fine individuals. Surely without the work of the numerous students of the Reconstruction era, particularly those who have published over the past three decades, I would never have been able to write this book. Dr. Gene Lewis of the University of Cincinnati has guided and taught me since my first days as a graduate student. He is more than a scholar, teacher, and mentor; he is a trusted friend who deserves credit for any growth I have made as a historian. Frances Hensley and David Duke of the History Department at Marshall University graciously read the entire manuscript and provided valuable comments, insight, and encouragement. I also benefited from the cooperation and knowledge of the staffs of many research libraries. In particular, I would like to thank the good and friendly people at the Manuscripts Division of the Library of Congress, Oberlin College Archives, the Ohio Historical Society, the Western Reserve Historical Society, and the Cincinnati Historical Society. Their knowledge opened several doors and saved me many errors and hours of potentially fruitless searching. Finally, I thank my family for its support, love, and even the distractions which were helpful in refreshing my brain despite the times I may have grumpily begged for quiet.

Although all these folks have major roles in enhancing the value and quality of this book, I alone am responsible for its faults and errors.

I also thank the publishers of *The Old Northwest* and *Civil War History* for permission to include material that previously appeared in those journals.

INTRODUCTION

Of all eras in American history, perhaps none has been more universally criticized as a failure than the years after the Civil War when the nation struggled with the tangled web of issues that arose from the war. The overall disgust, dismay, and disappointment with Reconstruction is apparent in the titles of scholarly and popular studies of the period—*The Tragic Era, The Age of Hate, A Compromise of Principle, White Terror, Black Scare,* to mention only a few. Eric Foner contends in *Reconstruction: America's Unfinished Revolution* that the nation failed to complete a revolution that the war had begun.[1] What these and countless other books suggest is that policies adopted during the Reconstruction era failed to produce the results the authors believe were critical to the national welfare, that Reconstruction programs and policies failed to solve the problems they addressed. Whether one focuses on the terms of reunion, the treatment of the freedmen, the fate of the Confederates, national finances, the near removal of a president, or some other significant issue, the dominant impression is that national leaders proved incapable of fashioning appropriate and lasting solutions.

It is possible, however, to look at Reconstruction from another perspective, that of contemporary northern political opinion. To assess the various Reconstruction policies and programs, which, after all, were actually peace terms, it is necessary to understand what the victors sought from them and how the victors viewed the results. This book focuses on one northern state to see what politically active Ohioans wanted Reconstruction to accomplish. I do not choose this approach to counter the judgment of generations of historians—and I include myself in that group—who have wished that Reconstruction might have yielded more progressive, juster solutions to postwar problems. To understand, however, why the nation refused to do what many twentieth-century Americans later wished it had done, why it failed to live up to promises it seemed to have made during Recon-

STATE OF OHIO

struction, we need to have a clearer picture of what nineteenth-century Americans wanted and expected from their elected officials.

By early 1865 most Ohioans could see that the Union forces would soon crush the rebellion and that the nation would then need to direct its attention to restoring the Union and solving the myriad problems related to the emancipation of the slaves. By fall 1865 Ohio Republicans, who formed a slight majority of politically active Ohioans, had a reasonably clear idea of what they expected from a Reconstruction policy. Accepting the idea that the southern planters had led the South into secession and rebellion, they believed that the planters' political and economic power must be curbed in order to protect the nation from further rebellion. Political rights should be granted to former slaveholders only if they provided proof of their loyalty to the United States. A fair number of Ohio Republicans believed that freedmen were entitled to certain rights, up to and including suffrage, on moral and humanitarian grounds. The majority, however, looked on the freedmen as a counterweight to the planters. They believed that the nation should extend to the former slaves enough civil and economic rights to guarantee their new status, primarily because these rights would keep the planters from regaining economic dominance over the South. Nearly all white Ohioans fully intended to maintain white supremacy.

With amazing consistency Ohio Republicans held to these positions, and by the end of 1868 they believed that the fundamental tasks of Reconstruction had been accomplished. The results did not please everyone, nor quite likely did they approach anyone's ideal solutions, but most Ohio Republicans thought Reconstruction had come quite close to securing what they most wanted, a peaceful union with white supremacy still intact. Reconstruction for many Ohioans who lived through the era was thus not a failure but a qualified success.

By early 1869 Ohio Republicans concluded that the nation no longer needed to concentrate primarily on Reconstruction issues. In part, that decision reflected their sense that with Grant safely in the White House, Republicans still holding majorities in Congress, and most southern states restored to the Union under Republican leadership, the nation need not worry about another southern rebellion. They also recognized that Reconstruction questions had lost their power to determine election results in Ohio. Ohio voters were ready to move on to other matters, and the Republicans believed that they must focus on the new issues if they hoped to continue winning elections in Ohio. In short, Reconstruction ceased to dominate the political landscape in Ohio after the 1868 elections.

The situation was somewhat different for the Democrats in Ohio.

Although they resorted to some of the most vicious race baiting in all American history, the Democrats were unable to dislodge the Republicans from office as long as Reconstruction issues dominated elections. Throughout the era discussed in this book the Democrats remained a minority, desperately seeking issues with which to return to power. By 1870, as Ohioans increasingly turned their attention away from Reconstruction, the Democrats were ready to challenge the Republicans. The future, viewed from the perspective of 1870, probably appeared at least as promising as at any time in the previous decade.

In this book Ohio Republicans receive most of my attention, chiefly because they enjoyed a numerical majority in the state. In addition, because of their control of Congress, Republicans had far greater opportunity to influence national policy and had the responsibility of developing programs. Thus the views and actions of Republicans seem to be more crucial than those of the Democrats. As the party of opposition, the Democrats must carry less weight.

Focusing on one state has obvious drawbacks. Utilizing information about any single state, including Ohio, to draw sweeping conclusions about what northerners in general sought in a Reconstruction policy is hazardous at best. Neither Ohio nor any other northern state can be considered "typical" of the region as a whole. Nevertheless, as Stephen Maizlish has convincingly argued, during the 1840s and 1850s, its location, population composition, economic importance, and political clout made Ohio a key northern state.[2] In fact, in the middle decades of the nineteenth century Ohio was arguably one of the most important states in the Union. In 1860 it was by far the most industrialized of the midwestern states, ranking fourth nationally (behind New York, Pennsylvania, and Massachusetts) in capital invested in manufacturing, value of manufactured products, and number of people employed in manufacturing.[3] Ohio was also an agricultural leader.[4] Combining manufacturing production with agricultural output, Ohio trailed only New York and Pennsylvania in overall contribution to the economic well-being of the nation.

Ohio also merits study because of its population, the third largest in 1860 and extremely diverse in composition. A high percentage of Ohioans who lived in the northern half of the state, particularly those who resided near Lake Erie, had migrated from or were descended from those who had migrated from New York and New England. These people overwhelmingly supported the Republican party and endorsed more advanced positions on issues related to slavery and the treatment of the freedmen. In contrast, a significant number of Ohioans living close to the Ohio River had southern roots and tended to approach national issues from a distinctly southern perspective. A large number of foreign immigrants, particularly from Ireland and Germany, further enhanced the mix of people in Ohio, forming a reasonably close approximation of the population composition of the United States as a whole. In many ways one can perhaps conclude that views expressed in Ohio were representative of attitudes held throughout the country.

One yardstick of Ohio's perceived importance in the Civil War and Reconstruction eras, albeit simplistic, is the number of candidates for president and vice-president who were Ohioans. In 1864 the Democrats nominated George Pendleton of Cincinnati for vice-president. Four years later he nearly secured the Democratic presidential nomination. His opponent would have been Ulysses S. Grant, who was born in Ohio but certainly had other, far more compelling political attributes by 1868. In 1876 and 1880 the Republican nominees, Rutherford B. Hayes and James A. Garfield, both Ohioans who had also served in Congress, captured the presidency. This list suggests that nineteenth-century Americans considered Ohio a key political state, one that neither major party could afford to lose if it hoped to elect its presidential candidate.

Ohio also merits study because its two political parties were so evenly matched. In 1855 and 1857 Republican Salmon Chase was elected governor of the state in three-way contests, but in each case he received less than 49 percent of the vote. In 1859 in a two-way election for governor, Republican William Dennison secured 51.9 percent. The following year 52.3 percent voted for Lincoln. Thus as the Civil War approached the two parties had nearly equivalent strength. Republicans had won the allegiance of a small majority of the state's voters, largely by relying on national issues. During the war, the Union party coalition of Republicans and some Democrats did somewhat better, securing between 56 and 60 percent of the vote in statewide elections in 1861, 1863, and 1864. The volatility of Ohio politics was underscored in 1862, when the Democrats, relying heavily on racial fears aroused by the preliminary Emancipation Proclamation and the dismal performance of the Union armies, won all the statewide contests and fourteen of nineteen congressional seats. By the end of the war, though, a majority of politically involved Ohioans again supported the Union coalition.

The success of the Union troops soon placed the future of that coalition in doubt, so that by April 1865 neither party could guess what the future held. The Democrats hoped that enough former Democrats would return to the party to give them the margin of victory. The Republicans had to face that potential loss and the realization that the basic issue that had held the Union party together—opposition to the extension of slavery—had been settled. The party that could convince the voters that it could best heal the nation's wounds and secure a peaceful, united future would almost certainly win majority support.

The Republicans had one tremendous advantage: they were the party of Union and victory. As long as Reconstruction dominated the political debate, they did very well. In fact, their support increased in the fall of 1865 and again in the fall of 1866. After that, however, the intrusion of other issues, particularly economic and racial issues, which the Democrats manipulated brilliantly and venomously, resulted in dwindling Republican margins. Thus, between 1865 and 1870 the Republicans tried to keep the voters focused on Reconstruction while the Democrats tried to persuade them to determine their votes on other issues. The Republicans enjoyed initial success; by 1870 the Democrats were closing the gap.

Racial questions were definitely the most emotional and politically explosive issues of the Reconstruction period. In Ohio they played crucial roles in debates and political contests between 1865 and 1870. Although virtually every white Ohioan believed in white superiority, Democratic and Republican attitudes and behavior differed tremendously. The Democrats employed mean-spirited and vicious rhetoric to appeal to voters' basest prejudices and fears. Buzz words and phrases such as "nigger-lovers," "Sambo," "thick-lipped wenches," and "dusky devils" peppered editorial after editorial and speech upon speech for years. Most Ohio Republicans, by contrast, supported some basic rights for blacks—for example, control and enjoyment of the fruits of their labor, the right to be secure in their property, and such basic legal rights as the rights to sue, be sued, and testify in court. Republicans divided sharply on the question of black suffrage, however. In 1865 few endorsed it; by 1869 it seemed to be a necessary step. When Republicans worked for black rights, they usually did so for reasons other than a humanitarian concern for blacks. Frequently, these reasons had more to do with their perception of national interest or local political interest. Whatever their motivation, the fact remains that Ohio Republicans sometimes insisted on black rights that Democrats refused even to consider.

A study of political opinions in Ohio, therefore, can yield valuable insight into the minds of a large group of northerners. On some issues the dominant attitudes may have reflected the views of the northern majority; on others they probably did not. Nevertheless, by learning more about them we can learn more about why Reconstruction evolved as it did, leaving so many problems with which future generations of Americans would be forced to deal.

1

LOOKING FOR SOLUTIONS

> I repeat again, the people of the United States have the right to say when those rebels may again exercise the rights and powers of States in the Union, and, in my judgment, should see that they are not so restored except upon conditions of *security for the future*, if not also of *indemnity for the past.*
>
> —John A. Bingham, 1865

Nearly bursting with pride, thanksgiving, relief, and more than a trace of self-righteousness, an Ohioan from Sandusky wrote in mid-May 1865, "The great war is now virtually closed & if we read it aright, it has taught us an important lesson. I think too it is felt to be so by the whole nation, i.e. that God rules. In my view the Jews of old were no more God's peculiar people in their day, than we are now." [1] As sure as he was that God's hand had preserved the Union and that God would continue to watch over the country as it attempted to reunite itself, the author of this letter gave no evidence of favoring any specific Reconstruction plan. Nevertheless, if he resembled the typical politically aware Ohioan, he probably had some ideas about the best means to restore national unity. In fact, throughout the late spring and early summer of 1865 Ohioans vigorously debated Reconstruction issues.

Ohioans began their first widespread discussion of Reconstruction immediately after they learned that Robert E. Lee had surrendered. At the many public celebrations, such as the one held in Cincinnati on April 14, most speakers urged reconciliation with the defeated South. For example, Henry Stanbery, later Andrew Johnson's attorney general, asserted that the South had suffered far more than the North and needed a helping hand to regain its prosperity, so it could contribute to the future of America. He hoped northerners would "forget, if you can, but at least forgive" southerners.[2]

Other Ohio orators and editors took a harsher line. They wanted the leaders of the rebellion punished, and they advocated permanent disfranchisement, for they believed these men were fully capable of leading the South into renewed rebellion if their political and economic power were not curbed. W.H.P. Denny, editor of the *Circleville Union*, declared that "this revolt is the greatest crime recorded in history, and was wholly unprovoked and unjustifiable." He laid the blame squarely on the leaders of the Confederacy and hoped that "the least punishment to be inflicted on them would be disfranchisement and perpetual banishment."[3] One of Congressman James A. Garfield's correspondents seconded this view, urging that Congress punish with political disabilities "that deep rooted aristocracy [slavery] has nurtured and which is almost untouched. Let it go under now."[4]

W.D. Bickham, editor of the *Dayton Daily Journal*, raised another crucial issue. Though he advocated the execution of several Confederate leaders, Bickham indicated his support of a federal policy that "would be magnanimous to repentant rebels" because he believed they had been "duped and forced into the crime of rebellion by their masters."[5] Ohio Republicans generally emphasized this distinction between loyal masses and traitorous southern planters, upon whom they placed almost the entire blame for secession. According to this widely held view, the landed aristocracy had used its economic and political power, based on slavery, to mislead the otherwise loyal southern masses into supporting secession. Conservative Republican Rush R. Sloane reflected the dominant wish when he urged Senator John Sherman to "excuse the sincerest people when they renew their allegiance to the old flag—*but never their leaders.*"[6]

This belief had immense significance for Reconstruction because Ohioans of both parties insisted that a large reservoir of loyal whites existed in the South. In their view, to restore loyalty and peace in the rebellious states, the nation need only secure pledges of future good conduct from a fairly small number of southerners of the planter class. Republicans and many War Democrats were adamant that no reunion must occur until the leading traitors had accepted their defeat and promised future loyalty, but this process might be speedily accomplished. In the meantime the loyal whites—those who had opposed, given grudging support to, or been forced to fight for the Confederacy—could control the South. Lincoln and Johnson also accepted this view as a basis for their Reconstruction policies.[7] Unfortunately, future events proved these assumptions to be quite wrong. For the moment, though, the citizens of Ohio celebrated the end of the war and looked forward to a reunited nation.

John Wilkes Booth's assassination of Lincoln abruptly ended the postwar euphoria in Ohio. Northern anger toward the Confederates increased significantly, and views on Reconstruction hardened, raising the distinct possibility that the southerners would live to regret the day Booth tried to be a hero.[8]

Some Ohioans, like so many northerners, blamed the South for Lincoln's assassination and advocated taking a full measure of revenge on the Confederates. An Ohio volunteer claimed to express the views of the army when, from his unit stationed in Alabama, he wrote his wife that he felt "like staying in the army for three more years and fighting for reveng[e], yes, fighting until every Cursed Rebble [*sic*] is exterminated."[9] Journalist W.D. Bickham reacted similarly; he angrily announced that "the finger of a madman sped the fatal bullet, but it was slavery that did the deed."[10] Other Republican editors accused southern leaders, particularly Jefferson Davis, of complicity in the murder. One, believing he had discovered a connection between the leaders of the Confederacy and northern Democrats, informed his readers that "we have no doubt that the plot to assassinate President Lincoln and his Cabinet, originated in the late rebel capital, and its execution given over to their faithful friends of the Knights of the Golden Circle and Sons of Liberty."[11] One Ohioan concluded that "the whole feeling of the people appears to be changed" because of the assassination, and they now "swear for vengeance."

Nevertheless, despite the early anger, little evidence has been found to suggest the tragedy had any significant long-term effect on the basic Reconstruction requirements proposed by any Ohioans. Apparently, most Ohioans, like most northerners, as Eric McKitrick has shown, understood the irrationality of blaming the entire South for Booth's deed.[12] Although this anger was transitory, however, the death of the president did have a profound effect on Reconstruction, for it gave the country a new chief executive. Andrew Johnson, former Democratic senator from Tennessee, whose diligent efforts on behalf of the Union cause in Washington and as military governor of Tennessee had earned him the Union party nomination for vice-president in 1864, now succeeded to the presidency.

Ohio Republicans nearly unanimously rallied behind the new president. They tended to emphasize his wartime Unionist activities and to discount his prewar record as a states' rights Democrat. Many people in Ohio appear to have placed considerable reliance on Johnson's statements in March and April 1865, in which he promised to make treason "odious." Nobody knew exactly what policy Johnson meant to pursue, but almost all northern Republicans, some northern Democrats, and even a sizable number of southerners were convinced that the new president would endorse actions of which they approved.[13]

The most prestigious and influential Republican newspapers in

Ohio echoed each other in their praise for and support of the president. The *Cleveland Leader*, the powerful radical voice of the Western Reserve, stated that Johnson "is supported by the entire people with a unanimity and cordiality as surprising as it is novel and unprecedented." Its editor, Edwin Cowles, confidently concluded "that the executive office is safe in his hands, and that his course will at once bring assurance of it to the country." William T. Coggeshall of the *Ohio State Journal*, the official state Republican organ, based in Columbus, and Richard Smith, editor of the most influential Radical Republican paper in southern Ohio, the *Cincinnati Daily Gazette*, agreed.[14] Influenced by the rumor that Johnson was an alcoholic, Murat Halstead of the conservative Republican *Cincinnati Daily Commercial* gave the least enthusiastic endorsement of any of the major Republican papers in the state. "We have high hopes and some confidence," he wrote, "that the President will prove himself, in the end, worthy of the warm approbation of the people."[15]

Republican weeklies from throughout the state also supported Johnson, praising what one editor called his "unswerving integrity and sterling patriotism." Most editors, expecting that his wartime record would prove to be the best guide to Johnson's future actions, believed the president would basically follow Lincoln's Reconstruction plans. Several writers approvingly suggested that Johnson would deal fairly, yet more sternly than Lincoln had with the South. A Western Reserve correspondent declared that "unless we greatly mistake the character of the man, the rebels will rue the day they assassinated Abraham Lincoln."[16]

In addition to the blessings of Republican editors, Johnson could rely on the assistance of many leading Republican politicians and citizens of Ohio. Tobias Plants, congressman from Pomeroy, pledged his "most cordial support." Congressman James Ashley of Toledo, who would later try three times to impeach Johnson, wrote to the president, "The prayer of every heart in the nation is, that God will bless, preserve and keep you from all harm. . . . May God strengthen you and aid you in the discharge of your every duty." Realizing that Congress was not scheduled to meet until the following December, Ashley gave even stronger evidence of his faith in Johnson's wisdom and ability to deal with Reconstruction issues by expressing his hope that "*no* extra session of Congress will be called."[17] Like many of the most radical Republicans, Ashley believed that the new president would deal more harshly with the South than had Lincoln. Even Radical Republican Senator Benjamin F. Wade indicated that "if Johnson will surround himself with able, bold, earnest and resolute spirits like himself, as I think he intends to do, he will give us the best, most popular and magnificent Administration that this nation has had." Many others concurred.[18]

Considered as a group, Ohio Republicans provided Johnson with an amazing amount of support during his first months in office. Given the subsequent hostility between the president and that party, this early backing seems almost inexplicable, but at the time it made perfect sense. The Republicans, after all, had elected him to national office, and he now represented them and their party as president. Of vastly more importance, Johnson had shown almost no evidence of any major disagreement with the majority of Republicans over Reconstruction issues. In early 1865 neither they nor he knew precisely what the other desired in terms of a Reconstruction policy, but both considered peaceful reunion with guarantees that would ensure future security to be the primary objective. When differences did emerge clearly in the winter and spring of 1866, Republicans insisted that Johnson, and not they, had shifted ground. At least, as *they* perceived the president's policy, they were correct.

Not unsurprisingly, Democrats in Ohio did not heap such praise on Johnson as did the Republicans. Undoubtedly Johnson's wartime desertion of the Democratic party played a role in their attitudes, but at the same time, some Democrats certainly were pleased that the archfoe Lincoln had been succeeded by a lifelong Democrat. The editor of the *Marietta Times* expressed the views of the most optimistic Democrats when he confidently announced that Johnson would return to his prewar principles and base his administration on states' rights doctrines. Washington McLean of the *Cincinnati Daily Enquirer*, probably the most influential Democratic paper in the state, reacted to Johnson's elevation with a definite lack of enthusiasm and only grudgingly accepted Johnson as president; the paper virtually ignored him during his first month in office. The editor of *The Crisis* (Columbus), like many Democrats, adopted a wait-and-see attitude toward Johnson.[19] The ambivalence of the Democrats—some heartily endorsing him, others giving lukewarm approval, and still others in open hostility—would continue throughout 1865 and into 1866, when Johnson's vetoes of crucial Reconstruction legislation would draw their support.

Thus, as Johnson assumed the presidency he had the support of most Republicans in Ohio, who believed they would approve of his as-yet-unannounced Reconstruction policy. The Democrats could not agree on whether to endorse him or not. Some expected to back the new administration, while others chose to withhold judgment until they had a chance to assess Johnson's policies. On the whole

Andrew Johnson in the spring of 1865 enjoyed strong political support in Ohio.

Once they decided that Johnson would serve the nation well as president, politically involved Ohioans gave more attention to possible plans to reunite the divided country. In their quest for a policy that would lead to successful and secure reunion, most Ohioans assumed that the North could and should dictate the terms. Many believed, quite logically, that one way for Confederates to prove that they had learned never again to challenge federal authority was to accept, through democratic processes, the requirements for readmission that the nation established for them. Thus, southern acceptance would be evidence of repentance and willingness to resume being "good Americans." In addition, most Ohioans thought that common sense and constitutional restrictions on the power of the federal government prohibited any attempt to force the rebels to abide by federal directives. They would always have the option of rejecting federal requirements, but most Ohioans seem to have believed that the rebels, perhaps some with their teeth gritted, would see the wisdom of accepting the terms offered them. Few could foresee that southerners might say no, might prefer to remain unrepresented in Congress rather than acknowledge the right of the North to dictate to them.[20]

Certainly, though, Ohioans who accepted such views were creating a dilemma for themselves. On the one hand, they longed for peace, quiet, and a return to normalcy. On the other hand, they demanded guarantees of future loyalty and good behavior before rebels were readmitted into the Union. Future events proved that these goals were mutually exclusive and forced Ohioans to decide which was the more critical. Virtually every Republican opted for a secure future. Ironically, by insisting that southerners recognize and renounce the evil of their war against the nation, they and northern Republicans in general allowed southerners to dictate the speed and timing of national reunion.[21]

Despite their differences, Ohioans of all political positions recognized the need to develop some definite Reconstruction policy. Reunion, the most basic Union war aim, was taken for granted, but other questions generated considerable controversy. Some Ohio Republicans advocated such strong and potentially revolutionary measures as confiscation of rebel property and exile for southern leaders. Many Democrats responded that the devastation of the war was sufficient punishment to alert southerners to the folly and wickedness of secession and urged immediate restoration of the Union.

Typical Ohio Republicans desired a policy between these extremes. They longed for a speedy unification but adamantly insisted that slavery must never again exist on American soil and that the future must be secure from any recurrence of southern secession. The editor of the *Eaton Weekly Register* expressed the common desire for peace: "Let there be no hurry. Let our statesmen reconstruct as cooly, as firmly, and as deliberately as our boys whaled them. . . . We *must have security for the future.*"[22] In practical terms these requirements meant that the leaders of the rebellion must not be allowed to regain control of the South or to participate in political decisions until they had renounced secession, abolished slavery, and pledged future loyalty. Until the ratification of the Thirteenth Amendment in December 1865, Ohio Republicans expected southerners to agree to emancipation by amending their state constitutions to prohibit slavery. The primary motive behind the demand for the abolition of slavery was fear that southern planters would again threaten the nation unless their power base, the slave economy, was destroyed. Richard Smith of the *Cincinnati Daily Gazette* stated the point with crystal clarity:

> We may blind our eyes, if we will, . . . but we have to deal with men who though subjugated in power are still malignant rebels in heart, who are the ruling class in the South, and if allowed by us will continue to control its political action as absolutely as they have in the past; and with whom the question of reconstruction is how they may turn their military subjugation into political domination; how they may make the Union subject to them, and reestablish their rule so that they may hold it as before by the menace of the destruction of the nation.[23]

Although Ohio Republicans also insisted that the defeated section renounce the doctrine of secession, they differed somewhat on the repudiation of the Confederate debt. Most thought that nobody should benefit materially from having given financial support to the rebellion.[24]

Much sentiment also existed in favor of the disfranchisement of southern leaders, but two major problems confused this matter. Tremendous differences of opinion existed over what group or class of rebels should lose the vote and how long the disability should last. Most persons favoring disfranchisement argued that only the leaders of the rebellion—by which they usually meant all military, civil, and diplomatic officers of the Confederate and state governments—must forfeit this right. Murat Halstead of the *Cincinnati Daily Commercial* favored such limits and figured that such a policy would deprive about a thousand men of their right to vote.[25] Other Ohio Republicans were more vague; they wanted all "known traitors" or all the "disloyal" disfranchised, or they believed that all planters, a category rarely well defined, should lose the right to vote because they had been the primary leaders of the secession movement.[26]

The Republicans who favored disfranchisement disagreed over how long it should last. The most radical Republicans advocated a permanent penalty, but most proposed a fixed period of time.[27] In order to keep from quarreling among themselves, proponents of disfranchisement often sidestepped the issue by insisting that to regain the vote penalized southerners must repent their "crimes."[28] Such vagueness had much appeal because it forced southerners to determine by their own actions how long their disfranchisement would last, but more important, it revealed the persistent fear of another rebellion. Nearly all Ohio Republicans were convinced that southerners could not be trusted until they renounced secession and rebellion and proved that they deserved a share in the political process. They applauded loudly when Johnson's Amnesty Proclamation effectively put Confederate leaders on political probation.

Many Ohioans, nearly all of them Democrats, opposed any political restrictions on southerners. Declaring that the South required no reconstructing, they urged justice and mercy in northern treatment of their fellow countrymen. The Democrats had a great deal to gain politically from rapid restoration of the South into the Union. In fact, as northern Republicans well understood, the Democrats' best hope of regaining control of national politics required the readmission of the South.[29]

Some form of disfranchisement, therefore, not only served the Republican version of the national interest but also aided the party's political interests. Republicans were not unaware that disfranchisement of southern leaders might deprive the South of experienced men to rebuild the state governments and to accept whatever Reconstruction policy the country would require. They relied, however, on the accepted myth that thousands of loyal white southerners had been forced to support secession and the rebellion against their wishes and that these men would step in to do the job. Surely, they bravely insisted, there were enough trustworthy white men to run the new state governments of the South.

The discussion of what group should have political power in the South forced consideration of the role of the freedmen in Reconstruction. With the exception of some Democrats, who simply refused to acknowledge their humanity, most agreed that the freedmen had been loyal to the Union. Firmly believing that the slaveholders' economic power had made secession possible, Ohioans demanded the end of slavery and basic civil and economic rights for blacks in order to prevent their reenslavement. Most Ohioans, however, wanted to grant the freedmen only enough rights to keep them from falling under the control of the planters, who could then reassert their economic and political hegemony over the South with potentially disastrous results for national unity.[30] Almost no Ohioans had any intention of granting the freedmen social or political rights that would endanger white supremacy in Ohio.

These attitudes, unfortunately, did not fully answer the troublesome question of the role the freedmen should have in reconstructing the South. Specifically, Ohioans and other northerners had to struggle with the difficult and politically explosive issue of the enfranchisement of the freedmen as a means of peacefully reuniting the country.

Some Ohio Republicans had concluded that successful Reconstruction required black suffrage. Richard Smith presented the case for permitting loyal blacks to join loyal whites in governing the South. These two groups would form a "legal majority in every secession State; then the problem of reconstructing civil governments would be solved, and military supervision and all arbitrary measures might be withdrawn. In this view, [black suffrage] appears a short road to the restoration of domestic tranquillity and law, with the security of the national authority." Unless the freedmen voted, Smith feared, the disloyal planter class would regain control of that region and again attempt to destroy the country. Another Republican wrote succinctly of the Confederate leaders, "We do not need their counsel or their aid. There are plenty of loyal whites and loyal blacks there to do the voting, hold the offices and carry on the government, both State and National."[31]

In mid-June, Senator John Sherman ably presented a similar view in a speech at Circleville in which he insisted that control over suffrage was a state prerogative; the only prerogative of Congress was to ensure that each state had a republican form of government. On precisely that basis, he suggested that Congress could and probably should demand black suffrage in the South. Astutely rejecting the idea that the mass of white southerners had in fact been loyal to the Union, Sherman declared, "It is a sad fact, but a very true one, that the number of such people in the Southern States would form a very narrow foundation for a Republican Government." Because they had fought for the Union and because of the lack of other loyal voters, blacks, although "ignorant, docile, easily led, and not safely trusted with political power," should vote in the South. Furthermore, this solution would be a far less expensive means to reconstruct the Confederacy than military occupation. On another occasion Sherman stated the point more bluntly, "If we can put negro regiments there and give them bayonets, why can't we give them votes? Both are weapons of offense and defense. Votes are cheaper and better."[32]

The need to confront such options as restoring the political rights of rebels, spending millions on an army of occupation, or enfranchising the freedmen must have distressed the senator almost beyond belief. Next to remaining in office, his greatest political concern was the financial well-being of the nation. Yet, he could not accept the idea of immediately returning control of the South to the leading secessionists. Sherman must have gulped hard before swallowing the medicine of black suffrage in the South. Undoubtedly, he did so only because he believed that black suffrage represented the cheapest route to a secure future. "We must," he declared at Circleville, "have security for the future."

Soon enough, his doubts about the wisdom of enfranchising the freedmen came to the fore, and he retreated from his advanced stand. Later in 1865, for most of the first half of 1866, and in retirement from public life, Sherman praised as "wise and judicious" Johnson's Reconstruction program, which left the matter of suffrage to the states being reconstructed. In Sherman's view, Johnson had extended to the freedmen "in every case full and ample protection," while wisely refusing to press for black suffrage. Given national racial attitudes, Sherman thought, "such a provision, if it had been inserted, could not have been enforced, and, in the condition in which slavery left the negro race, it could hardly be defended."[33] It is apparent that only the national crisis compelled him to endorse limited black suffrage, and then only for a short period.

While Sherman worried about the financial cost of Reconstruction, other Ohioans and northerners feared the damage Reconstruction policies might do to their laissez-faire political ideology. Many Republicans, as well as nearly all Democrats, adhered to a philosophy that severely restricted the role of the federal government in protecting or enhancing the welfare of individual citizens. They were dismayed that a massive federal presence might be needed to secure the freedmen's safety, for it was impossible for them to accept such intervention without rejecting major portions of their political ideology.[34] Some Republicans, therefore, endorsed the enfranchisement of the freedmen as a means to make them responsible for their own protection. Certainly this rationale for black suffrage lacked deep commitment to the welfare of the freedmen and could readily be jettisoned whenever it become politically desirable to do so. At the same time it reflected a nearly blind faith in the ballot as a panacea that supposedly would guarantee black freedom. In particular, it obviated the need to consider a program of economic assistance and landownership for the freedmen.

Many northerners, including some Ohioans, seem to have been convinced that arming southern blacks with the ballot would guarantee their personal safety and lead to their economic elevation to a level approximately equal to that of the poorest white farmers. Indeed, some based their advocacy of enfranchisement on the improvement of the freedmen's economic situation.[35] But this argument proved unpersuasive because the majority in the Buckeye State had little interest in raising the economic or social status of blacks. Most Ohio Republicans ultimately insisted on basic civil rights for freedmen but had little patience with plans to grant social, economic, or political equality.[36] Some thought that black votes would also protect the lives and interests of white southern Unionists. Salmon Chase was among those who believed that to "insure ample and complete protection to all loyal citizens of the United States within the restored states," the freedmen must receive the ballot.[37]

A rather perverse analysis of potential national problems led one Ohioan to advocate the franchise for the freedmen. According to S.A. Bronson of Sandusky, the future conflicts in the country would involve not sectionalism or race but "Protestants and Romanists." He had no trouble whatsoever insisting that God favored the former. He believed that the success of the Union armies provided the solution to stopping the supposedly growing and dreaded influence of Catholicism in America. Bronson proposed that black voters could function as "a Protestant barrier to the Romanizing tendencies of foreign immigrants." He concluded that white Americans "are doubtless to owe our salvation as a free people to the aid of negro votes. So wonderful are the ways of God."[38]

A small minority of Ohioans held the moral high ground, contending that suffrage was a natural right or that the former slaves should be given the vote as a reward for their service in the defeat of the rebellion.[39] Almost without exception these appeals to humanity, brotherhood, and justice as reasons to enfranchise the freedmen came from the Western Reserve, the northeastern corner of the state, where migrants from New England or their descendants fought a losing battle in their attempts to convince the rest of Ohio of the decency and correctness of their advanced positions on racial issues.[40]

Among the minority of Ohioans who favored black suffrage, a

split developed over what qualifications should be required. Many tended to favor universal manhood suffrage in the South, but few advocated the same privilege in Ohio. Some Republicans preferred either an educational qualification for the former slaves or some form of impartial adult male suffrage, with a property or education restriction for both whites and blacks. The educational requirement had an additional attraction because, by forcing them to become literate and thus potentially better informed on issues, it might encourage blacks to become better citizens if they wanted to vote.[41]

The distinction between universal and impartial suffrage had important ramifications. Universal suffrage would grant voting privileges to all males of a certain age, except those who had forfeited their rights by crimes or rebellion. Impartial suffrage was much more restrictive, requiring only that all races (in reality only white and black, for Ohioans refused to recognize any rights for Indians or Orientals) be treated alike. Thus, impartial suffrage might include property or educational restrictions. It attracted the support of many Ohioans who did not really want to enfranchise the freedmen but, for whatever reasons, felt compelled to pretend they did. They could advocate impartial suffrage, while trusting that high property or educational requirements would effectively keep blacks from the polls. Impartial suffrage could also serve to bar from the polls many uneducated or propertyless immigrants, whom many Ohioans considered a blight on American democracy.

The majority of concerned Ohioans, however, largely because of their belief in the inferiority of blacks, refused to endorse either impartial or universal manhood suffrage in the South or in Ohio. Advocates of black enfranchisement recognized the prevailing prejudice and attempted to overcome it by stressing the need to control the supposedly traitorous planter class. One such proponent of black suffrage pleaded:

> Let those who still harbor a prejudice that leads them to despise the Negro, remember that in the reconstruction of the Union, there is far more at stake than the mere question of negro suffrage. The question to be now decided is, shall the defeated oligarchs who despise labor, be permitted to mold our institutions to suit *their* ideas of civil liberty? Shall additional power be placed in *their* hands, to be used in degrading the workingmen of the North who have just asserted the dignity of their calling by their ability to conquer? We answer no! If they are not yet whipped into complete submission, let us finish the work that was too soon abandoned. We need not

> do this, if we will give the loyal negro the ballot, and withhold it from their traitorous master.[42]

Many Republicans appear to have been willing to trust the judgment of returning veterans on the matter of the blacks' ability to vote intelligently. Surely most of these Ohioans already knew that contact with the freedmen had "increased instead of diminishing [the army's] pride and prejudice of race."[43] Well aware that the veterans, the vast majority of whom (81 percent) had voted for the Union party during the war,[44] might hold the balance in future elections, a large number of Ohio Republican politicians not only opposed suffrage extension but even attempted to stifle any discussion of the issue. They hoped to remove this explosive issue from the political arena in Ohio by maintaining that the Constitution reserved to the states the power to control voting requirements. Neither Congress nor any state, they argued, had any right to tell or order any other state to enfranchise anybody.[45]

Many Republicans rejected the argument that the freedmen needed the ballot to protect themselves from their former masters. They believed black economic power, not the vote, would force white southerners to treat the freedmen fairly. After all, these Republicans confidently declared, without the blacks' labor, the landowners would starve. The freedmen had only to use wisely the power their labor gained them and they would do just fine. One such Ohioan revealed an astonishing lack of concern for the freedmen, considering that his party was supposedly dedicated to helping the freedmen, even if that committment remained quite vague. He cavalierly suggested that the freed slaves "may no doubt suffer some wrongs and abuses at first, but these will be corrected by time and an open and healthy competition."[46]

Other Republicans wanted to wait and see. One suggested that "our colored people ought to be satisfied for a while with what they have already acquired. The change from slavery to freedom is enough for one day. If time proves that they are capable of participating in the government of the country; and the people can *see it*, why of course, the right of franchise will be extended to him, but at present we do not believe a majority of the people see it."[47] This writer hit on the matter exactly. For many Ohio Republicans the issue of enfranchising the freedmen was terribly difficult and, given the relatively equal strength of the two parties in Ohio, politically frightening. Their party had earned the credit for emancipation but now was unsure what to do with the freed slaves. Their belief in white superiority had emerged from the war either intact or enhanced, but Republicans still felt some, albeit vague, responsibility to the freedmen. Because most Ohioans opposed enfranchising them, those Republicans who agreed with the majority but did not or could not admit it could hide behind the democratic argument that they should and would abide by the wishes of the majority. Yet, the nagging doubts and confusion often remained, as the previously discussed case of John Sherman typifies.[48]

Ohio Democrats felt few such qualms about the freedmen's fate. They denounced most attempts to aid the former slaves, relying almost exclusively on blatant racism for self-justification, while inciting whites' worst fears about black competition and domination. Democrats argued that the vote would not enhance the freedmen's status but would only degrade the ballots of white men. Contradicting their own logic in warning whites of the danger of black competition, they asserted that "mental and physical peculiarities" would prevent blacks from successfully competing with whites. Any attempt to help them would result, therefore, in lowering the status of whites. Others argued that the "habit of obedience to superiors, born with the negro and concentrated in him by centuries of servitude" guaranteed that if granted the vote, he would become "the willing and obedient slave of the meanest demagogue."[49] Certainly no one could fail to discern the political affiliation of that "meanest demagogue." Similarly vicious racist appeals had served the Democrats rather well in elections in the years immediately preceding and during the war and they showed every indication that in postwar elections they would again rely heavily on white bigotry and fear.[50]

Like many Republicans, Democrats declared that only the states could determine voting qualifications. Unlike the Republicans, however, they claimed that white southerners knew best how to handle the freedmen. Most Democrats, in fact, wanted to allow the Confederates to do whatever they wished with the freedmen.[51] Some of the most reactionary even suggested reenslavement, or worse. For example, Washington McLean, a political leader of Hamilton County, argued that blacks had "accepted" slavery and then baldly announced, "Slavery is dead so they say, but the negro is not; there is the misfortune. For the sake of all parties, we say: Would that he were."[52] Such declarations were appallingly common, as McLean and other Democrats tried to fan racial prejudices in Ohio.

By late spring general attitudes on Reconstruction had coalesced. Very few in Ohio advocated a vindictive policy toward the South. Radical Republican hopes for land confiscation, execution of Confederate officials, and land for the freedmen aroused little support. The overriding concern was to reunite the country and ensure a secure, peaceful future. To accomplish this end the Republicans wanted to keep the leaders of the Confederacy from regaining political or economic control of the South. Thus they favored the disfranchisement of the planter aristocracy, which they held responsible for the Civil War. To crush that group's economic power, Ohio Republicans insisted upon the destruction of slavery and the protection of basic civil rights for the freed slaves, but not equality. Republicans generally believed that enough loyal whites lived in the South to establish new state governments and guide the states back into the Union. Disloyal southerners would have to pledge future loyalty before regaining their political rights.

In late April 1865 General William T. Sherman tested Ohio Republicans' commitment to their emerging terms of Reconstruction. On April 18 he and Confederate General Joseph E. Johnston signed a cease-fire agreement that ordered the Johnston's forces disbanded but allowed his soldiers to keep their weapons until they reached their home state capitals. Sherman also allowed Confederate state governments to remain in power, denied the North's right to disfranchise or otherwise punish the rebels, and asserted that slavery had not ended and that southerners might be permitted to keep their human property.[53]

To most Ohio Republicans these terms amounted to a completely unacceptable status quo ante that rendered worthless the immense sacrifices of the previous four years. They cried out in anguish and frustration at "General Sherman's Great Mistake," as one headline called it, and abuse poured in on the hero from Ohio. Edwin Cowles of the powerful *Cleveland Leader* spoke for many when he denounced the agreement as so lenient that it could lead to another rebellion and correctly declared that it "will rouse the people of the entire North with indignation and alarm."[54] Although many Democrats praised Sherman's terms, the general view seems to have been that the pact was far too mild and potentially dangerous.[55] The Sherman-Johnston agreement would have left the power of the planter class completely intact; this Ohio Republicans could not accept. They approved President Johnson's rejection of the memorandum and his order to Sherman to resume hostilities.[56]

Meanwhile Johnson worked to develop his own Reconstruction policy. During his second day in office he indicated its probable basis when he announced to a group of Unionist senators, including Benjamin Wade of Ohio, "I hold that robbery is a crime; rape is a crime; murder is a crime; *treason* is a crime, and *crime* must be punished. Treason must be made infamous, and traitors must be impoverished." Shortly thereafter Johnson told a delegation from Illinois that his past actions and principles would guide his future policy.[57] Given his pro-Union sentiments and his tenure as military governor of Tennessee during the war, most Ohioans expected that the president would pursue policies similar to Lincoln's.[58]

Johnson did not lack advice from Ohioans. From the Western Reserve came a plead to ensure "*indemnity* for the past and Security for the future." The writer also urged that race cease to be a determinant of voting eligibility. Such opinions on suffrage surely had little effect on the president, who firmly held that the Constitution reserved the right to set voting qualifications exclusively to the states.[59]

Johnson, however, did listen carefully to the suggestions of one of his most frequent Ohio correspondents, Lewis Campbell of Hamilton, with whom Johnson had long been acquainted. After four terms in Congress as a Whig, Campbell had joined the Union party during the war and served under Johnson while he was military governor of Tennessee. A conservative Unionist, Campbell would consistently support Johnson during the various Reconstruction crises.[60]

In May 1865 Campbell applauded the president for declaring that his past actions would guide his future policy. Campbell endorsed Johnson's contentions that the states must control voting qualifications and that the southern states, however far removed from their correct relationship with the federal government, had never left the union. Fearing attacks by Radical Republicans and Democrats that might endanger his widespread support, Campbell urged Johnson not to announce his plans prematurely.[61]

On May 29, Johnson inaugurated his anxiously awaited policy by issuing two proclamations. The first granted amnesty and the restoration of all property, except slaves, to certain southerners if they would take an oath of allegiance to the United States. Johnson specifically excluded fourteen groups of southerners—basically military, political, and diplomatic leaders of the Confederacy—from the amnesty offer, and he denied a pardon to any southerner who owned over twenty thousand dollars' worth of taxable property. This last exception clearly revealed Johnson's notion, with which most Ohio Republicans agreed, that the planter class had been primarily responsible for secession and had duped the southern masses into participation in the rebellion. All persons denied the right to take the oath could apply directly to the president for amnesty.[62] The president thus provided all southerners with a means to regain their political rights.

Johnson's other proclamation established the procedure by which North Carolina could be restored to the union. Under its provisions only persons who had taken the amnesty oath and who met the state's prewar franchise requirement could vote for or serve as delegates to a constitutional convention. This convention or the new state legislature would determine permanent voting qualifications. In short, Johnson had refused to encourage or demand black suffrage in North Carolina, and he officially expressed his conviction that the federal government could not set voting requirements.[63] The process he outlined gave southern states the opportunity to rejoin the union as rapidly as their citizens chose, provided that they elected only loyal or pardoned men to office.

Politically involved Ohioans responded enthusiastically to Johnson's proclamations. Many Democrats were disappointed, as were the most radical Republicans, who had hoped the president would require black suffrage, but most Ohioans generally endorsed both of his proclamations. They attached more immediate significance to the Amnesty Proclamation, however, especially approving of the twenty-thousand-dollar property exemption. Throughout the Buckeye State, Republicans described Johnson's proclamations as "a generous offer," "wise and just," "good," and "worthy of Lincoln." They praised the "wisdom and generosity of the President."[64] Even the most radical Republican sheets in the state approved of Johnson's pardoning process. They expected him to deal sternly, yet fairly with those who asked for special pardons. Most Republicans did not anticipate immediate widespread granting of presidential pardons.[65] They agreed with the assessment of a Springfield newspaperman: "The stringency of its requirements and the just exceptions which it makes will be regarded with satisfaction by all who have not a sneaking sympathy with the rebellion or the cause of the rebellion."[66]

About the only genuine criticism of the Amnesty Proclamation came from the Democrats. One writer denounced it because Johnson had excluded too many southerners but consoled himself by sarcastically concluding "that this policy is the wisest and best that could be expected from its source." Other Democrats approvingly noted that Johnson had not accepted Radical Republican doctrines but wished he had acted with greater leniency. The *Cincinnati Daily Enquirer*, for example, gave the president its conditional approval, viewing the proclamation as merely a step in the right direction and calling on him to restore the writ of habeas corpus to southerners and open the civil courts.[67]

The president had now made his views on Reconstruction public. First, Johnson had rejected the "state suicide" theory, which held that the southern state governments had committed suicide by attempting to leave the union. In order to return to the union, according to this theory, the Confederates would have to fulfill whatever requirements Congress established. Johnson insisted that secession had not occurred and that the southern states were merely out of their proper relationship with the federal government. Once the states had legitimate, republican governments that fulfilled the terms of the North Carolina and subsequent proclamations, southerners would deserve and receive full rights, including representation in Congress. Ohio Republicans endorsed these ideas.

Because nearly all Democrats also approved of it, Johnson's position on suffrage received even more widespread support. The president had signaled his intention to follow the Constitution and leave voting requirements to the states. A typical Republican editor praised the president, noting, "Of course, the blacks will not be allowed the right of suffrage. The inevitable negro is still upon us, and will be a source of trouble until we either colonize him or make him a citizen."[68] This writer implied that he favored the former alternative. Democrats, with virtually no regard for black rights, cheered Johnson's stance.[69]

Although most Ohioans in both parties endorsed Johnson's rejection of black suffrage in the South, some of those who favored enfranchising the freedmen voiced their dismay. Realizing the vast popularity the president enjoyed, however, they made their criticisms gingerly. Even the most radical Republicans meekly suggested only a reconsideration of his position.[70]

By hinting at a possible change in policy, these men referred to one other controversial aspect of the plan. Future events would show that Johnson had firmly established the terms of the North Carolina Proclamation as his policy for all the southern states, but at the time, nobody knew for certain if he considered it a fixed policy or an experiment subject to change. Those who approved of his position on suffrage restriction tended to view the document as a final, set policy. The Republicans who favored enfranchising the freedmen declared his policy an experiment open to modification. They confidently expected that events would reveal the necessity of black suffrage in the South. Believing Johnson would ultimately accept enfranchisement and having no other apparent differences with him, these Republicans continued to support him.[71] George Hoadly reflected the attitude of the most radical Ohio Republicans in a letter to William Henry Smith: "If the North Carolina project of Pres. Johnson is a finality and not an experiment, I am ready to quit supporting him with my vote, and go out into the cold once more."[72]

By early June, Ohioans and Andrew Johnson had determined their desires and plans. Although Ohio Republicans and Democrats differed on nearly all key issues, both groups tended to support Johnson.

Because they were the president's party and the majority party in Ohio, the Republicans' endorsement seems more crucial. They approved of his position on slavery and tended to believe that the planters, as the major force behind secession, must not regain control of the South or influence in the nation until they had proclaimed their willingness to be loyal citizens by taking the amnesty oath. The nation's future security required nothing less than the destruction of the planters' economic and political power. In the meantime the wartime southern Unionists should determine the destiny of their region. Still, moderation reigned supreme, with no confiscation of land or widespread trials of Confederate war leaders anticipated. The president and most Ohio Republicans also appeared to agree about the fate of the freedmen. To deny economic control to the planters, the freed slaves should be granted certain civil rights, including the right to sue and testify in court, marry, and own property, but genuine economic, political, or social equality was neither desired in the North nor required of the South. Despite some significant differences within and between the two political parties, most Ohioans had little intention of using Reconstruction as a vehicle for a social revolution. It seemed far more important to ensure a peaceful future.

Thus as the summer of 1865 approached Johnson enjoyed unusually strong support from both parties in Ohio. Given the very real disagreements between these parties, that situation could not last for long. The tensions aroused during the coming fall elections would begin the process that would within a year find the unity between Johnson and the Republicans completely destroyed.

2

THE ENDORSEMENT OF JOHNSON'S POLICY

> The great mass of the Union party and nearly the whole of those who have been in the Army will stand by you if you remain firm in your present policy. For every Chase radical who leaves you at least ten fair minded Democrats will flock to your standard.
>
> —Lewis Campbell, 1865

In August 1865 conservative Republican Lewis Campbell of Hamilton, Ohio, wrote reassuringly to President Johnson.[1] The letter, written just as the campaign to elect a new governor and state legislature in Ohio began, accurately reflected political views in the state. In a campaign dominated almost entirely by Reconstruction issues, both parties endorsed Johnson's policies. Ohio voters, however, understood that real differences existed between the parties on Reconstruction, and they gave the Republicans a significant victory.

The Democratic and Union parties did not enter the campaign of 1865 on an equal footing. Both enjoyed certain advantages and labored under some liabilities, but the Unionists had won the allegiance of a slight majority of Ohio voters in the last years before the war and had continued to attract their support since then. The Unionists also had the enormous prestige of having been the architects of the victory. In fact, Republicans and some Democrats had created a coalition called the Union party with the express purpose of suppressing the rebellion. After the war most Democrats who had joined the Union party quickly returned to their former party, but throughout 1865 Ohio Republicans continued to refer to themselves as Unionists. In this chapter *Unionist* and *Republican* refer to the same party.

Of course, individuals of all political affiliations had contributed to the northern victory, but the Ohio Democratic party had officially adopted the peace doctrines of Clement L. Vallandigham, an outspoken Peace Democrat from Ohio whom Lincoln had ordered deported in 1863 for his criticism of the Union war effort. Thus, the

Democratic party had forfeited any right to claim a share in the military triumph.[2] An accurate assessment of the value to the Unionists of being the party of victory would be virtually impossible, but without question they believed it gave them a political advantage, and they ceaselessly reminded voters for most of the rest of the century of the party's role in the war.

Along with bearing the prestige of victory, the Unionists also benefited from being identified with all the sacrifices of northerners on the battlefronts and at home.[3] Eric McKitrick has described these feelings in words that are as accurate as they are poignant:

> Republican principles could be personified and objectified in ways that touched the experience of a nation in agony: the boys in blue, the flag, the Union, and the martyred Lincoln. The shrines and memorials that came to be erected at every crossroads village were symbols of sacrifice that the Democrats could not claim; politically, the vacant chair and the empty room were beyond their reach. The military and political fortunes of war had made them all symbols invulnerable and had delivered them into Republican custody. It was this that made political and moral authority so inseparable and had committed them so fully into Republican keeping.[4]

Moreover, having controlled the state political bureaucracy for several years, the Unionists also had the advantages that accrued to those who wielded the power to appoint and who controlled the financial apparatus of the state. Association with an immensely popular president, whose Reconstruction policy a majority of politically active Ohioans apparently approved, further increased Unionist expectations.

The party, however, did face some serious obstacles. As a wartime coalition, the Unionist party could be expected to fragment at least somewhat now that victory had been achieved. During the war, the party had won overwhelming majorities from the soldiers, apparently even from those who had been Democrats before the war. In the absence of an immediate national crisis, at least some of these temporary allies would return to their prewar party affiliation. If the Union party survived these defections, it would have to face the fact that Union armies had also destroyed slavery, the cement that held together the potentially fragile coalition of ex-Whigs, ex-Democrats, ex-Know-Nothings, ex-Free-Soilers, and others that had coalesced into the Republican party in the mid-1850s. Beyond a dedication to stopping the expansion of slavery, each of these groups had its own agenda. If these other issues gained priority, the Union party certainly had the potential to disintegrate.

Indeed, according to Felice Bonadio, factionalism and the pursuit of personal political power dominated the postwar Union party in Ohio to the extent that in the five years after the war "ideology had little place in the political struggles." Bonadio further suggests that "Ohio's political leaders were less concerned with a sincere discussion of Southern reconstruction and Negro rights than historians have commonly assumed." Instead, Bonadio says, Ohio Unionist politicians manipulated national issues for factional or personal goals.[5] Undoubtedly Unionist factionalism existed and presented serious problems for party leaders; however, Bonadio vastly underestimates the commitment of Ohio Republicans to some basic principles of Reconstruction. Unionists at times quarreled furiously and sometimes viciously over party nominations or offices, but they remained dedicated to a Reconstruction program that would ensure the nation a secure future. Bonadio seems to have overlooked or at least discounted the possibility that successful political organizations usually contest nominations quite sharply. Nominations, after all, have no value at all if the candidates have no chance of winning. In that sense party strife reflected party strength.

The Democrats in Ohio faced a far more uncertain future than their political opponents. During the war they had adopted the Peace Democrat position that demanded an end to the war even if it resulted in southern independence. The party had nominated Clement L. Vallandigham for governor while he was in Canada, where he had traveled after being deported from Ohio to the Confederacy for his antiwar speeches. The odium of treason would be a heavy burden for the Democrats, not just in 1865 but for many years thereafter.

In Ohio the Democrats suffered from a lack of good leaders who had not been tainted with Copperheadism. George H. Pendleton, Allen G. Thurman, and Vallandigham—all wartime peace advocates who had dominated their party in the early postwar years—were as attractive and capable as any Unionist politicians, but they proved nearly impossible to elect because of their wartime activities. The Unionists easily could, and did, remind voters that the Democrats had deserted the nation in its most serious crisis.

Like the Unionists, Ohio Democrats had to contend with factional disputes. As Joel Silbey has indicated, Democratic organizations throughout the North were divided into two camps. Those he calls "Purists" wanted to keep the party faithful to its long-established principles, for example, states' rights and limited government. Those Silbey calls "Legitimatists" wanted the party to adjust to the changed political environment that emerged from the war. The Legitimatists might endorse such policies as black suffrage in order to attract more votes.[6] Democrats in Ohio at times divided precisely as Silbey has described. Nevertheless, party loyalty was usually so strong that they, like the Unionists, almost invariably supported the party's nominees in general elections rather than vote for the opposition.

Despite these very real handicaps, Democrats in Ohio and the North believed they had an excellent chance to win the 1865 elections. They realized that many northerners had deep concerns about the expansion of federal powers and possible constitutional violations that had occurred during the war. For example, Vallandigham's 1863 exile resulted from defying a military order in Dayton, Ohio, while that city and much of southern Ohio were under martial law. In addition, he was tried by a military court even though civilian courts were also open. Many Ohioans worried that a federal government that could declare martial law in Ohio, which had so little hostile military action during the war, had simply grown too powerful. The Democrats had stressed that issue with some success during the war and would return to it again whenever possible. They also hoped to benefit from public discontent over wartime taxes and the vastly increased national debt. While the Unionists worried about probable defections by war veterans, the Democrats relished the prospect. Frequently they catered to the veteran vote and attempted to overcome the loyalty issue by nominating veterans for offices.

The Democrats could also exploit the most promising of all factors, racial prejudice. Even though Ohio had given the Republicans/Unionists majorities in almost every statewide election for a decade, most Ohioans, like most Americans, firmly believed in white supremacy.[7] Republicans were no exception, even though they generally thought that the freedmen had the right to benefit from their own labor. Certainly the Democrats believed that describing their opponents as the party of the "damned darkeys" and the "nigger lovers" would aid their quest for votes. With the return of peace the Democrats wasted little time in springing to the offensive and charging that the Unionists meant to destroy the white race throughout the country by forcing black domination, often called "nigger equality," on the nation.

For months before the parties held their 1865 state conventions, each understood that Reconstruction issues, particularly black suffrage, would dominate the campaign. Even though Ohio Unionists agreed that the freedmen required basic civil rights, the matter of suffrage deeply divided the party. During the first five months of 1865 a sizable number of Radical Republicans had endorsed either impartial or universal suffrage for adult male freedmen; some urged the enfranchisement of black males in Ohio. These and other like-minded Republicans had hoped that President Johnson would require black suffrage in his Reconstruction policy and had exerted pressure on him to do so. Indeed, in the weeks before Johnson issued the North Carolina Proclamation optimism had greatly increased among the Radicals.[8]

Support for suffrage extension may have been increasing throughout the North in the weeks before Johnson announced his Reconstruction policy, in part because some lukewarm advocates of black enfranchisement had heard that the president would insist upon at least impartial suffrage in the South.[9] When Johnson issued the North Carolina Proclamation without any mention of black suffrage, some Radical Republicans became alarmed but continued to work for ballots for the freedmen. Others, who had endorsed black voting as a cheap and effective means to reconstruct the nation and protect the freedmen's rights, concluded that without presidential support black suffrage would not be enacted. As noted, they quietly acquiesced in the president's plan, hoping that Reconstruction could succeed without black political participation or that events would later force enfranchisement. Some who favored enfranchisement remained quiet because they feared that stressing the issue would lead to political disaster for their party. One such Republican confided to his diary, "Color as a basis of suffrage is absurd, but a party that in Ohio would now commit itself to negro suffrage would inevitably be defeated."[10]

A.F. Perry of Cincinnati typified those Republicans who accepted the apparent need to avoid the suffrage issue. In early June he wrote to General Jacob Cox. Perry declared his "own tendency" to rely "upon the principles of natural justice" and thus grant the freedmen the right to vote. He admitted, however, that "the doubts and hesitations involved in any sober view of the question are such that if I should see and experience what you have, my decision might be the same as yours."[11] General Cox had had extensive experience with blacks before and after emancipation. At his request, less than three weeks later, Perry would serve as Cox's spokesman at the Union State Convention, working against a party endorsement of black suffrage.[12]

A majority of Ohio Republicans had almost assuredly never sought suffrage extension in the South. They insisted that this issue was too politically sensitive, that the soldiers would desert the party if the matter were pressed, that control over suffrage requirements rested with the individual states, and that blacks needed to be educated before receiving the vote. To the Radicals' argument that successful Reconstruction necessitated black suffrage, one Unionist answered, "If Southern society can only be saved by the votes of Negroes, we fear it is a lost society."[13] Without question these men believed that the Union party must at all costs avoid making a declaration on the issue in its platform.

Even many of those who favored black suffrage agreed that the party convention should avoid the suffrage issue. Nevertheless, several of the most radical fought successfully to have the matter brought before the delegates when the party met in Columbus on June 21, 1865. Their hopes that the party would adopt a strong and advanced position on suffrage would be dashed on the rocks of political reality.

On April 5 the Central Committee of the Union party had met with party members serving in the state legislature and Congress and made a decision that would critically affect the state convention. They agreed to apportion 143 of the 575 convention seats to army veterans. Each Ohio regiment, separately organized battalion, and independent battery would be allowed to send one delegate.[14] The presence of the soldiers promised to give the convention a conservative flavor, especially on the suffrage issue, and assured that the more radical members of the party would not control the meeting.

The decision to allow army delegates had one major effect on the party before the convention even began. Governor John Brough, a Democrat who had joined the Union party during the war, had irritated many Ohio soldiers by declaring that army promotions must be based on seniority rather than merit.[15] When he learned that soldiers would make up about 25 percent of the convention delegates, Brough thought seriously of declining to run for another term. Some Unionists immediately sprang to Brough's defense and urged him to seek reelection.[16] Brough, however, apparently decided that he had no chance to be renominated and withdrew less than a week before the convention.

Brough's withdrawal virtually assured that Major General Jacob Dolson Cox, the sole remaining active candidate, would receive the gubernatorial nomination. Cox had attended Oberlin College, where he absorbed the antislavery attitudes that permeated the Western Reserve. After he married a daughter of the abolitionist Charles Finney, Cox practiced law. Just as the party was being organized in Ohio, he entered politics as a Republican. In 1859, largely because of his strong antislavery views, Cox won a seat in the Ohio Senate. Then, shortly after the Civil War began he joined the army and ultimately rose to the rank of major general.[17] His Oberlin training, military background, and antislavery sentiments were appealing political attributes.

The general's supporters had been working for months to persuade him to run and to ensure his nomination. By mid-May one confidently informed Cox, "The prospect now is that we shall make you Governor of Ohio." With the active backing of the soldiers; William Dennison, a past governor of Ohio and now Johnson's postmaster general; and President Johnson himself, his nomination was almost certain. Cox agreed to accept that nomination as long as the platform did not endorse suffrage for the freedmen. He told his campaign manager, Aaron F. Perry, that he would withdraw his name if the convention demanded enfranchisement.[18]

Cox's ultimatum indicates the split within the Union party on key Reconstruction issues, the two most critical of which were the president's announced policy and black suffrage. In part because of the presence of the army delegates, five of whom sat on the twenty-four-man platform committee, and also because the overwhelming majority of Unionists approved of it, Johnson's plan received an unequivocal endorsement by both the committee and the entire convention.[19] The deliberations on the suffrage question proved far more interesting.

Judge William Dickson of Cincinnati, an advocate of black suffrage but also one of those who urged Cox to run for governor, presided over the turbulent committee meeting. A vocal minority stated the case for enfranchisement of the freedmen, but moderate and conservative Unionists joined with the soldier delegates to write a platform that did not even mention the suffrage question. One delegate succinctly summed up the discussion, "State Convention met. . . . Negro Suffrage pressed—Yielded. I worked to put it out of the Platform."[20] To appease the Radicals and to keep them from submitting a minority report, the committee added a vague resolution stating "that the experience of the last four years shows the absolute necessity of keeping steadily in view the great principles of our Government as set forth in the Declaration of Independence." Perhaps realizing that this resolution was the best they could secure, the Radicals relented, and the platform received the unanimous approval of the convention.

The endorsement of Johnson's Reconstruction program put the party on record against any federal attempts to force black suffrage on the South. It was not a renunciation of black suffrage so much as an indication that the Union party intended to give Johnson a chance to try his plan. In any case Unionists generally agreed that Johnson's Reconstruction program was only experimental and that he would modify it in whatever fashion the national interest dictated.[21]

Politics also played a key role in the decision to avoid a statement on the suffrage question. A solid majority of Unionists, regardless of their position on suffrage, desperately wanted to keep that issue out of the 1865 campaign either because they believed that states should continue to set voting requirements or because they worried that the Democrats would gain votes by denouncing them as the party of "nigger equality." In other words, the Unionists feared the power of Democratic appeals to the voters' racial prejudice. More specifically, as the nomination of a general for governor suggested, the Unionists believed that they needed the veterans' votes to win the election. They feared that any hint of black suffrage would drive the soldiers into the wide open and ready arms of the Democrats.[22]

The remainder of the Union platform suggests how issues related to the war and Reconstruction dominated Ohio politics in 1865. The Unionists demanded the "overthrow and eradication" of slavery "as our only safeguard against the recurrence of like evils in the future." Thus, although this plank stated that slavery defied "the dealings of Providence," the emphasis was on future national security as a justification for the destruction of slavery. The same plank, by referring to the war as "the slaveholders' rebellion," also made clear Ohioans' general belief that planters had caused the war.

The Unionists also insisted that Reconstruction, while it should not be unduly delayed, should "be at such *time* and on such *terms* as will give unquestioned assurance of the peace and security, not only of the loyal people of the rebel South, but also of the peace and prosperity of the Federal Union." The plank accurately reflected the Unionists' belief that the North should set the terms and that the South would have to prove its loyalty before returning to the union. And the party declared in another plank that it expected President Johnson to lead the way to a secure, happy, and prosperous future.[23]

If the convention delegates had anticipated that all Unionists would quietly accept the platform, particularly its position on suffrage, they were almost immediately disillusioned. Edwin Cowles, editor of the *Cleveland Leader*, for example, though he unenthusiastically endorsed the platform, expressed his disappointment "not in what it says but in what it fails to say." Cowles had hoped for a "bold and explicit declaration" in favor of black suffrage because "it can't be dodged. It is *the* issue—almost the *only* issue—of the day."[24] One would have to search long and hard to find a cooler endorsement of a party's candidates than that given them by the *Portage County Democrat*, which grumbled, "The ticket is said to be a good one. It is to be presumed it is." The paper's editor then warmed to the task and ripped into the convention delegates for being

> manifestly under the sway of a timid conservative spirit. Conservatism is always cowardly—is always afraid to do right, fearing somebody will not be prepared to sanction the right.
>
> The Platform is a didactic emasculation—unworthy of the convention—unworthy of the stern demands of the hour. *It enunciates* no vital, living principle,—unless, perchance, the foggy reference to the Declaration of Independence, may be regarded as such. Yet, we do not so much dissent from the Platform, smooth and crafty in its verbiage as it is, but we do complain of palpable and deliberate omissions.[25]

Of course, the platform had its defenders. Aaron Perry, logically enough, found the "merit" of the platform in these very omissions. "If it could not say what every man wished to have said, it does the next best thing. It omits to say what every man wished to have omitted." Other party members from across the state noted the platform with satisfaction.[26]

Even though some advocates of black suffrage realized that most Ohioans disagreed with them, they refused to let the matter rest. Throughout the summer various Unionists continued to speak out for enfranchisement. Most of them carefully avoided condemning either their party or President Johnson, but nonetheless their views were clear.[27]

By far the most important postconvention development related to the suffrage issue concerned Jacob Cox. Ohioans knew little about his position on suffrage extension, but some considered his Oberlin College background and strong antislavery views sufficient evidence to conclude that he favored black suffrage, at least in the South. Many Radical Republicans hoped—and Democrats charged—that he did. By contrast, moderate and conservative Republicans wanted to believe that Cox opposed allowing the freedmen to vote or at least would have the good sense not to make suffrage extension a campaign issue.[28] As early as July 3 Cox had received a request from a group of Ohio veterans to state his position on the suffrage question. Perhaps to help him decide, they informed Cox that they supported Johnson's plan and would never agree to black voting in Ohio.[29]

All of this greatly distressed Cox. He realized that his mixed background of Oberlin training and military experience made many conclusions about his position possible; yet, he believed his personal views had little role in the election, and he hoped to avoid the issue as much as possible during the campaign. Despite Democratic charges that Cox actually favored black suffrage and was only hiding from the voters until after the election, when he would push for suffrage extension in both the South and Ohio, Cox's stance made sense. In the mid-nineteenth century the chief executive of Ohio, lacking even the veto, had little real power over the legislative process. That fact, plus his strong desire to maintain party unity at almost any cost, not just to win the election but primarily to keep the Democrats, whom Cox and most Ohio Unionists considered virtual traitors, from gaining control of the state, explains the general's reluctance to clarify his views. Cox was particularly irritated at Radicals from the Western Reserve who refused to abide by the party platform and leave the suffrage question out of the campaign.[30]

The Radicals finally forced him to make a public statement on the suffrage issue. On July 25 the candidate received a letter from E.H. Fairchild, an Oberlin College professor, and Samuel Plumb, mayor of Oberlin. These men, who called themselves the Oberlin Committee, had heard rumors that seemingly originated in Warren, Ohio, that Cox opposed enfranchising the freedmen. They demanded that the candidate state his position on suffrage extension as a requirement for the readmission of the southern states.[31]

Just two days earlier Cox had written to a longtime friend, John Ellis, that the freedmen's salvation required the separation of the races. Cox predicted that black enfranchisement would lead to a race war, which the freedmen could only lose. He further asserted that if Congress demanded more than the Thirteenth Amendment as conditions of restoration, southerners would reject the terms and northern voters would elect a Congress that would enact milder requirements.[32] When Cox received the letter from the Oberlin Committee, he apparently concluded that Ellis had not respected the privacy of their correspondence, and therefore, he decided to respond publicly to the committee.

The candidate immediately wrote a lengthy and, as soon became clear, extremely controversial reply to Fairchild and Plumb.[33] He began by lecturing them and whatever group they purported to represent on the merits and necessity of political organizations. Parties, the general suggested, "are founded upon a mutual waiving of some articles of personal belief for the sake of securing united and effective action upon others." In other words, the party had decided not to take a position on the suffrage matter, and all good Unionists should accept that decision. Their refusal to agree to such a basic fact of political reality clearly raised his ire.[34]

After chastising the men for failure to endorse the party's platform, Cox defended the work of the convention. The delegates, he informed them, had not endorsed a suffrage plank because Ohioans had not yet determined the best way to deal with the question of black suffrage in the South. The party had merely chosen to wait for future developments before committing itself. The candidate announced that he intended to run on the platform and to continue to support President Johnson. Cox feared that to press the issue now would split the Union party, perhaps destroying it, and might allow the dangerous and untrustworthy Democrats to regain political control of Ohio and, possibly, the entire nation.

Had Cox ended his "Oberlin letter" at that point it almost certainly would not have become the major issue it did. Instead, however, after revealing his unwillingness to demand black enfranchisement in the South as a prerequisite to restoration, Cox elaborated his "private views on reconstruction." Based on many years of carefully watching racial attitudes in the North and four years of "close and thoughtful observation of the races where they are," the general concluded that northern whites hated blacks almost as much as southern whites did and that the war had greatly exacerbated race relations in the South. Thus, the suggestion that the inherent power of the ballot could protect blacks' freedom struck Cox as utter nonsense. In fact, he despaired that black suffrage would instead lead to intensified racial antagonism and possibly a war for racial supremacy. In such a conflict the general saw no possibility of success for the blacks, whose survival, he suspected, would be at stake. Cox therefore concluded that only the separation of the races would protect the freedmen's rights. He suggested reserving for black settlement the coastal portions of South Carolina, Georgia, Alabama, and all of Florida, where they would have complete political and economic control and would enjoy all the rights, including suffrage, that any other Americans had. Cox envisioned no need to coerce the freedmen to move to that area because the absence of hostile whites, who would not be allowed to vote in black areas, and the chance to run their own affairs would persuade them to settle there. In addition, blacks would be discouraged from remaining in white areas because they would not receive equal economic or political rights there. The candidate acknowledged that many people would consider his ideas unworkable, but he stressed that he had pondered the racial situation for years and firmly believed that he had arrived at the best solution.[35]

Cox's proposal of a separate territory for the freedmen followed in the long American tradition of trying to colonize blacks anywhere they would not upset white Americans. The freedmen had few better friends in Ohio than James Garfield, but even he shared the general dismay over the ultimate significance of black suffrage and the common desire to be completely rid of blacks. He confessed to "a strong feeling of repugnance when I think of the Negro being made our political equals and I would be glad if they could be colonized—sent to heaven or got rid of in any decent way it would delight me. But colonization has proved a hopeless failure everywhere."[36] Indeed, Cox's idea was hopelessly impractical. Implementation of the plan would have involved the massive movement of thousands of blacks and, even more impracticable, thousands of whites, nearly all of whom would undoubtedly prefer to have the blacks settle somewhere else and leave them and their property alone. And the transfer of millions of dollars' worth of property from whites to the incoming blacks would have been even more difficult to accomplish. Cox, understandably, presented no clear ideas on how to execute or pay for his proposal. Nevertheless, he had two excellent reasons for dropping this bombshell on Ohio at the start of an extremely critical political campaign.

Cox was an intelligent and thoughtful human being whose resettlement plan represented his sincere conviction and reasoned solution on how best to solve one of the most critical problems facing the nation. He genuinely believed that the two races simply could not live together in harmony.[37] As a classic liberal with a deep commitment to limited government, Cox could not accept the enormous expense of the massive federal presence in the South that he believed would be required to protect the freedmen if the races were forced to try to live together. He also feared that federal attempts to intervene between the freedmen and their employers would destroy the functioning of the free market and thus do perhaps irrevocable harm to the economic system of the nation. Unlike many of his fellow Republicans, Cox realized the severe limitations of the ballot as a protection for black rights. Yet he believed almost devoutly in a laissez-faire economic system that could be disrupted or even destroyed by federal attempts to provide blacks with the economic wherewithal to compete with whites. Cox, therefore, faced almost equally unsatisfactory alternatives—turn the fate of blacks over to the white southerners or watch the federal government try to protect them at the possible cost of destroying the country's economic system. Even though his proposal violated his own principle of laissez-faire, Cox believed the separation of the races could solve his dilemma.[38] He announced his plan when he did because he thought it would help the nation deal with a difficult issue.

Political considerations also motivated Cox. He hoped his letter would help keep racial issues out of the campaign. Quite simply, he feared that forcing racial questions into the campaign would endanger the chances for a Unionist victory, and he was convinced that victory was essential for peaceful reunion and a secure future. Unionists must retain control of the state and federal governments because only they understood that to protect national security southerners must give guarantees of future loyalty before readmission to the Union. Cox and most Unionists were convinced that the Democrats were fully capable of undoing the work of the war and thus setting the stage for renewed armed sectional conflict. The country simply could not trust its future to the Democrats, because of their role in the secession crises and their wartime record of Copperheadism. Cox feared that the Radicals' constant pressure for black suffrage would drive Ohio war veterans from the party and thereby give the Democrats the election. Convinced that the veteran vote would determine the election result, Cox expressed his racial views because he thought the veterans would agree with him and then vote for Union candidates.

The general fully understood that this proposal might alienate some Radicals, and he suggested that they had every right to disagree privately but not to endanger the nation with their differences. For example, Cox assured Congressman James Garfield that the Radicals "are crazy to make [black suffrage] an issue. They can gain all they desire in the way of advocacy of their opinions without making them tests for me or others and can let the suffrage question remain open till Congress meets." While desiring the Radicals' votes and assistance, he thought that the situation demanded that the Union party seek a moderate, middle ground on Reconstruction questions.[39]

The remarkable controversy that ensued when editors across Ohio published the Oberlin letter during the first week in August provides insight into Ohioans' views on suffrage and the role they envisioned for blacks in America. A fairly substantial number of Republicans endorsed Cox's proposal, praising the "novelty of the proposition" and his "boldness of thought and independent spirit."[40] Cox received letters that verified his contention that soldiers opposed granting the ballot to the freedmen. His defenders further asserted that his proposal discouraged the Democrats, who had been making serious attempts to attract votes from Ohio veterans. Some said that the whole issue mattered not one bit because Cox had pledged to support the president and Congress in whatever they decided was required to protect the nation's future.[41]

Other responses to the letter exposed the deep divisions between Unionists who favored and those who opposed suffrage extension.

Some of those who conveyed their approval of Cox's ideas also used the opportunity to take a swipe at the Radicals. Lewis Campbell, a conservative Republican who had successfully worked at the party convention for a plank that endorsed Johnson's Reconstruction policy, graphically expressed his disgust that in Oberlin "the population think that when Oberlin takes snuff the whole world must sneeze" and his joy that Cox had taken the Radicals down a notch or two.[42] The Radicals, for their part, did not hesitate to differ with Cox. Some followed the course of James Garfield, who quietly and gently informed Cox, "I cannot agree with all the positions you take," because the proposal "appears to me hopelessly impractical." The congressman then added startling evidence of how frustrating and disturbing the whole racial matter was to thoughtful Unionists, "If neither your plan nor political interfusion are possible then it may well be questioned whether it were not better to amend our error and re-enslave the negro." Another Republican noted in his diary, "This plan of solving the negro problem will not be approved. I earnestly warned [the] General not to allow himself to be construed as against [the] extension of suffrage.[43]

Other Radicals expressed their dismay with and anger at Cox. One Republican editor wrote, "If anything were needed to increase our regret that the Union Convention of Ohio should omit all mention of the absorbing question of negro suffrage, it would be found in the attempt of our candidate for Governor to supply that unfortunate omission." Another called Cox's position "embarrassing" but not particularly worrisome because Ohio governors had so little constitutional authority or power.[44] In general, though, party Radicals supported him. They really had little other choice, and besides, his views would not dictate to the party in either Ohio or Congress.

Nearly all Republicans seemed to agree that Cox's letter would hurt the party little, if at all, in the fall elections. Some even predicted it would result in a net gain for the Unionists.[45] In all probability the Republicans were correct. Except for the impracticality of his plan, Cox's basic conclusions seem to have been quite compatible with those of most Ohioans, who believed in white superiority and had little desire to live with blacks or extend to them full political or economic equality. The whole episode, however, did show that issues related to the freedmen would not go away and that, no matter what a majority in the Union party wished, racial matters would be discussed in the 1865 campaign.

The Democrats in Ohio certainly intended to use racial issues to whatever advantage they could. From the earliest days after the end of the war, their strategy had been clear. The Democrats incessantly charged that the Republicans would not stop until they had forced "nigger equality," miscegenation, and amalgamation not only on the South but also on Ohio. The Democrats proudly portrayed themselves as the white man's party and urged all to join them in the struggle against the "Black Republicans."[46] They resurrected all the familiar arguments against black suffrage, tending to focus on a state's right to regulate suffrage; blacks' alleged intellectual unfitness to vote and other natural liabilities (frequently they came very close to charging that blacks were subhuman); and the probability that Republicans would manipulate black voters. These accusations amounted to little more than race baiting. The *Cleveland Plain Dealer*, for example, concluded that "mental and physical peculiarities" made the freedmen "totally unfit to enter, successfully, into competition with the dominant races," and so any attempt to elevate the freedmen would in fact require the degradation of whites. Other Democrats agreed that "prejudice, education and nature" ordained white superiority.[47] The Democrats added little to the intelligent discussion of an issue that vitally concerned most Ohioans, nor did they try to do so. They sought not to educate the voter but to frighten him or take advantage of his ample prejudices.

After the Union party convention refused to endorse black suffrage, the Democrats took almost perverse joy in taunting the Unionists to quit lying to the electorate and admit that they really intended to enfranchise the freedmen. Democrats charged that the Unionists did not declare their true goals because they lacked the courage to do so and because they knew that Ohioans would reject them if they acknowledged their ultimate plans.[48]

Although they could not agree on the significance of Cox's Oberlin letter, the Democrats uniformly asserted it would help their cause. Washington McLean, editor of the *Cincinnati Daily Enquirer*, crowed, "In the letter of General Cox, we find our vindication. . . . General Cox ought to have been a Democrat. He would have been doubtless, but for the African atmosphere in which he was educated." A few Democrats argued quite correctly that Cox did not say he would fight against black suffrage, and they claimed, therefore, that Cox was part of the Republican attempt to "dodge" what they considered the most vital issue of the campaign.[49]

Meanwhile the Democrats moved closer to an endorsement of Johnson's Reconstruction policy. In early June one Democratic editor, reflecting the hesitancy shared by many in the party to take back the prodigal president, nonetheless pledged to support him "whenever he, in our opinion, is right, as we will certainly oppose him whenever we believe him to be wrong." Although this hardly amounted to a ringing endorsement, it showed the general Democratic movement in the direction of backing the president. Within weeks that editor praised Johnson for pursuing a "line of policy in conformity with the views of the great mass of the American people." [50] The state convention would reveal that other Democrats were traveling the same path.

In late June party leaders met in Columbus to schedule the state convention and discuss campaign strategy. Recognizing the existing political volatility in the nation, these Democrats concluded that they could gain some political advantage by waiting as long as possible before holding their convention, which they decided to convene in late August. The June meeting failed miserably in its attempt to develop a unified party position on Reconstruction issues. Those in attendance reflected the split in the party between those who sought to remain loyal to time-honored Democratic principles, such as states' rights, and those who argued for a more flexible approach that might gain new Democratic voters. This relatively liberal wing more or less won the debate, but not without temporarily driving the conservatives from the party. These extreme states' righters held their own convention, but they had a neglible effect on the election. They nominated former congressman Alexander Long for governor, but the voters so completely ignored him that the official election results did not even mention him.[51]

In the absence of the right-wing critics in their own party, by August the Democrats had developed a three-part strategy. The party intended to support Johnson's Reconstruction program, to capture the critical veteran vote by nominating a soldier for governor, and to rely during the campaign almost exclusively on arousing Ohioans' racial prejudice.[52] Disregarding and distorting the attitudes of their political opponents, the Democrats planned to assault the voters with a constant barrage of racist diatribes aimed at convincing the electorate that the Unionists intended to legislate black political and social equality.

Democrats had decided long before their state convention that to win in October they would have to nominate a veteran to head the ticket. They initially sought to bestow the honor on General William T. Sherman, a genuine war hero but also widely known for his antipathy toward blacks. In mid-July, however, Sherman announced his refusal to run for any political office.[53] The chagrined Democrats quickly found a suitable alternative. By virtue of a stinging harangue against black enfranchisement on July 4, 1865, General George W. Morgan proved his qualification for the nomination, and he quickly became the front-runner after Sherman withdrew.

In his Independence Day speech Morgan previewed the basic

thrust of the entire Democratic campaign. The general warned that miscegenation, which the Republicans supposedly sponsored, would destroy the United States. Morgan also denied that the phrase "all men" in the Declaration of Independence included blacks and argued that they were inferior beings incapable of becoming voters, officeholders, jurors, or anything except unpropertied laborers. He concluded the virulent attack on the freedmen by urging his listeners to "resolve that the white race must remain as created by [the] Deity, unadulterated and supreme."[54] The party could scarcely overlook a man so representative of the attitudes of its membership. At the state convention on August 24 the delegates duly nominated Morgan for governor.[55]

The convention delegates also wrote the other two phases of their strategy into the platform. They demanded that the Confederate states immediately regain representation in Congress and, because Johnson's policy looked as if it would facilitate rapid restoration of the Union, agreed to support the president in "all constitutional efforts to restore the States to the exercise of their rights and power within the Union." This slight hesitation to endorse any policy the president might adopt revealed a residual mistrust, a lingering fear that he might demand black enfranchisement in the South as a condition for readmission to the union. In another plank the Democrats stated their belief that only individual states could set voting qualifications. They considered any attempt by the federal government to grant suffrage to anybody completely unconstitutional. The party pointedly expressed its opposition to black suffrage, which it said would "overthrow popular institutions by bringing the right to vote into disgrace." The party of the people also insisted that the state legislature stop black migration, which it described as a "growing menace" to Ohio.[56]

Despite the fact that both parties had endorsed Johnson's Reconstruction policy, they differed vastly on this major issue. The Democrats believed that the southern states deserved immediate restoration to the union and that the country could trust the leaders of the Confederacy (most of whom, of course, had been prewar Democrats) with the political future of the South and the nation.[57] The Unionists, by contrast, insisted that only loyal southerners, that is, those who had opposed the rebellion or had signed an oath of future loyalty to the federal government, should have a voice in governing the South. They refused to allow secessionists to regain political rights until they had given concrete evidence of future loyalty.[58] The Unionists expected that Johnson's program would accomplish this end, and therefore they supported him. Most of them believed that the president shared their view that his policy was experimental, and they thought he would hasten to change it if southerners proved unwilling to fulfill its requirements.[59] These critical differences between the parties became much more apparent when reconstructed southern states elected unpardoned individuals to state and federal offices, thus proving to Unionists that they were still unrepentant and undeserving of readmission. The Democrats saw little wrong with the elections held under Johnson's policy and urged the immediate seating of those elected to Congress when that body would meet in December.

Although both parties had endorsed Johnson's Reconstruction policy, issues related to the reunification of the nation dominated the campaign. Rather than rely on positive discussions of how they would best ensure the nation a peaceful and secure future, however, both parties attempted to convince the voters that their opponents would endanger the social and political fabric of the country if allowed to control Reconstruction.

The Democrats continued to wage a campaign of fear. Their spokesmen and candidates consistently distorted Unionist attitudes beyond recognition, warning that a Unionist triumph would lead directly to black political, social, and economic equality throughout the nation. They charged that if Ohio enfranchised blacks, hordes of freedmen would flood into the state, take jobs away from whites, and violate white Ohioans' daughters. The Democrats fully understood the racial insecurities of the typical Ohioan and relentlessly played upon them.[60]

Faced with the nearly universal appeal of the Democrats' racist rhetoric, the Unionists took the offensive. They charged that during the war the Democrats had supported the Confederacy, and if elected now, they would pursue the same goals the rebels had sought by bullets and bayonets. The war, with its immense sacrifices, would then have been fought for nothing. The Unionists accused the Democrats of seeking the reenslavement of the freedmen and of planning to allow unrepentant secessionists to resume their positions in Congress, where they would unite with equally traitorous northern Democrats to regain control of the federal government. The nation would then find itself in exactly the same situation in 1865 as it had been in 1860 and could expect just as disastrous a future. The Unionist message, simply stated, was that "only loyal men should determine the fate of the South and the nation and that the Democrats have proved they are traitors."[61]

This "waving of the bloody shirt" may have served some positive purpose in 1865 that it would not in the 1870s and after. With good reason, many Ohioans were most anxious to secure a peaceful future. They feared that the tragic suffering during the war might prove fruitless if the South regained political influence. The Democrats, by continued adherence to a states' rights philosophy and by insistence on immediate restoration of the southern states, appeared willing and even eager to let this happen. The possibility of national disaster appeared very real to the Unionists, and they felt justified in alerting the voters to this possibility. Given the actions of the Democratic legislature elected in 1867, which among other reactionary steps attempted to rescind Ohio's ratification of the Fourteenth Amendment, the Unionist charges hardly seem extreme.

In addition to attacking the loyalty of their opponents, the Unionists worked diligently to calm the voters' racial fears. Party spokesmen repeatedly insisted that they did not support black suffrage in any state and that it was simply not an issue in the election. The Union party advocated protection of the freedmen's civil rights, but its members were far too convinced of white superiority to seek black political, social, or economic equality. Most Unionists emphasized that the greatest national priorities were reunion and a secure, peaceful future. Of course, they said, only their party could accomplish these objectives.[62]

Even though most of the Unionist supporters of black suffrage acknowledged their minority position within the party, some still refused to be silent on the matter. In an occasional letter, editorial, or speech they reminded Ohioans that blacks had earned the vote by their role in war, that black votes were necessary for peaceful reunion, or that basic justice dictated extending suffrage to male freedmen. These Radicals accepted the Unionist position to the extent that they did not make the suffrage question a major campaign issue, but neither would they ignore an issue that for many was a matter of principle.[63]

An examination of Unionist county platforms clarifies somewhat the relative strength of the prosuffrage element within the party. A sample of twenty-six county platforms from all areas of Ohio reveals that seven conventions (those in Lorain, Trumbull, Geauga, Summit, Astabula, Mahoning, and Preble counties) endorsed some form of black suffrage in some portion of the country. Of the seven, four supported black suffrage in both Ohio and the South, one favored extending the franchise only to the freedmen, and two approved strong prosuffrage planks that did not specify the geographic area to which they would pertain. Six of the seven counties were located in northeastern Ohio and Cox carried all seven, winning 67 percent of the votes compared to his statewide percentage of 53.5.[64]

Ten Union conventions (those of Coshocton, Clermont, Pickaway, Morgan, Fulton, Williams, Franklin, Henry, Hamilton, and Cuyahoga counties) passed a variety of resolutions, most of which expressed support for Johnson and the state Union platform but made no reference to black suffrage. Cox carried six of these counties with 56 percent of the votes; in the four he lost, he garnered 43 percent. If the results for all ten counties are combined, Cox won 53 percent of the votes cast.[65]

Nine of the twenty-six conventions (those of Clarke, Crawford, Lawrence, Washington, Muskingum, Montgomery, Erie, Union, and Huron counties) passed no resolutions. Eight of them went for Cox by a combined 55 percent. He received only 38 percent of the vote in Crawford County.[66]

As a group the twenty-six counties gave Cox 56 percent of their votes, slightly more than his statewide percentage. It would be reasonable to conclude that these counties were slightly more Unionist than the average Ohio county. Yet, only seven of them endorsed black suffrage. Thus, even granting the randomness of the sample, the platforms seem to indicate that most Ohio Unionists opposed suffrage extension and believed that Reconstruction could succeed without it.

Most Unionists preferred to ignore the suffrage issue and instead to speak or write about their support of Johnson's Reconstruction program. They assured the electorate that the president was leading the nation wisely and that the Union party enthusiastically backed his efforts.[67] In the fall of 1865 few Ohio Unionists had decided to abandon Johnson or his program.

Yet, the behavior of southerners during the summer and early fall concerned them, and some almost inaudible grumbling and consternation among the more radical Unionists could be heard. Without question the election of unpardoned former Confederates to state conventions and national offices raised the worry among some Ohio Republicans that Johnson might be proceeding too quickly. For example, Ohio Senator Benjamin Wade privately reported that the situation looked "gloomy" because Johnson had been overly lenient with southerners and had issued too many pardons. Some who agreed with Wade put their faith in Johnson's willingness to amend his policy; for his own part, Wade looked forward to the convening of Congress, which would assume its constitutional role in Reconstruction. Other nervous Unionists conveyed their perceptions directly to the president. The few newspapermen who printed editorials critical of the course of Reconstruction usually blamed the troubles not on Johnson but on southerners for their unwillingness to abide by his requirements.[68]

On election day Ohio voters gave Cox and the Union party a solid

Table 1
Ohio Gubernatorial Elections, 1855-1865

Year	Republican (Union) Party	Democratic Party
	Percentage (Candidate)	Percentage (Candidate)
1855	48.6 (Chase)	43.4 (Medill)
1857	48.7 (Chase)	48.2 (Payne)
1859	51.8 (Dennison)	48.1 (Ranney)
1861	57.7 (Todd)	42.3 (Jewett)
1863	60.4 (Brough)	39.3 (Vallandigham)
1865	53.6 (Cox)	46.4 (Morgan)

SOURCE: *Annual Report of the Secretary of State of Ohio* (1868), 100-109

endorsement. Cox garnered 53.6 percent of the vote and the party gained a two-to-one majority in each house of the Ohio General Assembly. Cox's percentage of the vote exceeded that of any previous Republican gubernatorial candidate, except those elected during the Civil War. Thus, the 1865 election marked the most significant peacetime Republican victory to date in Ohio.

The party had cashed in on its popularity as the party of military victory. It achieved success because its platform had accurately gauged majority opinion in the state on the best way to deal with the Reconstruction crisis, that is, follow the president's leadership. Although both parties had endorsed Johnson's policy, Ohio voters apparently discerned that only the Unionists would demand the safeguards they believed necessary, and the voters also preferred the party that had won the war.[69] The election was a victory for those who wanted reunion, a secure future, and protection of the freedmen's basic rights, but who opposed black social, economic, and political equality.

Thus, the policies advocated by the Unionists had won the approval of the majority of voters in Ohio. With Congress scheduled to convene in early December, Ohioans would not have long to wait to determine if Congress and Johnson would heed their recommendations and desires. Regardless, Ohio Republicans had gained majority support for their view of the requirements for a successful Reconstruction policy.

3

JOHNSON'S POLICY REJECTED

> I see that he has again become raving—He is very virulent. He is determined to "write himself down an Ass"—If it is his purpose to play downright Traitor to the Union party that elected him, I am glad he goes it strong enough to furnish, in the general distrust he creates, an antidote to his poison.
>
> —B.F. Hoffman, 1866

Balmy, springlike temperatures greeted members of Congress on Monday, December 4, 1865, as they headed up Capitol Hill to convene the first session of the Thirty-Ninth Congress. The weather might have reflected the hope of most northerners, including Ohioans, that the long nightmare of sectional strife might end reasonably soon. Less than two months earlier these Ohioans had underscored their insistence that the Reconstruction process must defuse the threat of further conflict by voting for the Union party, which had endorsed President Johnson's Reconstruction policy. In early December the president remained enormously popular and trusted in Ohio. Soon, however, the storms would break in Congress, and by the following summer, the president would find himself abandoned by his party. For that predicament he would have only himself to blame, for he would ignore or reject the messages he received from Ohio Republicans and other northerners until they completely lost faith in him. Actually, though, Johnson's problems had begun before Congress met.

During the summer and fall of 1865, under the direction of Johnson's provisional governors, southerners had begun the process of recreating their state governments. In general they had grudgingly accepted some of Johnson's requirements. Nevertheless, the refusal of some southern states to abide by all the president's directives, proved to many Ohioans that the former Confederates remained too rebellious to be trusted with a major role in Reconstruction.[1]

Johnson's interpretation of the Amnesty Proclamation also concerned many Ohioans. When the president excluded a significant number of southerners from the general grant of amnesty, Ohio Republicans and many Democrats readily endorsed his proposal, but they expected him to give few special pardons. Instead, he granted so many that some observers concluded he was less interested in ascertaining the loyalty of the applicant than in forcing them to beg for the pardon. Regardless of his motives, many Ohioans expressed grave concern that the president seemed to have forgotten his promise to make treason odious. They feared that Johnson's actions could deny the nation the dearly purchased fruits of victory and endanger the future.[2] In short, Reconstruction might fail unless some remedial actions were taken.

The president may have granted far more pardons than some Ohioans desired, but southerners nonetheless managed in the fall of 1865 to elect to state and federal offices many who remained unpardoned and thus ineligible to hold public office. These elections dismayed many northerners, for they seemed to display the impudence of the former Confederates, indicating that they could not be trusted to resume their place and role in the union. Even more alarming was Johnson's seeming indifference to them. His acquiescence seemed to suggest that he neither appreciated the gravity of the national crisis nor understood the desires of the northern public.[3]

The treatment of the freedmen also raised serious questions about southerners' willingness to accept the verdict of the war. In late fall 1865 newly elected southern state legislatures grappled with the complicated issues related to the demise of slavery. Southern whites seemed to be most concerned with securing a stable, subservient labor force and with legally defining white-black relationships. To deal with these matters southerners passed legislation that became widely known as black codes, which granted the freed slaves some rights, such as the right to marry and to sue in court, but denied them many others, carefully spelling out the relationship between the races. White southerners may have considered these regulations the height of generosity toward the former slaves, but much of the northern public, including nearly all Republicans and many Democrats in Ohio, considered the black codes little more than transparent attempts to reenslave the freedmen. The codes flew in the face of many Ohioans' conviction that the freedmen must receive sufficient rights to protect their freedom and to prevent the planter class from using them to regain hegemony over the South. Ohio Republicans in particular absolutely refused to accept the black codes.[4]

By late 1865 these examples of southern intransigence persuaded many Republicans in Ohio that Johnson must amend his Reconstruction policy to give greater protection to the freedmen and ensure that only loyal southerners participate in Reconstruction. Probably a majority of Ohio Republicans disagreed with the president's insistence that southerners had accepted his guidelines and deserved to regain their places in Congress. Yet, because he also carefully acknowledged that only Congress could judge the qualifications of its members, most of them tended to refrain from criticizing Johnson. Their hope and expectation that Johnson would work with Congress to correct the flaws that had appeared in his policy further increased their confidence that Reconstruction would succeed.[5]

Johnson's first annual message to Congress, delivered in December 5, 1865, enhanced the optimism for a speedy yet secure reunion. The president defended his policy and the manner in which southerners had fulfilled it but stated that Congress would have to determine when southerners would return to the national legislature. Johnson reaffirmed his view that the federal government had no right to force black suffrage on any state or group of states, but he also announced "that good faith requires the security of the freedmen in their liberty and their property, their right to labor, and their right to claim the just return of their labor." Undoubtedly these declarations reassured those Ohioans who had watched the treatment of the freedmen and the passage of the black codes with ever increasing dismay. They probably assumed that Johnson would continue to endorse the activities of the Freedmen's Bureau in helping blacks adjust to their freedom. Yet, Johnson ominously also asserted that "the public interest will be best promoted if the several States will provide adequate protection and remedies for the freedmen."[6]

The vast majority of concerned Ohioans approved of Johnson's message, agreeing with one Republican editor who announced that "every word . . . bespeaks the patriot and the statesman." Of this annual message one Ohioan even gushed, "Never has there been one written that will be read with so great a degree of satisfaction by the great mass of the loyal people of the United States." Republican Representative James Garfield was less enthusiastic; he reported that the more radical members of the Ohio congressional delegation found the "message is much better than we expected."[7] Although some Republicans continued to insist upon black suffrage, most expressed confidence that Johnson had accepted congressional involvement in Reconstruction and that the two branches would cooperate on issues related to the reunification of the nation. In particular many applauded Johnson's apparent willingness to alter his Reconstruction policy as much or little as public safety required. Many

Democrats, continuing the movement begun in the summer of 1865 to claim Johnson as their leader, also endorsed the message.[8]

Immediately after receiving Johnson's message Congress showed its belief that Reconstruction was not completed and that it expected to participate in the process. On the first day of the session southerners elected to the House and Senate from states that had seceded were refused their seats. Ohio Republicans, who hoped the president and Congress would work together on Reconstruction issues, responded to this congressional action with "general rejoicing."[9] Within two weeks Congress also created the Joint Committee on Reconstruction to study Reconstruction and make recommendations to Congress.

As southerners had gone through the restoration process outlined by the president, Ohio Republicans had discerned three serious problems. First, the former Confederates, with Johnson's tacit approval, had not dealt adequately with loyal southern blacks and whites. Ohio Republicans, who counted on these groups to form a nucleus of loyalty in the South, demanded that they receive greater protection. Second, emancipation had brought confusion over the basis of representation in Congress and the electoral college. If each freed black was now to be counted as a whole person, rather than three-fifths of a person as the Constitution counted slaves, southern states would receive a windfall increase in the number of congressmen apportioned to them, and a corresponding increase of influence. Nearly all Republicans opposed this reapportionment, believing it would amount to a reward for having tried to destroy the Union. Thus, some new basis of apportionment was needed. Third, most Ohio Republicans thought Johnson had attempted to reconstruct the South too hastily and that too many rebels remained unrepentant and untrustworthy. They urged Congress to create safeguards against the return of the South until it had given compelling proof of its loyalty, and consequently, these Ohioans supported the exclusion of southerners from the Thirty-ninth Congress.[10]

Thus, most Ohio Republicans by early 1866 doubted that Johnson's policy would sufficiently safeguard the future, but in no sense had they abandoned the president. His apparent pledge to work with Congress seemed to ensure that whatever problems arose would be quickly resolved. In fact, some Ohio Republicans often harshly criticized more radical party members, such as Thaddeus Stevens and Charles Sumner, who seemed intent on creating a Reconstruction policy far more extreme than Johnson's. For example, Murat Halstead, the conservative editor of the *Cincinnati Daily Commercial*, declared with obvious exasperation that Union soldiers "did not fight to give Thad. Stevens a *carte blanche* to amend the Constitution, and they hold his sneers at the fathers of the Republic in contempt." Even the radical Richard Smith, editor of the *Cincinnati Daily Gazette*, who agreed with many of Stevens's ideas, still believed that for political reasons, "it would be well if Stevens and Sumner could be kept more in the background." Most Republicans considered continued Republican control of the nation essential for future security and thus dreaded any action that threatened party harmony.[11]

Ohio congressmen understood the basic position of their constituents but also had the opportunity to judge the president and Reconstruction from a different perspective from that of an Ohio resident. As a result some of the Republicans, who held seventeen of Ohio's nineteen seats in the House and both Senate seats, tended to be somewhat more critical of Johnson than the typical party member in Ohio. In the first two months of the congressional session, however, relations between the president and the Ohio delegation remained positive. Moderate Republicans, such as John Bingham and Rufus Spalding, endorsed the president's actions. Congressman Bingham, for example, announced that Johnson's policy was "in exact accord with the position of this House."[12] Even the far more radical John Ashley accepted the president's plans. Acknowledging their differences over the suffrage issue, Ashley nonetheless agreed to compromise his position and support the president for the sake of the party and the nation.[13]

Other Republican congressmen from Ohio stated their approval of Johnson and his policies in several speeches in which they also outlined their own ideas on Reconstruction. In early February, William Lawrence, speaking for the most conservative Republicans, called for the repudiation of the Confederate debt, securing the rights of every citizen, and unqualified loyalty as the basic necessities for a return to an "era of fraternity," but he considered "unconditional loyalty" the only indispensable prerequisite of readmission into the Union. Sharing a similar viewpoint, Columbus Delano declared that the southern state governments had virtually completed the Reconstruction process, and therefore, he sought only additional guarantees of decent treatment of the freedmen. He considered Tennessee and Arkansas ready for immediate readmission but urged a continued military presence in the rest of the South until the rebels provided clearer proof of their loyalty. Martin Welker expected more. He advocated a federal constitutional amendment that would ensure fundamental civil rights for the freedmen, would base representation in the United States House of Representatives on the number of voters, and would require repudiation of the Confederate debt. Welker wanted to make readmission contingent on ratification of such an amendment.[14]

Representative Samuel Shellabarger, struggling with the legal status of the defeated Confederate states, advanced the "forfeited rights" theory. Shellabarger contended that secession was impossible and therefore that the southern states had not left the Union. Nevertheless, they had destroyed their previous state governments, thereby forfeiting their right to congressional representation. Congress was thus required to fulfill its constitutional duty "to guaranty [*sic*] to each State a republican form of government." Although Shellabarger generally accepted the work done under Johnson's policy, he advocated a prominent role for Congress before Reconstruction could be safely ended.[15]

Republican congressmen from Ohio thus qualified their support for Johnson's Reconstruction policy. They retained great faith in the president, but they believed his policy stopped short of ensuring successful reunion. These representatives wanted Congress to assume a leading role in Reconstruction and to pass legislation to supplement and strengthen Johnson's program.[16] Because in his annual message to Congress Johnson had advocated nearly all the measures that these men considered vital, they saw no reason for the president to oppose slight modifications of his policy. In no sense did they reject Johnson as president or lose faith in him. Rather, these congressmen sought additions—particularly further protection for loyal black and white southerners—to a policy that events in the South were rapidly proving inadequate.

Ohio's junior senator, John Sherman of Mansfield, worried about a possible split between his party and the president over Reconstruction. He feared that two basic disagreements, one over whom the nation could trust to govern the South and the other over the protection of freedmen's rights, threatened party unity. Sherman worried that if Johnson refused to accept congressional modifications to his Reconstruction program, the Republicans might be forced to break with him. The senator worked diligently during the first months of 1866 to avoid exactly that.[17]

As much as Ohio Republicans worried about Reconstruction, before his February 19 veto of the Freedmen's Bureau Bill, no member of the Ohio congressional delegation and no significant number of Ohioans repudiated Johnson. They might have concluded that Congress must participate in Reconstruction, but they expected Johnson to work willingly with Congress.[18] The issue of freedmen's rights would test how much assistance Johnson would accept from Congress.

Under the provisions of Johnson's Reconstruction policy southern state governments controlled the freedmen's fate. By the beginning of 1866 concerned Ohioans had concluded that white southerners intended to utilize black codes to return the blacks to virtual servitude. In 1865 Ohio Republicans had insisted that black freedom not be abridged, and despite Johnson's refusal to denounce the black codes, nothing had changed their minds. With these Ohioans and other northerners expressing their concerns over the deteriorating situation for the freedmen, Senator Lyman Trumbull of Illinois prepared two additions to Johnson's policy designed to assist the freedmen. Trumbull and many other members of Congress thought these relatively minor changes, which he anticipated the president would approve, would enhance the chances for successful Reconstruction.

On January 5, 1866, Trumbull introduced the first of his two bills, commonly called the Freedmen's Bureau Bill, which sought to extend the life of the bureau and expand its functions. The most important, and controversial, increase of power contained in the bill gave the bureau specific authority to protect the civil rights of former slaves by ordering that civil rights cases would be tried in military, not civil, courts.[19]

By early February both houses of Congress had passed the bill. Ohio Republican members voted for it, and most Ohio political observers believed Johnson would sign it, so indicating his willingness to accept congressional assistance in the development of Reconstruction policy. They were wrong.[20]

On February 19 Johnson vetoed the measure, arguing that the extension of military power and the usurpation of the civil courts' jurisdiction exceeded peacetime constitutional limits. Reflecting the prevailing nineteenth-century abhorrence of governmental assistance to any downtrodden group for fear of creating dependency, Johnson declared that the aid to the freedmen envisioned in the bill would have "a tendency injurious alike to their character and prospects." He also denounced the cost of implementing the bill and the vast bureaucracy it would create; these would result in a dangerous centralization of power in Washington. Completely ignoring the black codes and thus dispensing with a basic purpose of the bill, Johnson saw no need for special protection for the freedmen. Perhaps most ominously for future relations with Congress, the president declared that that body should not legislate on matters dealing with the South while that section had no representation in Congress. In the absence of such representation, he announced, he himself would "present their just claims to Congress."[21]

Ohio Republicans generally reacted positively to the veto, accepting Johnson's contention that the bill was unconstitutional. They had not deserted the freedmen, but they found Johnson's arguments against this particular bill compelling. Many continued to believe that the president would demand protection of the freedmen, that he and Congress disagreed only over the best means to that end. One prominent Republican probably assessed the situation correctly when he asserted that "every member of the State Central Committee [of the Union party], every member of our county committee except one, every Union member of the Bar" endorsed Johnson's reasons for the veto. Rush R. Sloane, a conservative Republican, reported to John Sherman, "Since the veto, I have been *all* over the State [and] 7 out of 10 stand by the President." Several Republican editors echoed these sentiments. Many Republicans simply refused to believe that Johnson would abandon the freedmen and the Union party. For example, one member of the Ohio General Assembly informed John Sherman that "in this region no man can make anything by speaking harshly of the President. The people believe he wants to do right."[22] The editor of the *Ohio Repository* summarized the prevailing attitude among Ohio Republicans:

> Loyal men are found on both sides of this *supposed* great issue. For ourselves, we do not see the necessity for the bill. We already have a Freedmen's Bureau with ample powers and facilities, and *bound* to exist at least one year more if necessary. There is no fear that the President will abandon the negro to the tender mercies of his former master. He has given evidence of a disposition to deal fairly by the negro. We believe that the negro has no better friend than Andrew Johnson, and that the country contains no truer patriot. His sole purpose is to secure justice to the Union men, to the rebels, and to the negro, and to reinstate the Union as it *was* in Geographical limits as it *should be* in Constitutional rights and liberties for the whole people.[23]

These Republicans accurately asserted that the majority within their party favored the veto.[24]

Some Ohio Republicans were not as enthusiastic about the veto as their fellow citizens. Until the veto they had hoped that Johnson and Congress could develop a Reconstruction policy that would correct the flaws in the president's program. They had already abandoned the expectation that his plan would succeed unmodified, largely because Johnson appeared unwilling to demand that southerners abide by his terms of restoration. The veto, especially the part that denied the power of Congress to legislate for the unrepresented southerners, shook their conviction that Johnson would cooperate with Congress to write a new and more effective program. Some of the more radical Republicans concluded that Johnson had deserted the Union cause, but most retained some hope that the executive and the legislature could still agree on a policy and considered the veto insufficient cause to condemn the president.[25] As one editor from the Western Reserve showed, they could not believe that Johnson would destroy their greatly cherished hopes for harmony between the president and Congress. "Andrew Johnson has suffered and sacrificed too much for the preservation of the Union," he argued, "to be lightly denounced as unworthy of confidence, because his views in regard to the details of policy happen to differ from those of a majority of Congress." These Republicans made it abundantly clear, however, that if a split did occur, they would back Congress.[26]

Democrats in Ohio, unlike their political opponents, reacted to the veto with unconcealed glee. They ridiculed the bill as "the most violent and scandalous measure introduced in the present disreputable Congress" and compared the veto to Andrew Jackson's glorious veto of the bill to recharter the Bank of the United States. Many Democrats praised the president's adherence to a states' rights philosophy and his refusal to expand federal powers. They concluded that the long-lost Jacksonian was ready to return to the fold. Making no attempt to hide their pleasure at the prospect, the Democrats triumphantly announced that warfare had commenced between Johnson and the Radical Republicans, by which the Democrats meant all Republicans. Ohio Democrats concluded that with their aid the president would "become master of the situation" and the "revolutionaries'" doom would shortly follow.[27]

Johnson thus emerged with his Republican support virtually intact in Ohio, though in some cases the veto caused considerable anxiety. Meanwhile, his position with the Democrats was substantially enhanced. Some historians have asserted that northern backing of the president declined precipitously after the veto. This seems not to have been the case in Ohio.[28] The overwhelming majority of Ohioans approved of the veto, and even most of those who did not still thought that Johnson and Congress could reach an agreement on Reconstruction policy. Events in the South since the previous fall had certainly introduced doubts in the minds of many Ohio Republicans about Johnson's plan and his willingness to execute it. Many no longer considered it adequate but still believed that the president would see the need to force the South to give evidence of loyalty and would accept enough congressional assistance to achieve a speedy and secure reunion. Many Ohioans were drawing distinctions between support for Johnson's policy as the sole Reconstruction plan and support for the president as leader of the nation. By late February a growing number had doubts about the policy, but only a handful of the most radical Republicans in Ohio had rejected Johnson as president.

Johnson almost immediately challenged those who supported him when on February 22 he responded to the appeals of a crowd outside the White House with a stinging harangue against some of the most prominent Radical Republicans. Specifically, he stated that the goals Thaddeus Stevens, Charles Sumner, and Wendell Phillips were pursuing were just as treasonous in their promotion of disunion as those of Jefferson Davis and his partisans a few years before. When reports of the comments reached Ohio, Republicans could hardly believe what they read. Virtually none made any attempt to justify Johnson's remarks, although some did believe he had been provoked by Radical criticism. Most hoped the speech would soon be forgotten. A few Republicans may have taken the president's words as a declaration that he had renounced his party allegiance and rejoined the Democrats. Nevertheless, despite the frustration it caused those who wanted harmony within the Republican party, the incident appears to have had limited long-term effect on attitudes in Ohio.[29]

Despite the generally positive reaction to the veto, many Ohio Republicans were concerned about the apparent dispute between Congress and Johnson, and the speech no doubt worsened their consternation. Some blamed the Radical Republicans for the problem, arguing that they had abused Johnson and were pressing for too drastic Reconstruction measures. Others found fault with the president, citing his inconsistency. No matter who was blamed, the situation was worrisome.[30]

In an attempt to mediate the growing dispute, Senator John Sherman urged Governor Jacob Cox to go to Washington to talk with the president. Cox could then inform Ohioans of Johnson's views on working with Congress on Reconstruction legislation.[31] The veto apparently convinced the governor that he should accept Sherman's advice, and within days he went to Washington, where he stayed with Postmaster General William Dennison, another conservative Republican and a former governor of Ohio. Cox and Dennison decided that after discussing the issues with the president, Cox would write, with Johnson's approval, a public letter analyzing the president's Reconstruction policy.

In the letter, which appeared in Ohio newspapers in late February and early March, Cox reported that Johnson wanted the "earliest possible restoration of peace on the basis of loyalty." Speed was a primary consideration because the president thought that continued military rule would further alienate rather than pacify southerners. Johnson favored, according to Cox, the continuation of the Freedmen's Bureau as a means of stimulating good behavior in the South. The president intended to encourage white southerners to act responsibly toward the freedmen by promising to disband the bureau if they showed evidence that they would treat the blacks well. Johnson remained opposed to a permanent bureau because he felt it would foster hatred of both the Union and the freedmen. The president repeated to Cox his belief that the South had accepted his conditions and was ready for readmission to the Union. He suggested that Reconstruction would be complete when Congress seated southern representatives.[32]

Johnson's statements completely reassured Cox, who conveyed his optimism in a letter to the leader of the Ohio Union party: "If you could meet his straight-forward, honest look, and hear the hearty tones of his voice, as I did, I am well-assured you could believe with me, that although he may not receive personal assault with the forbearance Mr. Lincoln used to show, there is no need to fear that Andrew Johnson is not sincere in his adhesion to the principles upon which he was elected."[33] Many Republican newspapermen in Ohio also favorably reported Cox's conversation with Johnson. One for example headlined his analysis of Cox's letter "The President a Republican." A large number were reassured by Johnson's words on the issue of requiring proof of southern loyalty before readmission.[34]

The Ohio Republican delegation in Congress showed much less enthusiasm for Johnson and their governor, however. As part of their plan, Cox and Dennison sought their approval of Cox's letter and accordingly invited them to Dennison's home. After the governor read his letter, a fierce discussion erupted. Rufus Spalding, a moderate, quickly cut through Johnson's rhetoric and, in complete agreement with the facts, declared that the president had not changed his position at all. Congressman John Ashley reportedly added, "Not a damned bit." James Garfield summarized, "Cox has only put a decent suit of clothes on Johnson's nakedness."[35] Everything considered, Cox and Dennison had a rough and unsuccessful evening.

Senator John Sherman did not share this hostility toward Johnson. Throughout the late winter of 1866 he struggled to keep the Republican party together. At the same time that Governor Cox met with the president, Sherman finished a speech he hoped would restore harmony between Johnson and Congress. On February 26 he rose from his seat in the Senate and presented a lengthy plea for unity. He reaffirmed that Congress must judge the qualifications of its members but reminded his audience that the president had never challenged that right. He skillfully equated Johnson's Reconstruction policy with Lincoln's and praised the president's actions in protecting the freedmen. Sherman accepted Johnson's argument that he had no power to confer suffrage on the freedmen and then chided Congress: if it was so convinced that blacks should vote, then it should enfranchise them in the District of Columbia, where it clearly had the power to do so. In this plea to avoid a deeper split between Johnson and Congress, Sherman implored the Senate to agree with him that Johnson had the nation's best interests at heart. Nevertheless, Sherman acknowledged his concerns about the question of congressional apportionment and declared that he would "never yield that test oath to enable any man whose hand is stained with the blood of my fellow-countrymen to take a seat on the floor of the Senate." In addition, although he did not foresee such an event, he warned that "if I believed for a moment that he would seek an alliance with those who by either arms or counsel or even apathy were against their country in the recent war, and will turn over to them the high powers intrusted to him by the Union party, then, sir, he is dishonored, and will receive no assistance from me."[36] Significantly, Sherman announced that he would do nothing to drive the president away, nor would he support others who did.

The response to the speech must have raised Sherman's spirits. Nearly fifty Ohioans wrote to him. One denounced his speech; the rest congratulated him on a job well done and, more important, thanked him for his efforts to save the country, for the country is precisely what they saw at stake in the difficulties between Congress and Johnson. The laudatory phrases ranged from "productive of much good" to "a very remarkable & noble production . . . a grand, cool, logical production."[37]

Sherman's efforts seem to have encouraged those who longed for party unity. In early March several Ohio Republicans expressed restored hopes for greater harmony in the days ahead. They apparently were convinced that Johnson now had a better understanding of what they expected of him and that he would respond positively. They noted that there were limits to their indulgence, however, and warned that the efforts to work with Johnson must not require "any sacrifice of principle."[38]

In mid-March 1866 the Civil Rights Bill, the second of the two measures Senator Trumbull sponsored as amendments to Johnson's policy, precipitated a new crisis between Johnson and Congress. The bill provided for federal protection of the freedmen's civil rights. To forestall a veto on constitutional or any other grounds, Trumbull discussed the legislation with Johnson and concluded that the president approved the bill and favored its passage. Still, according to the same logic he had used to justify vetoing the Freedmen's Bureau Bill, it seemed likely that Johnson would reject the Civil Rights Bill, and of course, he did precisely that.

Some Ohio Republicans and most Democrats believed that the bill exceeded constitutional limits, but nearly all Republicans in the state favored action to protect the freedmen from virtual reenslavement under the black codes. Republican state senator E.B. Sadler reflected the dominant attitude in his party when he stated that the protection of the freedmen's civil rights was essential to national security and could not be compromised. He went a bit farther than most Ohioans when he concluded, "If the President vetoes the Civil rights bill, I believe we shall be obliged to draw our swords and throw away the scabbards." W.C. Howells, a journalist from the Western Reserve, made the point even more sharply, warning that if Johnson did not sign the bill, Republicans would have no choice but to "open the war with him at once and give him the hot end of the poker."[39]

Governor Cox realized the critical situation in Ohio and wrote the president a long letter urging him to sign the Civil Rights Bill. He warned Johnson that many Ohioans believed in the principle of fair treatment for blacks expressed in the bill, and they wanted it to be signed.[40] He admitted that they did not fully comprehend that the expansion of federal powers called for in the bill might be unconstitutional. Cox himself shared many of the president's doubts about the bill. Nevertheless, he suggested to Johnson that "under these circumstances, and especially of the fact that the persistent efforts which have been made by the extremists to create distrust of your motives and intentions are recoiling, and every day adds to the strength of your position before the country, I believe it would be well to *strain a point* in order to meet the popular spirit and impulse rather than to make a strict construction of duty the other way."[41]

Johnson, however, failed to heed this sound advice and vetoed the bill. By this action he destroyed most of the remaining Republican support in Ohio for his policy as the sole basis of Reconstruction. The vast majority of Republicans now looked to Congress for a policy that would reconstruct the South in line with the requirements they had set in 1865 and still held. Even though many of these Ohioans still expected that Johnson would remain a trustworthy leader, some Republicans also began to lose confidence in Johnson as the nation's leader.

Johnson accomplished these results more by the content of his veto message than by the veto itself. Many Ohioans agreed with Governor Cox that the bill dangerously enlarged federal power and doubted its constitutionality.[42] At the same time, one of the basic requirements of Reconstruction, in the view of Ohio Republicans, was that freedmen not be forced back into virtual bondage. The Civil Rights Bill, whatever its flaws, gave Congress the power to secure this objective, and thus many approved of the bill's basic goal. In his veto message Johnson did not merely attack the possible unconstitutionality of the measure; more significantly, he denied the right of Congress to legislate on matters related to the treatment of the freedmen. It was precisely this point that most antagonized the bill's supporters in Ohio, who agreed with the views expressed by the editor of the *Daily Zanesville Courier.* Johnson's objections were so sweeping, he stated, that they left the party with "but little hope that he will favor any national measure intended for the protection of the freedmen against State class legislation."[43]

For some Republicans the veto settled the issue of whom to trust with leadership of the Reconstruction program. They concluded that Johnson had deserted his party by vetoing the Civil Rights Bill and had clearly "thrown himself into the embraces of the copperheads and rebels." Congress alone could be trusted to lead the country safely through the Reconstruction crisis. Some who had tolerated or even endorsed the Freedmen's Bureau Bill veto now rejected Johnson completely and joined the small group that had already abandoned him.[44] State senator Warner Bateman's reaction typified the rejections of Johnson. "I have lost faith entirely with the President," he wrote. "He intends in my judgment to betray us. . . . I cannot but regard his vetoes as an escape from all his promises of protection to the freedmen on the hypocritical pretense of constitutional objection. His last message hands the freedmen over helplessly to the tender mercies of state legislation and his exasperated master. So we go."[45]

Although the number of Ohio Republicans who completely repudiated Johnson's presidency was growing and would increase dramatically over the next three months, care should be exercised not to exaggerate their numbers in late March and early April 1866. Conservative and moderate Republicans, who continued to hope Johnson and Congress would agree on a plan to protect the freedmen, approved of or at least tolerated the veto. Many hoped that Johnson and Congress would somehow avoid a complete break. A Cincinnatian, however, raised the ominous possibility that the struggle might take a definite turn for the worse; he pleaded with Ohio's junior senator, "For God's sake battle against any violence or conflict—any struggle of force between Congress and the President. Our country needs rest and repose." Rumors of violence had also surfaced in Cleveland and were reported to James Garfield. "There is some apprehension," the writer declared, "that Johnson, during the Summer Congressional interregnum, may attempt a coup d'état. I hope not. I can scarcely believe he will attempt so bold and dangerous a course. If he should try it, the radicals, backed by the governors of the loyal states, could wage fearful war against him."[46]

Immediately after the veto, then, President Johnson retained solid but declining political support in Ohio. Radical Republicans tended to reject both his Reconstruction policy and his personal integrity. The more numerous and influential moderate and conservative Republicans, however, generally had faith in Johnson as president, although they had concluded that by itself Johnson's Reconstruction policy would fail. Some moderate Republicans began to lose faith in Johnson as president. Still, had he cooperated with Congress, he could easily have regained their support.[47]

In fact, after Congress overrode Johnson's veto of the Civil Rights Bill, tempers cooled and hopes for better relations between the president and Congress rose again. For much of the spring some Ohio Republicans expressed optimism that Johnson would not unite with the Democrats and that the nation might yet enjoy peace and harmony. Those Republicans who had concluded that Johnson had abandoned them, however, expected only the worst from the man they were now openly calling a traitor.[48]

In addition to overriding the veto, Congress responded to the constitutional question by passing the Fourteenth Amendment as its alternative to Johnson's policy. Nearly all Ohio Republicans expressed satisfaction with the proposed amendment because it almost exactly mirrored their Reconstruction demands, first declared in mid-1865. For example, the first section—which defined American citizenship, made blacks citizens, and guaranteed them equal protection of the laws—perfectly fit the Ohio Republicans' requirement that the freedmen be secure in the enjoyment of basic civil rights. More important, the Republicans hoped that these rights would prevent southern planters from using the labor of the former slaves to regain political ascendancy in the South, becoming a threat to the country's existence once again. The amendment promised to accomplish this objective.[49]

The second clause dealt with the difficult problem of congressional apportionment. The legislators in Washington faced a fearful dilemma. They knew that northerners would not tolerate the nationwide enfranchisement of blacks. Yet, if total population remained the key determinant in apportioning the House of Representatives and if the freedmen did not vote but were counted as whole persons, southern representation in Congress would increase by up to fifteen members. This increase would allow northern and southern Democrats to wrest control of Congress from the Republicans. If that occurred, Republicans feared for the nation, the freedmen, and their own political futures, though not necessarily in that order.

Republicans in Ohio had anguished over this matter for months. Some advocated basing representation on total population, but others realized that that option did not solve the problem of the windfall increase southerners would receive.[50] Some supporters of black enfranchisement declared that the nation should simply demand that southerners grant black males the right to vote. Surely, one Ohioan declared, black voters would be as well informed as most Democrats, who "don't know any more about politics than the horse they ride to the election."[51] One Ohio Republican defended forcing black suffrage on the South while refusing to do the same in the North by insisting that national security required loyal black voters in the disloyal South but that no such need existed in the North.

Republican opponents of black suffrage spoke just as fervently against the extension of voting rights. They charged that blacks lacked the intelligence or education needed to cast reasoned ballots and, to refute the position that loyal black votes were needed to reconstruct the South, declared that "a party sustained by black votes will not grow old." Some also endorsed Johnson's argument that the federal government lacked the right to require black suffrage anywhere. Political considerations also dictated to some. One editor openly acknowledged his opposition to black suffrage because it "might have defeated the whole [amendment in Congress]. We are content for the present to accept that which is practical and obtainable."[52]

Indeed, most Republicans in Ohio found the notion of forcing black suffrage too radical. Many favored basing representation on the number of voters.[53] This strategy had the advantage of allowing individual states to decide the matter. Republicans hoped the incentive of greater congressional representation would persuade southerners to adopt some form of black voting. And if they did not, then they might actually lose some congressional seats, for not even three-fifths of the blacks would be counted. In addition, some Ohio Republicans optimistically asserted that this form of apportionment would remove the vexatious issue from future political contests. One from Ravenna stated the case for many: "Such an amendment would settle the Negro Suffrage question for if the South would be content with the meager representation they would be entitled to without negro suffrage, the North ought to be satisfied."[54]

In the end Congress fashioned a shrewd compromise, well within the Republican mainstream in Ohio. Representation would be based on total population. States would continue to set suffrage qualifications, but any state that chose to deny any group of adult male citizens the right to vote would have its representation in Congress reduced by the percentage of all adult males who were disfranchised.

This solution had enormous political attractions for most Ohio Republicans. It eliminated the windfall increase in southern representation that resulted from making blacks citizens. By allowing states to determine their own voting requirements, it provided the party with a defense against charges of being the party of black suffrage. At the same time, logic suggested that if southern states did enact black suffrage, the new voters would cast ballots for Republicans, and voting by loyal blacks, working with the Republicans, would help secure a future free of sectional strife. W.D. Bickham, editor of the *Dayton Daily Journal*, succinctly summed up the value of black votes to the Republican party in the South. The amendment, he wrote, "secures, we are confident, the supremacy of the Republican Union party for many years to come."[55]

Ohio Republicans thus endorsed a proposal that could lead to black voting, which they had refused to support in 1865. They were moved by the realities of Reconstruction. Ohio Republicans had insisted in 1865 that only loyal southerners might vote and hold office. They expected that a large number of loyal white southerners would move into the postwar political vacuum and take control of southern politics. Over the next year they learned that there were too few loyal southern whites to fill the gap and that Johnson was willing to let unpardoned and unrepentant traitors reassert their political muscle. Worse, the South might have greater representation in Congress than it had before secession. Given two imperfect options, these Republicans, despite their racial biases, chose to accept the possibility of black suffrage. Perhaps they also realized that Ohio, because of the relatively few blacks living there, could refuse to enfranchise blacks and yet avoid any meaningful penalty, which is precisely what happened in 1867 and after. Therefore, the amendment posed no immediate threat to white supremacy in Ohio. Furthermore, these Ohioans seem to have been convinced that the amendment was a Reconstruction measure and so would really be enforced only in the South. Requiring southerners, if they wanted increased representation in Congress, to enfranchise at least some blacks seemed to be a reasonable and necessary means to overcome Johnson's treachery and the shortage of loyal white southern voters. Republicans believed the provision would enable the nation to safeguard the fruits of victory.

After dealing with the sticky issue of representation, Congress addressed the matter of amnesty in the third section of the proposed amendment. Nearly all Republicans had criticized Johnson's leniency in granting pardons. They wanted more stringent requirements to protect the nation from the threat of a resurrected Confederacy. After protracted and often bitter debate among the Republicans over disfranchising white rebels or denying them the right to hold public office, Congress approved a more conservative third section that banned from state or federal officeholding any person who had previously taken an oath to support the Constitution and then participated in the rebellion against the United States. Only Congress, not the president, could remove this disability by a two-thirds vote in both houses.

Some Ohio Republicans sided with the Radicals in Congress, who worked for a voting disability, but most readily accepted the more limited restriction on officeholding only. It fit squarely with their demand that those responsible for the rebellion not regain political power in the South until they had provided proof of future loyalty, something that was sorely lacking up to mid-1866.[56] In fact, virtually all Republicans in Ohio approved the entire amendment. The provisions promised to remedy the flaws in Johnson's policy, to guarantee that nobody would benefit from having supported the rebellion, and to ensure peace. Most agreed with the editor of the *Marietta Register* when he wrote, "It is a long step ahead. No milder terms can be yielded to the ex-rebels, by people who have at heart the welfare of the country."[57]

One other critical factor influenced approval of the proposed amendment: Republicans understood that this Reconstruction plan originated in Congress and thus constituted the final conditions for restoration. Ohioans and northerners in general wanted as speedy a solution to the national crisis as possible considering the need to require appropriate safeguards. This amendment contained sufficient precautions and requirements. Furthermore, because Congress implied that southern ratification would result in readmission, it promised a quick end to the Reconstruction process.[58] The hope of an end to all the turmoil of war and its aftermath greatly appealed to most Ohioans. The editor of the *Sandusky Daily Commercial Register* expressed well the common longing for peace: "We are forced to read and talk at home and abroad of vital issues; we are forced to meet issues and to settle issues—a tax upon the vitality of a people which only a herculean race could withstand. . . . We are tired of rugged issues and earnest convictions. We are weary of this constant service at the front, and long for a quiet nook, out of range, where the thunder of distant battle cannot come."[59]

As the widespread acceptance of the proposed amendment implies, it was a moderate, compromise measure. Radical Republican congressmen had failed to force their ideas into the amendment.[60] Mainstream Republicans were therefore encouraged to support the proposal. With a sense of personal satisfaction, Governor Jacob Cox, whose conservatism had angered some of the Radicals, explained his advocacy of the amendment, "Since the party has made undoubted progress in my direction within the past year, I can afford to be easily suited."[61] Ohio Republicans hoped and assumed that southerners would realize that this policy was the will of the majority party, not the work of a radical fringe group, and that the South would accept its provisions.

Governor Cox understood that his constituents supported the amendment, and so he pleaded with Johnson to accept it. With good reason Cox was convinced that if he endorsed the amendment, the president could reclaim the personal support lost during the previous months and unite with moderate Republicans to overpower the radical wing of the party completely.[62] The Governor understood that the proposed amendment was quite similar to Johnson's original plan and that Ohio Republicans still had the same requirements of a Reconstruction program.

That so conservative a Republican as Cox favored ratification of the proposed amendment should have alerted Johnson to the state of the northern mind. If it did, he ignored the news. On June 22 the president informed Congress that Secretary of State Seward had forwarded the amendment to the states but that Seward's actions "are to be considered as purely ministerial, and in no sense whatsoever committing the Executive to an approval or a recommendation of the amendment to the State legislatures or the people." Johnson, in fact, urged southern legislatures to reject the proposed amendment.[63]

Johnson's actions undercut the efforts of those moderate and conservative Ohio Republicans who had worked to maintain party unity and backing of the president. A Columbus editor, for example, noted that he had been troubled by many of Johnson's vetoes and statements but, nonetheless, in the interest of party harmony, had not "printed anything offensive in reference to the President." Others tried in vain to bridge the growing gulf between themselves and the president.[64]

The decline in the president's support had resumed in late April when he made another intemperate attack on Republicans in Congress. Johnson's rhetoric again infuriated Ohio Republicans, one of whom reported that "my cheeks burn after each perusal" of Johnson's speech.[65] It was Johnson's position on the proposed amendment, however, not his public statements, that was destroying his relationship with Ohio Republicans.[66] Despite all that had transpired up to June 1866, Ohio Republicans would probably have continued to support him if Johnson had endorsed the proposed constitutional amendment, but he refused. After Congress passed what seemed to them to be a fair and reasonable compromise, Johnson, who had "veto on the brain," decided to use the power of his office to thwart the national will. Republican acceptance of Johnson's policy as the sole means of reconstructing the nation had long since disappeared. Now party support of the Tennessean as the leader of the nation virtually vanished.[67] Moderate and conservative Republicans, unwilling to abandon the president solely over the issue of freedmen's rights, rejected him because he tried to sabotage an amendment that they believed essential to successful, secure reunion. They joined the Radical Republicans, who had already rejected Johnson because of his stand against civil rights for blacks. Only one more step was required to shatter all remaining ties between the president and his party.

Three days after Johnson's message to Congress, a call went out with his knowledge and approval for a "National Union Convention." This meeting was the culmination of months of scheming and negotiating by some of Johnson's backers who hoped to establish a national party based on support for the president's Reconstruction policy. Johnson indicated his endorsement of the movement by announcing that he would work in the coming fall elections to defeat any Republicans who opposed "my policy."[68]

Former Congressman Lewis D. Campbell led the movement in Ohio to form the new party. Campbell had supported the Union war effort, but his states' rights and racial philosophies were more attuned to those of Johnson and the Democrats than to those of Ohio Republicans. He had pressed the issue of a new political alliance as early as January 1866, when he wrote to Johnson's son-in- law:

> The only practical question left is whether the impractical radical zealots who seem to be "instigated by the Devil and fatally bent on mischief" shall gobble us all up and run us on their infernal train to national perdition, or whether fair minded men will assert their independence and organize a party *on the basis of the President's patriotic policy* which is heartily approved by the mass of the people. The President himself can best give us a solution of this question. He must sooner or later accept the *fact* that the great Union party has *fulfilled its mission*—that although a beneficial institution in the *past* composed of elements that were in many respects

discordant, it cannot continue in the new order of things to do good in the future.[69]

Campbell also insisted that the success of Johnson's Reconstruction policy required a purge of all radical influence from the cabinet. "If [Johnson] has the remotest idea," Campbell further asserted, "that he will ever be accepted as a *leader* among the radicals (even if he could adopt their vagaries) he should at once be relieved of such a delusion. I know these men better than he does, and I know they hate him."[70]

Campbell hoped to create a new party, unaligned with either existing organization but drawing support from both. Many Democratic leaders in Ohio seem to have been quite interested in forging a political alliance with others who backed Johnson's programs. For example, George Hunt Pendleton, the 1864 Democratic vice-presidential candidate, told Johnson that the Ohio Democrats had "high hopes" for the president's Reconstruction policy. In February 1866 George Morgan, the defeated gubernatorial candidate in 1865, congratulated Johnson for "discharging your great trust" so well. Morgan and most Ohio Democrats wholeheartedly approved of the vetoes of the Freedmen's Bureau and Civil Rights bills and Johnson's denunciation of the proposed amendment.[71] Democratic editors also revealed a strong desire to claim Johnson as their president. Democrats rarely split over Johnson's vetoes, his virulent speeches, and his attitude toward Congress, as Republicans often did. They cheered his attacks on Radical Republicans. Some Democrats were reluctant to endorse Johnson because they believed he had usurped too many state prerogatives with his Reconstruction policy. Ultimately, though, even they, perhaps for lack of an alternative, backed the president. By July, when Johnson and the Republicans parted company, the Democrats had overwhelmingly accepted hs leadership.[72]

Campbell and R.P.L. Baber, another Johnson defender, realized that although more and more Democrats were rallying behind the president, a new party would succeed only if its basic allegiance come from the Republican party. They knew that if the public connected the movement with an attempt to rebuild the fortunes of the Democratic party, it would fail. Campbell and Baber, therefore, worked within the Republican party, seeking to keep the majority faithful to Johnson and at the same time to drive the Radicals out into the political wilderness.[73]

A key component of Campbell's strategy was to convince Governor Cox of the need for a new conservative party. He warned Cox in March that the gulf between Johnson and Congress was too wide to bridge and urged him to join a new political coalition. "If *we* do not pursue the course," he declared, "the Democrats will proceed with their organization and adopt the President's policy—thereby appropriating to themselves *our thunder.*" The governor, however, rejected Campbell's pleas.[74]

In mid-June the Republicans held their state convention; there Campbell continued his efforts to have the party follow Johnson's leadership. A fair number of delegates sought either an endorsement of Johnson or resolutions that would promote harmony between the president's supporters and those who favored Congress. Even Senator John Sherman apparently had lingering hopes for cooperation between the factions.[75] The few Johnson supporters, however, were quickly routed by the majority of the delegates who supported Congress and believed that the proposed Fourteenth Amendment offered the best hope for successful Reconstruction and for Republican victories in the fall elections. With Johnson's position on the amendment clear, the delegates readily endorsed Congress and the proposed amendment and implicitly repudiated Johnson.[76] Campbell, having lost in Columbus, denounced the party platform and joined others in concentrating on the National Union movement.[77]

Shortly after the Republican convention in Ohio, Johnson openly endorsed the National Union movement. Although the Ohio delegation to the National Union Convention included a handful of Republicans, for all practical purposes Johnson's support for the movement provoked nearly all Ohio Republicans to reject him completely.[78] The president had deserted Ohio Republicans.

The basic dispute concerned future security. Johnson argued that the former Confederates had proved their loyalty by fulfilling the requirements of his Reconstruction policy and thus merited readmission into the Union. Ohio Republicans firmly held that the South had not sufficiently acknowledged the wickedness of secession or given solid proof of future loyalty. They considered the National Union movement a threat to national welfare because it could return disloyal southerners to power in Washington. Johnson, these Ohioans concluded, had finally shown his true principles. He would not demand security for the future and so would allow the fruits of victory to be lost. The typical politically concerned Ohio Republican could not tolerate this situation, and he and the president split forever. The editorial Murat Halstead wrote in the *Cincinnati Daily Commercial* when he finally split from Johnson expressed the thinking of many:

> We have not heretofore been convinced that the President really accepted the doctrine of political equality of rebels

> with loyal men, and demanded the restoration of the people and States that were in the Confederacy, unconditionally to the full rights of citizenship and Statehood enjoyed before they experimented in treason. His drift, however, seems to be in that direction, and his footing in the dangerous current in which he is involved, precarious. Between the President in this questionable shape and Congress growing moderate from the leadership that wasted months in political intemperance, the choice is easy; and the almost universal support given by the people who were true in the trials of war, to the defined policy of Congress, rather than to the indefinite hostility of the President, is prompted no less by common instincts of patriotism than by clearest intelligence.[79]

The bitterness felt by many Republican editors who had stayed with Johnson in the hope that he would work with Congress burst forth from the editor of the *Scioto Gazette.* "Andrew Johnson, the man made President of the United States by John Wilkes Booth," he lamented, "has thrown off all disguise and boldly gone over to the party of which Booth was a worthy and honored member. . . . He stands forth now in his true colors, the prince of demagogues, the friend of rebels, the villifier of those who have saved the country in its hour of need."[80]

Warner Bateman, an important local politician from the Cincinnati area, also placed the blame for the final break squarely on Johnson in a letter to John Sherman: "When you last wrote me you were hopeful of Johnson and harmony between him and the Union party. Has not the last ground for such hope been at last removed—has not Johnson shown a determined purpose to reconcile no difference[?] The Democracy seem to have adopted him and he seems at last to be disposed to fall into their embrace." Bateman closed his letter with a most pertinent question, "How does Dennison stand?"[81]

As Bateman must have realized, the reaction of Postmaster General William Dennison would typify that of the most conservative Republicans who had stuck with Johnson until he embraced the National Union movement. Dennison resigned from the cabinet in protest. His departure left Secretary of War Stanton the only genuine Republican in that group.[82] The former governor of Ohio explained his abandonment of Johnson: "I waited patiently for a reconciliation between the President and our friends in Congress and spared no effort to that end. But the President's avowed opposition to the Constitutional Amendment and his approval of the Phil. [National Union] convention left me no room to doubt his purpose of separating from the Union party. To have longer remained in his Cabinet, under such circumstances, could only have been at the sacrifice of my manhood and duty to my party and the country. I therefore resigned and am satisfied I did right."[83]

Johnson thus found himself thoroughly isolated from his own party, and he had only himself to blame for this sad predicament. In 1865 Ohio Republicans had declared their requirements of a Reconstruction policy. Johnson failed to recognize how deeply these convictions were held. Instead, he pursued his own course. His vetoes of the Freedmen's Bureau and Civil Rights bills in February and March alienated the Radicals, who were sincerely concerned about the treatment of the freedmen. The majority of Ohioans cared much less about the blacks' fate and accepted the vetoes, but they could not be so cavalier on the issues of southern loyalty and future security. These were fundamental concerns. When Johnson urged southerners to reject the proposed constitutional amendment, which was specifically designed to address these fears, and when he approved the National Union movement, these Ohioans realized that the president had deserted them. The major cause of the split, then, was not Johnson's attitude toward the freedmen, exemplified by his vetoes, but his refusal to demand loyalty from the former slaveholders and thus to provide for a peaceful future. Ohio Republicans simply would not accept immediate, unconditional restoration of the South into the Union. They still believed that the terms they had endorsed in 1865, which were now incorporated into the Fourteenth Amendment, would result in successful reunion. The approaching 1866 congressional elections would provide Ohio voters with the opportunity to choose between Johnson's Reconstruction policy and that of Congress.

4
STANDING FIRM

> One great question to be decided is whether the people of this country shall continue, through their representatives in Congress, to make their own laws or whether this power shall be yielded to one man and he the friend, and sympathizer, and co-worker with those who lately sought and labored to destroy this free government.
>
> —*Miami Union*, 1866

Tremendous uncertainty about Reconstruction accompanied Johnson's desertion of the Republicans in the summer of 1866. Northern Republicans had to concede that Johnson had aligned himself with prewar Democrats in both the North and South, creating the possibility of a political coalition that would rally behind his Reconstruction policy. In the 1866 congressional election voters would have the opportunity to endorse the policy of either Congress or the president. Throughout the North, but particularly in Ohio, the elections would amount to a referendum on Reconstruction. No other issues intruded, and if contemporary Ohioans analyzed the election correctly, neither did factors such as religion, economics, or ethnicity. When the campaign ended, Ohio voters had endorsed the Fourteenth Amendment as the final terms of Reconstruction. By November 1866 the future seemed bright, if the South had the wisdom to accept the congressional policy.

Ohio Democrats began political activity in 1866 by holding their state convention in May. The struggle between Johnson and the Republicans in Congress led to great optimism among the Democrats; Clement Vallandigham, for example, claimed, "We have the game in our hands. Let us play it boldly and strongly." The Democrats hoped that many conservative Republicans would be disgusted with the actions of the Radical Republicans and would follow Johnson into the Democratic party when he completely broke with Congress. The party's call for its convention underscored their strategy by inviting all Ohioans who opposed the centralization of power in Washington and black suffrage to join them in "rescuing the country from the malignants." The convention translated that tone into a platform that endorsed the president's Reconstruction program and his attempts to gain immediate representation in Congress for the southern states. By the close of the convention the Democrats had agreed to campaign on three issues: support for Johnson, opposition to the enfranchisement of blacks, and the despotism of Congress.[1]

A few weeks later, on June 20, Ohio Republicans gathered at their state convention in Columbus in a highly charged atmosphere. The events of the spring had resulted in a nearly complete rejection of Johnson's Reconstruction policy, but the delegates realized that they could not merely denounce Johnson. They needed some alternative plan on which to campaign. Many had impatiently pleaded with their representatives in Washington to have Congress write a policy. When the proposed amendment passed in early June, most Ohio Republicans immediately recognized that it would make an ideal platform.[2]

The Republicans also debated whether they should formally endorse or attack the president. At the time of the convention he had yet to urge southerners to reject the Fourteenth Amendment, and a small but determined group of Republicans intended to seek an endorsement of his policy by the delegates.[3] The overwhelming majority of the delegates opposed such a stand, but they worried that Johnson's men might somehow succeed. One anxious member of the majority warned Congressman Garfield that "great efforts are being made to Johnsonize our coming state convention and to have such a program there laid down as will make it decidedly obnoxious to you and every true honest Union man in Ohio."[4] Party moderates also had to contend with the Radicals who sought platform planks that not only condemned the president but also advocated black suffrage.[5]

During the platform debates, Governor Cox persuaded Johnson's supporters not to press for a vote to endorse presidential policy, because, as Cox explained to the president, "the result would have been unsatisfactory in every way." At the same time the Radicals relented on their demands for black suffrage and denunciation of Johnson, and the party passed a short platform whose only significant plank endorsed the proposed Fourteenth Amendment "as a liberal, wise and patriotic" Reconstruction program.[6]

A.P. Denny, an editor from west-central Ohio, accurately analyzed the reasons the party chose to adopt a compromise platform: "Though many might have individually desired a more ultra platform, few can find fault. The Union party feels that the responsibility of the country's salvation rests upon it. It must therefore move steadily forward, it may be slowly, but none the less surely, to the high goal it keeps in view."[7] He might have added that the platform also fairly represented the wishes of the overwhelming majority of Republicans. With the moderates firmly in control, the party embarked on a campaign based almost exclusively upon approval of Congress and the proposed amendment as the solution to the Reconstruction crisis and the best means to gain the security that the majority of Ohioans so dearly wanted.

The party's decision did not please the president. Cox tried to placate him with an astute analysis of the platform:

> The platform adopted here is the result of this compromise, and is as I believe the best attainable at the present moment. It is better for what it omits than for what it contains. You will notice that it does *not* affirm that the acceptance of the constitutional amendment shall be a condition precedent to representation. It does not endorse any *expected* measures which Congress may add to its programme. It does not advocate or advise negro suffrage. It does not endorse any specific act of Congress whatsoever, but simply & solely the *amendment as it stands* & makes it a party measure in Ohio to vote for it.

The governor continued, noting that with prudence, patience, and an endorsement of the proposed amendment the president could yet win back the support of most Ohio Republicans. He suggested that "the friends of your administration can well afford to make no quarrels with the action of the convention, & to cooperate cheerfully in the state canvass."[8]

Johnson received precisely the opposite advice from Lewis Campbell and R.P.L. Baber, two of his most vocal advocates. Baber assailed the Radicals for avoiding the issues of black suffrage and southern representation in Congress, charging that they actually favored black voting and intended to deny southerners seats in the next session of Congress but did not have the courage to say so. He informed the president that the Radicals "should be defeated at all hazards by the union of those opposed to the obstruction policy." Baber was hinting that he and others were ready to work with the Democrats to defeat the Radicals. Campbell agreed completely. He told Johnson that the delegates had failed to support the president because the Radicals controlled so many patronage positions and the officeholders were afraid of losing their jobs if they defied them and because a Colonel Burnett had told the convention of a recent conversation with Johnson in which the president had stated that he would be satisfied with a platform that endorsed the proposed amendment. That announcement, Campbell said, "knocked all the calculations of your friends in the head, and completely disconcerted all the plans which I with others had been laboring for for many months."[9] Campbell believed that the president's friends could win congressional seats that fall only if Johnson began to wield his appointment power on their behalf.

In fact as early as January 1866 Campbell had recommended that Johnson check the Radicals' supposed control over patronage, beginning with a purge of cabinet members. The Ohioan assured the president that "your policy of reconstructing the *Union* will never prove a success, until you reconstruct your Cabinet and make it a *unit.*" Two months later Baber announced that the president's friends were "ready for the fight in Ohio but want our enemy deprived of the patronage." Baber explained to Secretary of State William Seward that

> the patronage of the Government should be used so as to oust the radical incumbents and place this lever in the hands of the friends of the Administration in each Congressional District and we will Secure the election of the *right* men in the fall elections. . . .
>
> The true policy is to fill all positions with competent Army men whom the Senate dare not reject. We can carry two thirds of the nominations for Congress with this help provided some constitutional law is passed to protect Freedmen in their rights denied by the State Courts.[10]

Johnson paid some attention to this advice, for by May some Ohio Republicans were complaining to their congressmen about Johnson's nomination of "rampant, foul mouthed Copperhead[s]" to federal positions in Ohio. Still, in the early summer the president's men urged greater exertions to reward his allies and punish the Radicals. Again Johnson responded, further widening the gulf between him and the mass of Republicans. By late summer 1866 virtually all Republican officeholders who had criticized the president feared that their tenure in office was about to end. They worried about the situation for personal reasons and because they agreed with Johnson's men that control over patronage jobs would help determine the outcome of elections. The issue continued to exacerbate relations between Johnson and the Republicans until he left office.[11]

Both Baber and Campbell realized that wise utilization of the patronage power alone would not result in the election of candidates who approved of the president's Reconstruction program. Both had been active, therefore, in the movement to create a new party whose basic purpose was to defeat anti-Johnson Republicans and restore the Union on the basis of Johnson's policy. Campbell understood that conservative Republicans must control and dominate the new National Union party. Given the general distrust of Democrats by northern Republicans, the National Union movement could not afford to be or appear to be merely an attempt to rejuvenate the Democratic party. Nevertheless, the movement could not succeed without the Democrats either.[12]

As their analyses of the Ohio Republican Convention indicate, Baber and Campbell had decided to continue the fight over Reconstruction by working with the emerging National Union party. On June 25 the six-member Executive Committee of the National Union Club announced a National Union Convention to meet in Philadelphia on August 14. It urged the participation of all who "sustain the Administration in maintaining unbroken the union of the States under the Constitution which our fathers established." More specifically, the National Union movement advocated immediate, unconditional restoration of southern states into the Union and full control by southerners over the freedmen. Proponents of the movement also denounced the "sad lack of statesmanship" in Congress for its refusal to admit representatives from the South. Movement leaders were so confident of success that one promised Johnson that "if we do not beat a majority of the radical members of Congress in Ohio this fall I will agree to maul rails for a livelihood."[13]

Only a few Ohio Republicans openly endorsed the National Union movement, but many Democrats in the state saw it as a possible way to rehabilitate their party, though they also feared that their party identity could be lost if they merged with the new party. Reflecting the uncertainty in Democratic ranks, the state central committee on July 12 refused to appoint delegates to the National Union Convention and then two days later reversed itself. The party appointed several prominent Peace Democrats, including former U.S. Senator William Allen, George Hunt Pendleton, and Clement L. Vallandigham, to serve as convention delegates, thus at least partly fulfilling Republican predictions that Coppperheads would control the convention. Despite official party support for the National Union movement, not all Democrats agreed to cooperate with the upstart organization.[14]

Reaction to the National Union Convention, which met in Philadelphia, August 13-16, generally followed party lines. Democrats typically praised, and Republicans typically condemned the movement.[15] Despite all the efforts and high hopes of its originators, the

National Union movement amounted to little more than "a farce and a fizzle."[16] About the only enduring effect of what might have been a formidable alliance was to convince a few Republicans that Johnson and Congress would never cooperate on Reconstruction.[17]

Other events, outside Ohio, helped determine the outcome of the second straight election in the state to be dominated by Reconstruction-related issues. On April 30 and May 1 a group of southern whites, assisted by some Memphis police, destroyed part of the black section of that city, killing forty-six blacks. The blatant murder of innocent blacks appalled Ohio Republicans and seemed to prove their contention that white southerners, left to their own devices, would never deal fairly with the freedmen. The episode thus intensified the conviction that the proposed constitutional amendment was essential to the freedmen's and the nation's future.[18]

In part because Johnson had a direct role, the riot that occurred in New Orleans on July 30 seemed even more appalling. That summer Louisiana politics were in turmoil. Former Confederates had used Johnson's Reconstruction program to regain control of the state. Meanwhile, loyal whites and blacks reconvened the state constitutional convention in order to gain readmission into the Union. With the president's apparent approval, white conservatives decided to arrest the convention delegates. Assisted by local police they attacked the convention delegates on July 30. Despite the delegates' attempts to surrender, the mob fired into the building and at delegates and others as they fled, killing 40 delegates and supporters—both black and white—and wounding over 130.[19]

The senseless murder of peaceful, pro-Union southerners shocked and dismayed northerners. The episode seemed to verify Republican fears that without federal protection loyal southerners of both races had little chance of survival in the South. Johnson's behavior seemed reprehensible. Rather than support the military in its peace-keeping function, he had undercut it and given the forces of violence a license to kill. The entire dreadful affair aided northern Republicans, who frequently reminded voters that the nation could expect more "New Orleanses" if the country voted for a Democratic Congress that approved of Johnson's plan of immediate restoration. Republicans could hardly have asked for better proof that the rebels had not yet accepted the verdict of the war or understood the basic position of the North on the treatment of loyal blacks and whites.[20] Like other northern Republicans, those in Ohio considered the New Orleans riot stark confirmation that Johnson's Reconstruction policy had allowed unrepentant, disloyal Confederates to regain political control of the South. The violence, called by some the logical "fruit" of Johnson's program, revealed the bankruptcy of the president's pledge to restore the Union peacefully. Riots such as the one in New Orleans proved that peace did not exist in the South. Indeed, at least one Ohio Republican concluded that the riot showed southerners must once again be crushed militarily before they could be trusted:

> Excitement is growing intense, and I fear we are on the eve of another war; and we must have another fight; the sooner the better for liberty, free speech & free press have no show now; and if matters continue as they are now going, in less than six months, no loyal man will be allowed to live in the rebel states. The terrible slaughter of union men in N.O., sanctioned & encouraged too by Andy Johnson, has sent a thrill through every loyal heart. And the late dispatches from the "White House" to the rebel Atty. Gen. at N.O. giving him sole command of the military forces to prevent the assembling of any union men, will certainly fire the heart of every loyal man throughout the North.[21]

The bloodshed further confirmed Ohio Republicans' conviction that only the ratification of the proposed Fourteenth Amendment could lead to successful reunion.[22]

The president created even more political problems for himself and his supporters during his famous "swing around the circle" in late August and September. Ostensibly traveling to Chicago to dedicate a memorial to Stephen A. Douglas, Johnson used the trip to campaign against the congressional Reconstruction plan. In several northern cities Johnson delivered speeches that removed any doubt about his desertion of the Republican party.[23]

Taunted and heckled by audiences nearly everywhere he spoke, the president struck back furiously. At Cleveland on September 3 he referred to Radical Republican members of Congress, declaring his readiness to "fight traitors at the North." While launching vicious personal attacks on his opponents, Johnson squandered excellent opportunities to hit the Republicans where they were most vulnerable—on racial issues. He simply did not exploit voter fears that Republican policies might lead to black equality.[24]

As also seems to have been the case in Illinois and Michigan,the entire pathetic display probably had little effect on the campaign in Ohio, for Johnson had said nothing new, and most Ohioans had already decided whether to support him or not.[25] For the first time, however, many of them could actually see and hear for themselves how far Johnson had strayed from the position of the Republican party. The embarrassing spectacle led even Johnson's supporters to "wish the President could be induced to give up his miserable speechmaking," while his foes sarcastically asked, "Isn't Andy doing finely?"[26] Ohio Republicans concluded that Johnson had "forfeited popular respect."[27]

Fully cognizant that these factors enhanced their campaign hopes, the Republicans nonetheless feverishly crisscrossed Ohio, sparing no energy to ensure victory in a contest many thought the most critical in the nation's history. As early as February, James Garfield had urged the party to begin to organize for the campaign because "the decision of that election will determine whether the fruits of war shall be lost or not." Months later, with the Republican victory secured, Governor Cox recalled his preelection anxiety that "to suffer any interruption in our control of the government, even for a single session of Congress, would lose to us all we have been struggling to attain: probably undoing even the abolition of slavery." Most Republicans agreed with this assessment and worked assiduously to ensure victory. Certainly, Senator Benjamin Wade pushed his aging body to the limit for the Republican cause, reporting that in three weeks of campaigning he had lot eight pounds. He concluded: "I shall expire when it is over & I would not do so much were it not absolutely necessary to beat the traitor Johnson & so save the country."[28]

Republican orators agreed that fundamentally the election would be a straightforward referendum on the proposed constitutional amendment, but they developed four basic themes in their speeches. Republicans argued that the "only issue" in the campaign was whether the nation had the right to demand of the rebels safeguards for future national security, as outlined in the proposed amendment, or whether the southerners must be readmitted with no guarantee of future good behavior. They insisted the requirements were essential for peace and that the Democrats' desire to restore the South without them would result in renewed rebellion. Republican speakers, thus, portrayed the amendment as essential to national peace and unity.[29]

The Republicans also constantly reminded their audiences that the moderates had written the proposed amendment. Senator John Sherman, for example, recalled how long he had worked to avoid a split with Johnson and how he had earned a deserved reputation as a conservative Republican. Yet, he told voters, he had played a key role in drafting portions of the amendment and had endorsed all of it. Sherman also carefully indicated precisely what the Radicals had sought and how they had been disappointed in the results, particularly concerning black suffrage. Nevertheless, all Republicans had agreed to rally behind the amendment as the nation's best hope for future peace.[30]

Proponents of the amendment also insisted that because it listed the final terms of Reconstruction, its ratification would result in a speedy reunion. Its adoption would, according to Governor Cox, end sectional strife, bitterness, and anxiety and allow the nation finally to enjoy peace and economic prosperity. As Cox suggested, the treatment of Tennessee, which had ratified the amendment and been readmitted into the Union, showed that the Republicans would make no further demands on southerners if they ratified the amendment.[31] This point was crucial, for although the voters wanted future security, they were also, as the Republicans knew, weary of prolonged crisis and eager for the speediest possible end to the troubled times.

Republican speakers also stressed the essential point that the amendment would protect the nation from the return to power of the antebellum planters. The officeholding disability in section 3 would prohibit the most notorious rebels from securing public office, and the first section would provide the freedmen with the legal rights necessary to protect their freedom. Congressman Samuel Shellabarger and Senator Benjamin Wade insisted the nation had the right and the need to deny the "chief architects" of the rebellion the opportunity again to "rule the Government they sought to destroy."[32]

Taking their cue from politicians, Republican editors and newspapermen throughout Ohio pounded home the party position. These men agreed that the election would determine the nation's future and that the major issue was the proposed amendment. Some editors called this the "who should rule—the loyal or the disloyal" controversy. Others saw it as a battle between Congress and a turncoat president who was usurping congressional prerogatives. Many writers considered the election simply a referendum on the proposed amendment. However they stated the issue, all were writing about the same thing. They insisted that Reconstruction could succeed only if Congress were allowed to insist on strict guarantees of future loyalty before reunification of the country. An editor from southern Ohio gathered the themes together and perhaps best defined the dominant Republican campaign thrust: "Will you reconstruct the rebels or will you submit to be dominated by their principles, which you, upon their defiance, rejected at the point of the bayonet. This is the main issue. It is forced upon you by a treacherous usurping President, backed by the rebels whom you forced to obey the majesty of the law, and their Northern allies who, during the rebellion, you so often defeated at the ballot box."[33]

When analyzing the proposed amendment, Republicans generally asserted that "every just man" readily endorsed all its sections except the second, which dealt with representation in Congress. In their discussion of that controversial section Republican editors followed the party decision to avoid the issue of black suffrage as much as possible. Instead, just as party speakers had, they stressed that the section would guarantee equal representation of whites throughout the country. In the Western Reserve Republicans grudgingly went along with the party decision to ignore the suffrage matter. In southern Ohio, however, where Democrats vigorously pressed the suffrage issue, silence was simply inadequate. In that area, Republican editors were occasionally compelled to discuss black suffrage, but they consistently followed the lead of the politicians in endeavoring to convince the electorate that the section would only equalize the votes of whites. W.D. Bickham of Dayton forcefully stated the prevailing Republican position:

> We tell the South that if you will say by the adoption of the Constitutional Amendment that you are willing that one white man in Ohio, or in all the Northern states, shall be the political equal of one white South Carolinian, or Virginian, you shall be restored to the Union. If not, you may take the alternative. For, after beating you into obedience, we will not cravenly write on our foreheads, *"one whipped rebel is the equal of two Ohio freemen."* The North would be doing exactly that thing if the South should be admitted on President Johnson's Copperhead policy.
>
> The Amendment *does not* require the South to adopt negro suffrage. It requires them to do nothing but acknowledge that one freeman of the North is the political equal of one ex-rebel of the South. That is all. They are free to adopt or reject negro suffrage. That's their own concern. If they want it, let them have it. It is a State Right. If they don't want it, we shan't quarrel with them about it.[34]

In part to defuse Democratic accusations that the Republicans were the real party of treason and disunion for their refusal to seat southern congressional representatives, Republicans hastened to promise Ohio voters that southern ratification of the proposed amendment would end Reconstruction. They insisted that southerners had only to supply proof of loyalty, which they could readily give by proper action on the amendment, and Reconstruction would conclude.[35]

While stressing their own commitment to reunion, the Republican press denounced the Democrats as the party of disunion and war. Journalists reminded Ohioans that Democratic southerners had led the secession movement and that many northern Democrats had opposed the war and now sought to readmit southerners with no guarantees or conditions.[36] They warned their readers that the election of a Democratic Congress would deprive the nation of the hard-won changes brought by the war. Even more ominously, writers charged that Republican defeat would result in a new outbreak of sectional warfare. The editor of the *Scioto Gazette* provides a representative sample of the general and apparently sincere fear. If the Democrats won, he cautioned, "all is lost for which we fought. We shall be bound hand and foot, and we shall be dared to elect another Northern President under penalty of another war more bloody than the recent conflict! All that has been done to secure a future peace will be undone and the South will be once more our merciless tyrant."[37] In his last issue before the election, the editor of the *Morgan County Herald* stated the same idea more succinctly, "Remember! that one day to the cause of your country now may save us from another deadly civil war. Give it!!"[38] In short, voting Democratic would return the nation to the crisis days of late 1860 and bring on even worse bloodshed than Americans had yet experienced. To a population whose major concern was a future secure from sectional strife, this was a powerful, even if not exactly accurate appeal. The Republicans exploited it masterfully.

Andrew Johnson also found himself under heavy attack from Republican pens. His actions during the summer and fall of 1866 exhausted the patience of nearly every Republican. They bitterly denounced his Reconstruction policy, which had evolved into one of immediate, unconditional restoration of the South. Some Republicans charged that Johnson might even stage a coup if voters refused to elect his supporters to Congress. Others did not go quite that far but accused Johnson of seeking "to overthrow our peace, won by such costly sacrifice," by his "revolutionary and treasonable policy" of unconditional Reconstruction. Furthermore, Johnson's role in the National Union movement led one editor, recalling the president's pledges of 1865, to accuse him of "forming an alliance with traitors and their friends. It is thus that he makes treason odious."[39]

Senator John Sherman probably best portrayed the total disgust many of the most conservative Republicans felt toward Johnson by the fall of 1866. After dedicating months of labor to bridging the gap between Johnson and the Republicans, in June, Sherman finally acknowledged that the president had deserted the Union cause. In late

September he ringingly denounced the man he had once hoped and expected would lead the country to successful reunion. Despite the president's promise to punish traitors, Sherman stated, Johnson now "used all his power to restore rebels to power and to make treason reputable." Once Johnson had pledged to be the freedmen's Moses, but the hard reality of 1866 was that "he has turned them to their former masters, already embittered by their loss as slaves, and taught by the prejudice of ages to treat them as a race of brutes. He has permitted them to be murdered and plundered when protection was in his power, and refuses to enforce laws for their safety." On top of all that, Johnson "now seeks to destroy the great Union party that elected him." Sherman called Johnson "a dangerous man" who could be controlled only by a Republican majority in Congress.[40]

Ohio Democrats meanwhile ran their usual, aggressive campaign. They pursued a multiphased strategy, developed by the Democratic members of the Ohio General Assembly, which began with an indictment of Congress for its behavior toward southerners and toward Johnson, whom they now accepted as their leader. The Democrats charged that their opponents were the party of disunion because the Republicans refused to restore the South despite ample evidence of its loyalty. The Democrats promised that if elected they would immediately and unconditionally restore the Union. They also tried to convince the electorate that the Radical Republicans and Congress were destroying the American system of government by a revolutionary concentration of power in the federal government at the expense of the prerogatives of state and local governments. Their most important issue, however, was their past and future favorite—the specter of racial equality.[41]

Early in the campaign the *Portsmouth Times* succinctly summarized the Democratic position in an editorial titled "The Issues":

> Support Congress and you sustain division, attack your government, and elevate the negro at the expense of your own race.
>
> Support the President and you restore the Union, preserve the government, and you protect the white man.
>
> On the one side are Stevens, Sumner, Agitation and Disorder.
>
> On the other, the President, the Union, peace and order.[42]

The editor seems to have been unconcerned about the irony of attacking for disunity a party that for five years had accurately called itself the Union party.

With a zeal fanned by five years of nearly unbroken election defeats, the Democrats brutally attacked Congress for usurping Johnson's prerogatives and for unconstitutional actions. Most Democrats welcomed Johnson as their savior, hailing him as "the Tribune of the people." Many cheered his "heroic" battles against the despotism of the "radical" Congress, which party politicians and editors frequently labeled a "rump" with no legal basis because of the exclusion of southern legislators. Democrats repeatedly assailed the Republicans for what they considered incessant attempts to centralize all power in Congress, thereby threatening the personal liberties of all Americans.[43]

In response to Republican accusations that held them responsible for the Civil War, the Democrats scathingly denounced their opponents for prolonging the national crisis. According to the Democrats, southerners had followed Johnson's program and deserved readmission into the Union. They insisted that it was Congress, not the Democrats, that was keeping the country split through outrageous demands made on the South. One Democrat said the voters would decide "whether the country shall drift on, under Congressional legislation, for years to come, in its present wrecked and disorganized condition" or be reunited, its sectional bitterness healed by a Democratic Congress. Some Democrats castigated the Republicans for putting party welfare above national welfare and stated that Congress was driving the country straight back to open sectional warfare. Thus, for neither the first nor the last time in American history, each party announced that the other's programs would destroy the Republic.[44] Probably such rhetoric resulted from the politicians' accurate perception that much could be gained from exciting the fears of the voters, who were nervous about a peaceful future.

The Democrats especially reviled Congress for demanding that the southern states ratify the proposed amendment before readmission into the Union. They correctly argued that no provision in the Constitution gave Congress the power to make such a requirement, which one editor called "an act of revolution."[45] Unfortunately for them, the Democrats were living through a situation never envisioned by the founding fathers, and their opponents controlled Congress. To a certain extent, at least in the absence of a test in the courts, the Constitution said whatever the Republican Congress decided it said. Hoping to overcome that reality, the Democrats advocated immediate restoration of the Confederate states and invited the voters to compare that plan to the Republican demand for more guarantees.[46]

The Democrats, however, vented their anger and frustration most vigorously in a determined effort to label their opponents the party of racial equality. The resolutions passed at the Jackson County Democratic Convention, for example, called the Republicans a "negro-loving combination." Many Democrats despaired that the disastrous results of the alleged Republican policy would range from school integration to miscegenation.[47] Democratic editors repeatedly asserted that the main issue in the campaign really was black suffrage and constantly charged their opponents with cowardice and lying for trying to dodge this "fact." For example, Washington McLean warned Cincinnati-area veterans, "Remember, Soldiers, that a vote for Egleston or Hayes [Republican congressional candidates] is an endorsement of Negro Suffrage."[48]

The possibility that the proposed amendment would enfranchise any blacks anywhere greatly aroused Ohio Democrats. It also lent, at least in their minds, much credence to their charges of "black Republicanism." General George Morgan, the 1865 Democratic gubernatorial nominee and a candidate for Congress in 1866, told a receptive audience at Coshocton that the

> object of this proposed amendment, then, is to create negro judges, jurors, and legislators, and if you refuse to make negroes your political equals, then you are to be partially disfranchised.
>
> I ask you, Ohioans, are you prepared for this? If you are, then vote for Mr. Delano [Morgan's opponent] and if elected, he will aid you in placing yourselves, your wives, sons, and daughters, on a level with the negroes.[49]

Undoubtedly, such racist harangues appealed to many Ohioans, who shared Morgan's attitudes, if not necessarily his well-cultivated paranoia.

Ten days before the election the State Central Committee of the Democratic party issued an open letter to "the Democracy and Conservatives of Ohio." The document clearly summarized the Democratic campaign strategy. The only question asked of the voters was whether "less than one third of the people [shall] despotically govern more than two-thirds." It predicted that if the Republicans won the election, they would start another civil war as a "pretext for disfranchising, if not exterminating, white men and confiscating their property."[50]

So stung were Republicans by such charges that they nearly trampled each other in their haste to deny them. Some praised congressional recognition of each state's right to determine its suffrage requirements. Others vociferously denied any desire to enfranchise blacks. Most, however, recognizing not only that the Democrats would try to make political capital of the issue but also that they could not agree among themselves, followed the party line determined in June at Columbus and insisted suffrage was not an issue in the campaign.[51]

Indeed, the Republican reaction to these Democratic attacks shed much light on the limits of the Republican commitment to the freedmen. For example, in the congressional debates on the proposed amendment, some Ohio Republicans advocated the enfranchisement of literate male freedmen and those who had served in the army during the Civil War. Nevertheless, on April 26 the Ohio Republican congressional caucus voted to oppose a clause in the amendment requiring black suffrage in the South. The supporters of the enfranchisement of blacks realized that Ohioans were not yet convinced that black suffrage was necessary for successful Reconstruction and modified their public stance accordingly.[52]

Rutherford B. Hayes was one of those whose public and private postures in 1866 were in conflict. On May 15 Hayes confided in his diary, "My decided preference: Suffrage for *all* in the South, colored and white, to depend on education; sooner or later in the North also—say, all new voters to be able to write and read." Reflecting how very difficult and sensitive this issue was, in his campaign speeches Hayes avoided even a hint that he supported impartial suffrage. Rather, in defending the equal representation clause of the amendment, he explained that its purpose was to correct for possible overrepresentation of white southerners in Congress.[53]

Congressman James Ashley, a genuine radical and friend of the freedmen, spoke glowingly in Congress of their right to vote. During the campaign, however, he accepted the party line and agreed that "the question of representation and suffrage will be discussed in the abstract" and that black enfranchisement would not be made a "direct issue." Unlike most Republicans, though, Ashley courageously acknowledged that he supported black suffrage, but because the party had decided against it, he would follow its decision.[54]

His colleague Rufus Spalding traveled a similar path. In Congress he stated his willingness to follow popular opinion, "I say, as an individual, that I would more cheerfully give my vote if that provision [the proposed amendment] allowed all men of proper age whom we have freed to join in the exercise of the right of suffrage in this country. But if I cannot obtain all I wish, I will go heartily to secure all we can can obtain." During the campaign, Spalding became so quiet about suffrage that some party members feared that he supported Johnson's policy.[55]

James A. Garfield reflected another hard reality. Many of those who favored black rights were not free of bias themselves. In Congress, for example, he spoke eloquently about the blacks' right to vote:

> First let me say I regret more than I shall be able to tell this House that we have not found the situation of affairs in this country such, and the public virtue such that we might come out on the plain, unanswerable proposition that every adult intelligent citizen of the United States, unconvicted of crime, shall enjoy the right of suffrage.
>
> Sir, I believe that the right to vote, if it be not indeed one of the natural rights of all men, is so necessary to the protection of their natural rights as to be indispensable, and therefore equal to natural rights.[56]

Yet, despite this unqualified endorsement of impartial suffrage, Garfield, like nearly all white Americans of his era, held racist attitudes. At a campaign appearance in Toledo Garfield said:

> But some one says, "That is not the point; tell me whether you would be willing for your sister to marry a Negro? " Well, I don't believe in dodging any question, gentlemen. Now I had always supposed that courtship and love and marriage were matters of taste, and if any Democratic or Johnson man is afraid that by giving the Negro a right to his life, liberty and property, he would therefore be marrying into the race, I will say to him if his tastes lie in that direction, that we have got a statute in Ohio that may help him. I remember when I was in the Ohio Senate, about seven years ago, that a Democrat who felt, I suppose, that he needed some restriction, proposed a law, and our people allowed him to have it passed, that in case any man or woman in the State of Ohio should marry one of the other race, they should go to the penitentiary for a certain number of years. I forget how many. I believe that law is standing on the statute books yet, as a sort of Democratic protection—but if any of your tastes should lead in that direction, there are the yawning cells of the Ohio Penitentiary, to spur your virtue, and better your taste.[57]

Even recognizing the political requirement of catering to the electorate, Garfield probably exceeded the necessity of the moment.

Perhaps the saddest example of how prejudice often combined

with radicalism was Senator Ben Wade, probably the blacks' most powerful and dedicated friend in Ohio. Time and time again Wade strove to push his party toward racial justice, including suffrage. His radicalism ran so deep that he was among a tragically small group of powerful politicians who endorsed women's suffrage. Yet, he complained to his wife, "The Niggers are the most intelligent part of the [southern] population but the Nigger smell I cannot bear." He even criticized the food which was "all cooked by Niggers until I smell and taste the Nigger." As late as 1873 he grumbled, "I wish that we could get a white woman of the English or Northern European breed. I am sick and tired of Niggers."[58] Unlike most of his contemporaries, however, Wade kept his prejudices private and rarely, if ever, catered to the views of his audiences. The fact of Wade's bigotry merely underscores the common attitudes of white America in the 1860s and makes one marvel at the courage of the Radical Republicans who strove for at least a semblance of racial justice in such a hostile environment.

The racism of the Republicans, however, differed substantially from that of the Democrats. Republicans generally believed in white superiority but acknowledged blacks' humanity and worked to guarantee their basic civil rights. Democrats, on the other hand, gave ample evidence of a desire to reenslave blacks or to allow their systematic annihilation by whites.

Republican editors shared the same fear of voter hostility toward black suffrage that the party leaders recognized. When they could no longer ignore the subject, they tried to convince the voters that the party did not favor ballots for blacks. W.D. Bickham reflected the nervousness of many of his colleagues when he almost pleadingly asserted:

> Negro suffrage is a political bugbear to excite the prejudices of unintelligent men, so that the rebels may accomplish by fraud what they failed to achieve by downright fighting.
>
> There is not an intelligent man in Ohio who does not know that negro suffrage is not an issue in this campaign. It is not expressed or implied in the State platform, nor in any one county Union platform in Ohio.[59]

While reminding his readers that the proposed amendment did not enfranchise anybody, Bickham and his journalistic colleagues carefully argued that its purpose was to guarantee that southern whites would not receive additional representation in Congress for nonvoting blacks.[60] They left little doubt that the goal of the amendment

Table 2
Percentage of Vote in Congressional Elections, 1860-1868

Year	Republican	Democratic
1860	51.57	48.42
1862	49.23	50.76
1864	56.36	43.64
1866	54.23	45.77
1868	51.26	48.74

SOURCES: *Annual Report of the Secretary of State of Ohio* (1864), 21-25; (1866), 34-38; (1868), 45-49.

was to end sectional conflict by restraining southern whites, not to elevate blacks to political, social, or economic equality.

In fact, most Ohio Republicans really cared little about the fate of the freedmen, except for one matter. The southern planter had endangered the nation's existence, using slavery as his power base. A major Reconstruction goal was thus to deny the planters the opportunity to use black labor to regain and retain political and economic control over the South as they had in antebellum days. In short, Ohio Republicans generally considered the freedmen pawns to be used to check the southern aristocracy in a chess game with immense national significance. Many of these Ohioans hoped that mere grants of freedom, the right to work for a wage, and minimal legal protection would undercut the power of the planters, thus allowing the nation to live in peace while maintaining white supremacy. The proposed amendment solved the problems both of Reconstruction and of the future role blacks would have in America.[61]

In the third largest voter turnout to date, exceeded only by the unusual 1863 gubernatorial and 1864 presidential elections, Ohioans gave the Republicans and the proposed constitutional amendment a solid endorsement.[62] Compared to the previous fall, over fifty thousand more Ohioans voted and the Republicans increased their percentage of the vote from 53.57 to 54.23. With the exception of the 1864 congressional elections, when the Republican-Unionists benefited tremendously from the success of the Union armies, Ohio Republican congressional candidates won a larger share of the vote than in any other congressional election from 1860 through 1868 (see Table 2). Republicans won sixteen of Ohio's nineteen seats in the Fortieth Congress. In the history of the Republican party in Ohio, from the mid-1850s to this time, only in the Thirty-ninth Congress, elected in 1864, did that party win a higher percentage of the vote and more seats in Congress (see Table 3). Thus a victory that might seem

Table 3
Composition of Ohio Congressional Delegation, 1861-1869

Year Elected	Republican	Democrat	Other
1860	12	8	1
1862	5	14	
1864	17	2	
1866	16	3	
1868	13	6	

SOURCE: *Biographical Directory of the United States Congress, 1774-1989,* Bicentennial Edition (Washington, D.C., 1989), 173, 177, 181, 185-86, 189-90.

modest by some standards can be considered decisive by Ohio standards.[63]

During the campaign Ohioans had confined their debates almost strictly to Reconstruction issues, especially the proposed amendment. If ever a general election could be considered a referendum on an issue, this one could. Without much doubt Ohioans cast their ballots based on their attitudes toward the amendment. The result was that five of every nine politically active Ohioans accepted the Republican position that the proposed amendment promised the nation the best means to a secure future. Certainly the Republicans believed the voters had "set their seal of approval, most emphatically, upon their action, as embodied in the Constitutional Amendment."[64]

The election had, indeed, hinged on which plan Ohioans believed would lead to a just and lasting peace. The events of 1866 had convinced a majority of politically active Ohioans that Johnson could not be trusted to secure the peace and that his policy could too easily result in renewed sectional strife. Such views placed Ohioans in the mainstream of northern attitudes in 1866.[65] Ohioans did not seek to recreate the South in the image of the North, but they did insist that southerners recognize the wickedness of the rebellion and provide ample proof of loyalty to the nation before readmission. Successful Reconstruction required nothing less. Voting for the proposed amendment became the vehicle for Ohioans to express that desire.

After the election most politically active Ohioans tended to believe that only one step remained before the nation could again be reunited on a secure basis. Southern ratification of the amendment would signify renewed loyalty and provide the necessary constitutional guarantees to ensure future harmony. This optimism would soon be leveled by the South's rejection of the amendment. Thus, 1867 brought not a positive end to Reconstruction but anxiety, doubt, and ultimately a whole new attempt to reconstruct the nation.

5

REINING IN THE REPUBLICANS

> I am trying to do two things, viz. be a radical and not be a fool—which if I am to judge by the exhibitions around me, is a matter of no small difficulty.
>
> —James A. Garfield, 1867

Ohio Republicans barely had time to savor their victories in the 1866 elections before southerners destroyed their hopes for a quick end to Reconstruction. Only four days after the election Texas refused to ratify the proposed amendment. Over the next four months the remaining nine Confederate states did the same. The Republican expectation that the proposed amendment would quickly conclude Reconstruction had evaporated.

Despite this setback, Radical Republicans in Ohio decided to push in 1867 for black suffrage in the South and in Ohio. They reasoned that the voters had endorsed a Republican plan of Reconstruction and, particularly in light of southern rejection of the proposed amendment, would approve another advance of black rights. They were wrong. In the fall of 1867 Ohio voters would overwhelmingly defeat a state constitutional amendment to enfranchise adult black males, would almost elect a Democratic governor, and would elect Democratic majorities to both houses of the General Assembly. The Radicals had certainly miscalculated. By allowing the debate to center on black suffrage, they ignored one of the key messages of 1866—keep the voters' focus on the South, and bury racial issues. Their defeat would send them scurrying for a safe, electable presidential candidate who could unite the party and whose nomination, they hoped, would guarantee a Republican in the White House and continued Republican majorities in Congress. At the same time, crumbling Republican support in Ohio and most of the rest of the North would prevent any additions to the requirements the South would have to meet to gain readmission to the Union.[1]

When Ohio Republicans analyzed the results of the 1866 elections they almost unanimously agreed that the voters had approved the congressional Reconstruction plan embodied in the proposed Fourteenth Amendment as the final terms of Reconstruction. Republicans generally expressed optimism that southerners would accept these terms, which Ohio Republicans considered fair to southerners and yet strong enough to ensure future national security.[2] Murat Halstead, the conservative editor of the *Cincinnati Daily Commercial*, accurately reflected their conclusions:

> The vote was taken on the main question—the approval or rejection of the amendment as it stands. The return to the Fortieth Congress of a majority of those who voted for the amendment, and of others who committed themselves to it unconditionally, is as emphatic a sanction as the amendment could have. It is the declared will of a majority of the loyal people of the country that the amendment shall form the basis of reconstruction and its terms be the bond of settlement between the Government and those who made treasonable war upon it.
>
> . . . The South ought to be given to understand that the amendment is a finality.[3]

Most Republicans confidently concluded that "unless we are greatly mistaken, the effect of these elections upon the South will be a most salutary one [and] will go very far towards the settling of all difficulties and the restoration of peace, order, and prosperity in the South on such a basis as to give assurance of permanency."[4] Probably most Ohio Republicans held Johnson responsible for southern intransigence and believed that the elections would convince the former Confederates that the president could not protect them from the will of the northern people. Thus, clear-minded southerners would surely see the value of following the congressional program.

Southerners quickly disabused Ohio Republicans of their optimism by unequivocally rejecting the proposed constitutional amendment. By February 1867 every southern state except Tennessee had voted against the amendment; indeed, it had received the paltry total of but thirty-three affirmative votes in all the southern legislatures combined.[5] Republicans in Ohio and throughout the rest of the North were shocked by what they considered stupidity and arrogance. Congress had presented the South with what northerners believed to be a fair and reasonable proposal and had been abused for its generosity. Many northerners sadly concluded that the South had once again refused to give proof of repentance.[6]

Southerners, however, having embarked on a policy that has been well described as "masterly inactivity," thought the rejection made perfect sense. They objected most strenuously to section 3, which denied some white southerners the right to hold public office for an indefinite time. Southerners believed this provision would replace their most experienced and best political leaders with greatly inferior persons—probably carpetbaggers and scalawags. Many believed, often with ample justification, that the motive behind this section was the establishment of Republican regimes throughout the South. The reward for ratification of the amendment was therefore to lose control of their state governments and to be represented in Congress by Republicans.[7] Almost no southerners considered that any great bargain; many clearly preferred to dominate local affairs and to remain unrepresented in Congress. Of course, southerners also rejected the second section, which threatened a decrease in any state's congressional representation if it refused to require impartial suffrage. According to Michael Perman, southerners not only flatly refused to discuss this section but never really debated the broader issue of ratification. They acted partly from the conviction that Congress had given them the option to accept or reject the amendment. Therefore, they were only declaring their basic rights in refusing the proposal. Southerners apparently thought they would dishonor themselves if they voluntarily accepted such despicable terms. Even if Congress later demanded harsher requirements, southerners comforted themselves by knowing that they had not willingly stained their honor but had been forced to acquiesce to the power of Congress.

Perman argues persuasively that by adopting "masterly inactivity" southerners had agreed that their political salvation would be best served by refusing to cooperate with any Republican-sponsored Reconstruction plan. Because they did not trust the Radical Republicans, southerners apparently believed that if they accepted any terms required by a Republican Congress, the Radicals would immediately demand more stringent terms. Southerners were convinced that the Radicals would ultimately demand universal black adult male suffrage because only that would give the Radicals any chance to create a stable and dominant southern Republican party.

The southern strategy was not totally passive, however. Southerners had calculated that if they rejected the congressional plan, northern Republicans would split over the future of Reconstruction and northern Democrats would be able to win control of Congress.

The new majority would then present southerners with far more favorable terms than the proposed amendment. Some southerners understood that a large portion of northerners would consider their actions further evidence of disloyalty, but most insisted that sooner or later the Yankees would tire of the strife, trouble, and taxes that accompanied Reconstruction. Then the political reaction against the Radicals would follow, freeing the South from the grip of the northern "destructives."[8]

The actions of southerners forced Ohio Republicans to acknowledge that a successful end to Reconstruction was not yet in sight. For some in Ohio and throughout the North the rejection of the amendment finally destroyed whatever remained of the cherished dream that loyal whites could and would lead the South back into the Union. Perhaps, indeed probably, many Republicans therefore concluded, some with great hopes, others reluctantly, that the time had come to require full participation by the freedmen in the political Reconstruction of southern society.[9] Other Republicans realized the political danger of such a position, citing campaign promises that the amendment represented the final terms of Reconstruction; they urged that the South be given a second chance to approve the amendment. In an era devoid of easy choices the Republicans faced great uncertainty. Fortunately the period of doubt was relatively short-lived, for Congress convened while southerners were still rejecting the amendment.

When the Thirty-ninth Congress began its last session in December 1866, it had to respond to the southern refusal to approve the amendment. The options ranged from doing nothing and letting the South stay out until it acquiesced to scrapping the entire structure of Johnson's state governments and developing an entirely new, or at least greatly modified, Reconstruction program. If Reconstruction were to begin anew, the most frequently mentioned possibility was to put the South under military rule until it accepted whatever plans Congress proposed. Such a policy obviously risked alienating vast numbers of northern voters who had wearily struggled through four years of war and two years of postwar chaos. Now in early 1867, only months after they had been led to believe that the nation would finally be reunited under the Fourteenth Amendment, Congress could hardly expect them to support a whole new and potentially far more comprehensive program of Reconstruction. Many conservative Republicans had enormous difficulty endorsing such a program themselves, much less asking voters to approve it. But the alternative of just waiting for a southern change of heart seemed just as bad and possibly worse. As much as some Republicans wanted to end Reconstruction on the basis of the proposed amendment, southerners still had to learn that they had lost the war and could not dictate to the nation. Future security and the memory of the countless sacrifices already made for the Union demanded nothing less.[10]

Almost immediately Republican congressmen introduced several bills that dealt with Reconstruction issues. The congressional debates on these bills forced Ohio's Republican members of Congress to make some difficult decisions. Most of them acknowledged that the state had pledged in the 1866 election to readmit the South if it accepted the proposed amendment. They hesitated to support additional requirements. Even when southerners spurned this offer, several Republicans hoped to avoid starting Reconstruction anew. Others relished the opportunity to press for the enfranchisement of the freedmen.

For example, Representative James Garfield, who at least since 1865 had favored some form of black suffrage, believed that a pledge of readmission had been made to the South. Writing on January 1, 1867, after seven southern states had already rejected the amendment, Garfield still thought that "if the Southern States should adopt the Constitutional Amendment within a reasonable time we are morally bound to admit them to representation." He gave a clear hint of the probable result of southern failure to ratify, however, acknowledging that "if they reject it then I am in favor of striking for impartial suffrage though I see that such a course is beset with grave danger." Garfield's dearest wish was to be done with the whole issue of Reconstruction: "I wish the South would adopt the Constitutional Amendment soon, and in good temper. Perhaps they will." Representative James Ashley and Senator Benjamin Wade adopted precisely the same position.[11]

Another House Republican, Rufus Spalding, insisted that in the fall of 1866 the people of Ohio had voted solely on the issue of the amendment and had spoken in favor of southern readmission upon ratification. But as early as December 20, 1866, he noted that if the South still refused, "it may become necessary, ere long, to place those revolted States in the condition of Territories. If that necessity shall be made apparent I shall not flinch from the work, though I would fain save the country from so great a strain upon its institutions of government." Clearly Spalding hoped the South would save everybody from harsher Reconstruction measures, and he declared his willingness to wait until March 4, 1867, when the Thirty-ninth Congress ended, for the South to reverse itself.[12]

On January 19, 1867, Representative Tobias Plants agreed with the substance of Spalding's position. Plants stated that he had voted for the proposed amendment as the final terms of Reconstruction, had so told the voters of Ohio, and still considered himself duty-bound to honor that pledge. Nevertheless, if the South continued to flout the nation's will, Plants said he would consider himself "released from all expressed or implied obligations created thereby, and free to adopt such other measures as the exigencies of the country might demand." In fact, Plants indicated that the tone of southern denunciations of the amendment had exhausted his patience. Plants was particularly disturbed that by rejecting "generous terms with the haughty and insulting bravado of assumed superiority," the southerners seemed to "demand that the nation submit to such terms as they dictate." Vowing never to accept such arrogance he announced his willingness to vote for stronger measures, including black suffrage.[13]

Senator John Sherman, surely one of the most conservative Republicans in Congress, also believed Ohio voters had made an implicit promise to southerners. As one southern state after another turned down the amendment, however, Sherman's frustration and concern increased dramatically. Writing to Governor Cox, he reflected the uncertainty of like-minded Republicans in mid-January: "The Amendment is rejected by the South. We must choose between the reorganization of the Southern States or the adoption of the Amendment by three-fourths of the adhering States. Why is this not sufficient? They [southerners] are ready to [acquiesce] in the Amendment as terms imposed upon them. Why is not this sufficient? Is it not better to secure reconstruction upon a basis approved by the people rather than endanger all by compelling organization of new State governments."[14] This statement reveals Sherman's clear understanding that southerners would accept a program that was forced upon them, though they would reject if given the option. It also shows how little enthusiasm he had for any action except patience toward southerners in the hope that they would soon ratify the amendment. Yet, as far back as the 1866 fall campaign Sherman had warned that southern rejection could lead to black suffrage. Indeed, his patience had its limit. Within a month of his letter to Cox, the senator helped draft compromise language that became the Military Reconstruction Act.[15]

Although Republican members of Congress from Ohio declared that the nation had pledged readmission for ratification of the amendment, all of them ultimately saw the need to put additional pressure on the South. Of the group Representative John A. Bingham held out the longest for a policy of outwaiting the southerners. During the first two months of 1867 he waged a bitter struggle against the Radicals and Thaddeus Stevens in particular to force Congress to stand behind the proposed amendment. He insisted that the amendment provided ample protection for white and black loyal southerners and would restore harmony between the sections, but he could not effectively counter the argument that southerners, in refusing the amendment, had shown intransigence, and thus something more had to be attempted. In February, Bingham relented, but he worked to keep the new Reconstruction policy as much in line with his views as possible.[16]

Governor Jacob Cox held an even more conservative position than Bingham's. He considered the amendment "the *people's ultimatum*" and had no intention of supporting any new plans that went beyond it. This stand placed him in the awkward situation of being more conservative than his party; yet he still believed that only the Republican party could save the nation. Therefore, he generally chose to state his views, which could be quite pointed, quietly and privately. For example, in January he expressed bitterness that "several members of Congress, who are men of sense though classed as Radicals, have said to me that they abhor the impeachment scheme, the territorial scheme for the rebel states, the refusal to regard the Constitutional Amendment as a finality. Yet I see by their votes that they are dragged along by men whose brains & whose motives they profess privately to hold in contempt." Even in mid-February, Cox felt sure that the nation should not change the terms of readmission and that the Republicans should "rest upon it as our party platform, 'for better or for worse.' . . . We could wait 10 years." With some logic he suggested that southerners would remain passive about the amendment until assured it would be the final and unalterable terms.[17]

Congressional Republicans fully understood the grave dangers involved in merely waiting for southerners to accept the amendment. Northerners were tired of turmoil, and any party in power that had no plan to solve the nation's major problem stood little chance of reelection. Some Republicans seemed willing to endorse nearly any policy that promised action. Ohio Congressman Rutherford B. Hayes received a letter that gave stark evidence of how desperate many politicians were:

> I am free to say that I feel deeply anxious and fear that serious mischief may follow the want of harmony among our friends in Congress. We are doubtless nearer a solution of our reconstruction troubles than we have been and yet I don't see the evidence. What is the fact? Will anything final be done by the present Congress? If nothing and the 40th Congress shall want on the 4th of March merely to organize, how will we

> stand at the coming elections? Will we rally on the Amendment as we did last Fall? Are we not in positive danger of entering upon the coming Canvass without an issue, approved by our own party? If so, will not the President be greatly strengthened. Please write me.[18]

This desire for action increased the possibility that Congress would pass a Reconstruction bill that incorporated a territorialization plan. In December 1866 Thaddeus Stevens had introduced such a bill, which also required black male suffrage in the South. After months of acrimonious debate, a compromise plan known as the Military Reconstruction Bill passed Congress. It became law on March 2, 1867, after Congress overrode Johnson's veto.[19]

The act ordered Reconstruction begun anew. The former Confederacy, except Tennessee, was divided into five military districts, each under the control of an army general. Southern states could return to the Union when they approved the Fourteenth Amendment and wrote universal male suffrage into their new state constitutions. Many leaders of the Confederacy were disfranchised and made ineligible to hold public office.

These provisions, more stringent than previous terms, did not represent a Radical victory. Moderate and conservative Republicans such as James G. Blaine of Maine, John Sherman, and John Bingham had succeeded in inserting language that expressly outlined the steps southern states would have to take to be restored to the Union and how they could fulfill the requirements.[20] Historians have argued persuasively that the plan reflected compromises by all parts of the Republican party.[21] Of all Ohio Republicans, only James R. Hubbell, probably the most conservative member of the Republican House delegation, voted against the bill, and even he voted to override Johnson's veto. Clearly, it was a moderate compromise.[22]

During the winter of 1867 while Congress struggled with Reconstruction issues, white southerners' behavior had forced Ohio Republicans to reassess their positions. Many Republicans believed they had an obligation to keep the campaign pledge to readmit the South if it ratified the proposed amendment.[23] Others vented their anger at Johnson and the Democrats for their roles in persuading southerners to vote against the amendment. W.D. Bickham reflected the irritation of those who were tiring of the notion of allowing the South to accept or reject the terms of Reconstruction and who blamed the Confederates for the rejection, announcing that southerners had "no rights excepting those the government may choose to accord them."[24]

Ohio Republicans had to face the fact that southerners were

rejecting the amendment. They frequently accused them of wasting the nation's magnanimity by rejecting the proposed amendment and demanded military rule "until they shall have learned to respect the authority of that government which they have vainly attempted to destroy."[25] By February 1867 most Ohio Republicans, whether enthusiastically or grudgingly, acknowledged the need for a stronger program.

The effects of southern intransigence and violence against loyal southerners on the views of Ohio Republicans can be observed in the opinions expressed by the editors of the two most influential party papers in the southern part of the state. The shifting positions presented in the *Cincinnati Daily Gazette* exemplified the opinions of Radical Republicans. Immediately after the 1866 elections the editor, Richard Smith, declared that "the work of reconstruction will be complete" when the South ratifies the proposed amendment. At the same time he cautioned that the nation had spoken, and easier terms would never be extended. One month later the editor reaffirmed his pledge that the amendment was the final terms of Reconstruction. When Congress met in December, Smith predicted that economic questions would be more critical in the forthcoming session than Reconstruction issues, and he opposed any new measures dealing with the latter. On December 13 the *Gazette*'s position began to change. Smith blamed President Johnson for the rejection of the amendment and stated that Congress had "just cause" to write a new Reconstruction policy. By the end of that month Smith had decided that the proposed amendment alone was "a policy imperfect" and urged Congress to impeach Johnson and then proceed to enact new legislation to territorialize the South. Finally, in early January he endorsed Stevens's Reconstruction bill. These drastic changes had resulted directly from southern action on the amendment, from the arrogant tone of the refusal to ratify it, and from the continued physical attacks on white and black loyal southerners.[26]

The changing views of Murat Halstead,the editor of the *Cincinnati Daily Commercial*, epitomized the struggles of the more conservative Republicans before accepting military Reconstruction. In December 1866 he demanded that Congress abide by the electorate's fall 1866 pledge of readmission if the South ratified the amendment. Six weeks later he asserted that "it is very doubtful whether the people demand any such extreme measure as the territorializing of the Southern States." By mid-February, Halstead informed the South that it had only itself to blame if Congress enacted harsher Reconstruction measures, but he still refused to endorse any. The editor's optimism soared in late February when inaccurate rumors circulated that President Johnson had decided to urge southerners to ratify the proposed amendment in exchange for dropping congressional plans for military rule. As the passage of a military bill became nearly a certainty, Halstead praised the conservatism of Bingham and Sherman. In early March, Halstead finally, but with a notable lack of enthusiasm, agreed with the "overruling necessity to do something without delay."[27]

By midwinter 1867, then, most Ohio Republicans had had enough of southern foot dragging and wanted action. A large portion of them had warned southerners that, though Reconstruction would end if their states approved the amendment, failure to ratify it would result in a more exacting policy. In early January an editor from the Western Reserve stated a view that a growing number of Ohio Republicans endorsed: "Certainly the people will not only sustain but demand such action as will give future security, and protect the poor freedmen in the enjoyment of personal and civil rights. We have conquered the rebels by superior prowess of our arms, now let it be seen to, that they do not overcome us by their superior strategy, even aided by a fossil court majority and a corrupt Executive." Within weeks a solid majority of them would, with one correspondent, "earnestly pray that Congress would pass the act reducing the rebel states to a territorial condition, so that the matter of reconstructing that hostile portion of our country can commence at the bottom of the question. Any other method will fail of its object."[28]

The Military Reconstruction Act, with its reliance on the army and insistence on black suffrage in the South, certainly exceeded Ohio Republicans' original demands for a secure reunion, but by March 1867 the situation had changed greatly. Southern stubbornness, abetted by Johnson, had resulted in a stalemate that most Ohio Republicans would not tolerate. Nor would they allow untrustworthy southerners to regain control of the South. The continued and, in many areas, increased harassment and abuse of loyal white southerners and freedmen further stiffened their determination to find a Reconstruction policy that would guarantee a secure future, free of sectional strife.

Ohio Republicans disagreed among themselves, though, about two issues raised by the passage of the Military Reconstruction Act. Some believed that only voluntary acceptance would demonstrate loyalty, that the decision must remain with southerners, as provided in the act. Others had seen enough of the results of such voluntarism and urged Congress to pass a policy "that shall not depend on the acceptance of the rebel states."[29]

The matter of black suffrage also divided Ohio Republicans. By

February 1867 they and most northern Republicans had accepted black suffrage as essential in the South.[30] In December and January many Ohio Republicans praised Congress for passing and overriding Johnson's veto of a bill that enfranchised black men in the District of Columbia.[31] Nevertheless, disagreement still existed over whether Congress should demand universal or impartial suffrage; the more conservative Republicans favored impartial suffrage because it would permit states to retain some control over suffrage requirements. Halstead, for example, wrote that "the denial of the ballot to the negro on account of race is indefensible," but he opposed giving the ballot to "ignorant men, white or black."[32]

Despite their differences, once Congress had overridden Johnson's veto, nearly all Ohio Republicans rallied behind the Military Reconstruction Act. Some insisted the South deserved no milder terms of reunion and suggested the act showed that northerners "are to be trifled with no longer." Several applauded the new policy specifically because it would protect loyal southern whites.[33] One editor approvingly concluded that the North had left the South little choice but to accept the terms or stay out of the Union. "The rebels," he declared, "must obey it or the bayonet will, if need be, be brought to bear to enforce it. If they desire to escape military government the way is provided by which they can do so and it is an easy one. They have their choice." Most Republicans thought that the only major difference between the terms of 1866 and those of 1867 was black suffrage and considered that a small penalty for the South's behavior since 1860, particularly in rejecting the proposed Fourteenth Amendment.[34]

Ohio Democrats responded predictably to the measure. Descriptions ran from the "infernal scheme" to "Polandizing the South" to "the embodiment of all that is malignant, wicked and revolutionary." Democrats generally referred to it as the "Military Despotism Act."[35] The use of the term *despotism* would prove politically rewarding for the Democrats in the fall of 1867. They understood that Democrats and a fair number of Republicans were troubled by the continued drift toward centralization of power in Washington. The Military Reconstruction Act certainly contributed to the decline of power held by the states, as the Democrats did not fail to remind voters.

At the same time as Ohioans were fretting over Reconstruction, they also had to confront black suffrage at home. While Democrats uniformly denounced the idea, Republicans split on the matter, although the trend was toward granting suffrage to blacks. A Republican from one of the two Ohio districts represented by Democrats in

Jacob D. Cox, Republican governor of Ohio from 1866 to 1868. Cox supported Andrew Johnson throughout his term, refusing to renounce the president, even after Johnson deserted the Republican party.

All photos courtesy of the Ohio Historical Society.

WHITE MEN'S DEMOCRATIC STATE TICKET

FOR GOVERNOR:

GENERAL GEORGE W. MORGAN,

Of Knox County.

FOR LIEUTENANT-GOVERNOR:

WILLIAM LANG,

Of Seneca County.

SUPREME JUDGE (FULL TERM):

PHILADELPH VAN TRUMP,

Of Fairfield County.

SUPREME JUDGE (VACANCY):

THOMAS M. KEY,

Of Hamilton County.

TREASURER OF STATE:

GEORGE SPENCE,

Of Clarke County.

ATTORNEY-GENERAL:

D. M. WILSON,

Of Mahoning Co.

SCHOOL COMMISSIONER:

Of Pickaway County.

BOARD OF PUBLIC WORKS:

CHARLES E. BOESEL,

Of Auglaize County.

CLERK OF THE SUPREME COURT:

DANIEL S. DANA,

Of Vinton Co.

From August 9, 1865, through election day in October, Washington McLean of the *Cincinnati Daily Enquirer* published the Democratic ticket daily under this heading, leaving no doubt where the party stood on racial issues.

George W. Morgan, The Democratic gubernatorial candidate in 1865, personified two of the party's key campaign strategies—nominate veterans and attempt to play on the voters' racial fears.

Washington McLean, editor of the most important Democratic newspaper in Ohio, the *Cincinnati Daily Enquirer,* promoted a powerful blend of racist diatribes and inflationary monetary policies that proved most successful in 1867.

Lewis D. Campbell, an ex-Whig congressman and conservative Republican, became Johnson's key political confidant in Ohio and directed the unsuccessful National Union movement in the state.

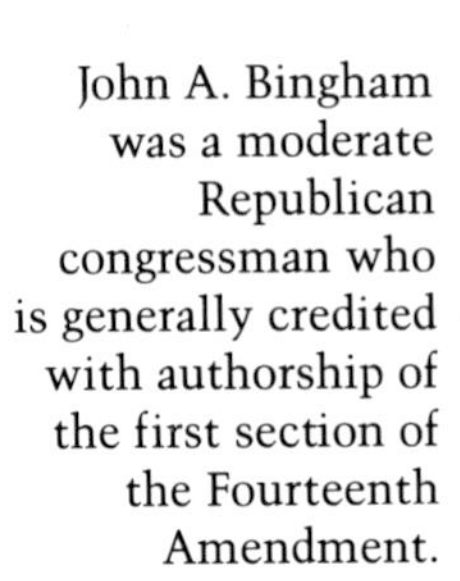

John A. Bingham was a moderate Republican congressman who is generally credited with authorship of the first section of the Fourteenth Amendment.

Above left, James M. Ashley, a Radical Republican from Toledo, traveled the familiar path from initial support for Johnson to implacable foe; ultimately Ashley became the driving force behind several attempts to impeach the president. Among the most radical of the Republicans in the Senate was Benjamin F. Wade, above right, who fought courageously for freedmen's rights before losing his seat when the Democrats gained control of the Ohio General Assembly in 1867.

Conservative Republican Senator John Sherman worked assiduously during the winter and spring of 1866 to keep his party united behind Johnson, but the president's denunciation of the Fourteenth Amendment convinced him that Johnson had deserted the Republicans.

Our Candidate for President.

U. S. GRANT.
ULYSSES SIDNEY GRANT.
UNION SAVING GRANT.
USUALLY SILENT GRANT.
UPRIGHT STATESMAN GRANT.
UNIVERSAL SUFFRAGE GRANT.
UNEQUALED SOLDIER GRANT.
UNAFFECTEDLY SIMPLE GRANT.
UNIFORMLY SUCCESSFUL GRANT
UNANIMOUSLY SELECTED GRANT.
UNDISTURBEDLY SERENE GRANT.
UNCONQUERABLE SPIRITED GRANT.
UNIMPEACHABLE SERVANT GRANT.
UNINTERMITTING SMOKER GRANT.
UNQUESTIONABLY SOUND GRANT.
UNFLINCHINGLY STEADFAST GRANT.
UNCONDITIONAL SURRENDER GRANT.
UNAMBIGUOUSLY STRAIGHTFORWARD GRANT.
UNITED STATES PRESIDENT GRANT.

Game to the Last

AND VICTORIOUS AT LAST

Many Radical Republicans resisted the momentum for Grant that developed in the wake of the Democratic victories in 1867, but once Grant's nomination became inevitable, even Radicals such as editor Edwin Cowles exuberantly endorsed the war hero, as shown in the *Cleveland Leader* of May 27, 1868 (above). When, after years of frustration, the Democrats won control of the Ohio General Assembly in 1867, editor Washington McLean could hardly restrain his joy, as seen in this clipping from the *Cincinnati Daily Enquirer* of October 12, 1867 (right).

Edwin Cowles, editor of the influential *Cleveland Leader,* was a consistent spokesperson for advanced Republican positions on Reconstruction issues, including black suffrage.

James Comly, editor of the *Ohio State Journal* and far more conservative than his Republican colleague Cowles, was among the last influential Republican editors to accept Johnson's abandonment of the party.

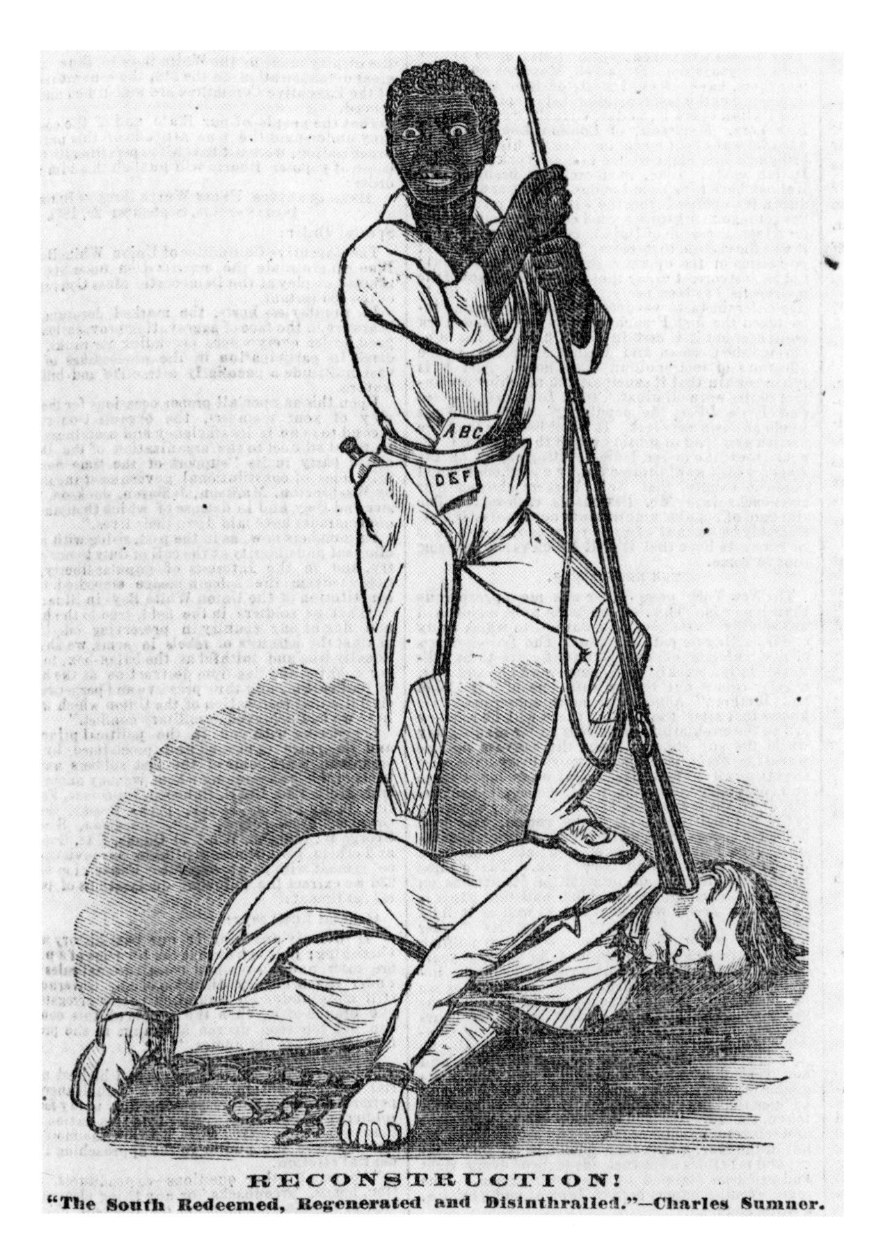

Ohio Democrats in general and Washington McLean in particular consistently portrayed the degradation of whites as the basic result of the Military Reconstruction Acts, as portrayed in this cartoon from McLean's *Cincinnati Daily Enquirer* of October 3, 1868.

the Thirty-ninth Congress reported that party members in his district were "opposed to Negro Suffrage in Ohio and would leave the party if this issue was forced upon them." Moderates and Radicals, however, generally favored granting the vote to blacks in the state. Even conservatives such as John Sherman and Murat Halstead had endorsed the idea of submitting to voters a proposal to remove the word *white* from Ohio's franchise requirement. Both believed that the time was right for such a referendum. Even Governor Cox hinted that he might endorse suffrage extension.[36] Other Republicans revealed doubts about popular opinion by advocating a referendum but at the same time suggesting that their party not take a position on it. At least two Republicans viewed the issue in blatantly political terms. The editors of the *Sandusky Daily Commercial Register* and the *Miami Union* straightforwardly acknowledged that they supported the enfranchisement of blacks because it would deprive the Democrats of one of their favorite issues, without which the Democrats "would have no foundation upon which to stand." Republicans would thus benefit from the removal from the political arena of the one issue upon which they were most vulnerable. With the matter put in that context, Ohio Republicans generally agreed that the suffrage issue should be decided as soon as possible by a statewide referendum.[37]

When the Ohio General Assembly convened in January 1867, Republican legislators decided to consider the subject of black enfranchisement. The moderates raised the suffrage issue in part because they had been stung by Radical denunciations of their past timidity. W.C. Howells, for example, sarcastically hoped that the legislature would "not leave it as a question for our next State Convention to frighten itself with."[38]

Republicans also were encouraged by their success in the fall 1866 elections. In October almost no Republicans had asserted that the elections could be interpreted as a mandate for black suffrage in Ohio.[39] Yet, as the weeks passed and Congress seemed to be moving toward a Reconstruction policy that would require the enfranchisement of blacks in the South, most Radicals and moderates decided that the time had arrived to move Ohio forward. Some undoubtedly were motivated by the desire to remove all race-related issues from future contests in Ohio. Others were sensitive to the hypocrisy of demanding from southerners what they refused to grant in Ohio. Some Republicans also calculated that the party could easily gain the support of the few thousand blacks who would be enfranchised in Ohio. In a state where elections tended to be quite close, those votes might be crucial.[40]

Consequently, some Republicans planned to seek an amendment to the suffrage clause in the state constitution. In December 1866 a Professor G.W. Shurtliff wrote to several key Republican leaders, including William Dennison, James Garfield, and Robert Schenck, urging them to put pressure on the General Assembly by publicly stating their support for black suffrage in Ohio. His pleas secured many positive responses.[41] On January 15, 1867, however, at a caucus of Republican legislators, party members divided so sharply that the issue was not brought to a vote. The split was primarily along geographical lines, with representatives from the southern part of the state opposed to a statewide referendum.[42]

Nonetheless, several bills to amend the state suffrage requirements were introduced in the first month of the session. One proposal, which reflected the widespread desire for a literacy requirement, granted the ballot to every male resident who had not fought against the Union during the Civil War and who could read the state constitution and write his name. Another would enfranchise all adult males except those who had fled the state to avoid the draft or had borne arms for the Confederacy.[43] Both were tabled and died in committee largely because of the presumed unpopularity of disfranchising white voters while giving the vote to blacks.

In late February a House resolution that called for a statewide referendum on the deletion of the word *white* from the state suffrage requirement was revived from the previous session. The Democrats attacked the proposal with their "old and favorite" argument that Ohio must always remain a white man's state. On February 26, before the House could vote on the proposal, John Rhodes, a Republican from Morrow County, offered a substitute resolution that enfranchised all adult males except those who had participated in the rebellion against the United States, fled their home to escape the draft, or deserted from the Union army. The Ohio General Assembly was empowered to remove any of those disabilities. Republican Jesse Oren of Clinton County then tried to amend the substitute by adding a literacy requirement, from which veterans and those currently eligible to vote were exempt. After some parliamentary manuevering, the House rejected Oren's amendment by a vote of sixteen to sixty-two. Immediately thereafter the House voted down Rhodes's substitute resolution by thirty-seven to forty-eight. Finally, the House voted on the original resolution to approve a statewide referendum. This too lost, by a vote thirty-nine to fifty. Twenty-three Republicans, most from Ohio River or western counties and none from the Western Reserve, joined with the Democrats to defeat the measure.[44]

These men, some of whom no doubt personally opposed black

suffrage, apparently believed they had an obligation to represent their perception of their constituents' views. When subjected to abuse from Radical Republicans such as W.C. Howells, who was "ashamed" that the legislature did not have "manhood enough" to vote for black enfranchisement in Ohio, these Republicans defended themselves.[45] For example, Alanson Davenport of Belmont County, located along the Ohio River, insisted he could not betray the mandate his constituents gave him in 1865 when suffrage was not an issue in the election. He lamely declared that because they had not spoken on the matter, he could not vote for the resolution. Davenport further asserted that a "large portion" of Ohioans were quite content to wait until the 1871 constitutional convention to tamper with state voting requirements.[46] John T. Clark of Guernsey County, located in east-central Ohio, shared precisely the same view. "We were elected to our positions denying that universal suffrage was or would be in question" he protested, "and many of us could not have supported the resolution without deceiving those who sent us here." Other Republicans who voted against the bill argued that the right to vote would attract blacks to Ohio; these new residents would compete for jobs with working-class whites, who, they insisted, would blame the Republicans and respond by abandoning the Republican party.[47]

Despite the defeat, the measure did not die. The Senate began consideration of a similar resolution the day after the House vote. On March 21, E.B. Sadler of Erie County spoke in support of a statewide referendum on the suffrage clause in the state constitution. He argued that all senators, whether for or against black enfranchisement, should agree to submit the question to the voters because "it is for the people to say and not for us to deny the right or privilege." He then strongly endorsed suffrage extension. He declared that suffrage was the right of all citizens and blacks were citizens. Furthermore, the senator asked, "Shall 'skedadlers' from the draft, Knights of the Golden Circle, rebels and enemies of the country be permitted to vote, while those who fought in defense of the government are denied the right." In short, blacks deserved the vote in exchange for service rendered to the Union cause during the war. Sadler did acknowledge the fear that a referendum would hurt the Republican party in the fall elections, and so he agreed that the matter need not be made a party measure.[48] Six days later, with some Republicans announcing that their positions had changed during the session, the bill passed by a vote of twenty-three to eleven more than the three-fifths necessary to submit it to the voters. Only one Republican, A.D. Combs of Highland County, joined the Democratic opposition.[49]

The House refused to accept the Senate bill and a select committee of one, Elijah Glover of Scioto County, was appointed to find a compromise solution. As the price for conservative Republican support, he added to the Senate bill a clause that disfranchised anyone who had fought against the Union, fled the draft or deserted from the Union forces.[50]

The debate on the new proposal took an unusual turn. Four Republicans who still opposed the measure tried to resign from the House. Clark, Davenport and A.W. Shipley of Muskingum County voiced their unwillingness to oppose their party further but also their refusal to acquiesce to it and so submitted their resignations. Scipio Myers of Darke County insisted that his constituents opposed the bill and that he wished to represent their views, but party loyalty denied him that opportunity. So he quit, or rather tried to quit. On April 3 the House rejected all four resignations and proceeded to discuss Glover's compromise proposal. Three amendments, almost certainly meant more to ridicule the agreement than to be taken seriously, were proposed: one to disfranchise anyone who had served in the Grand Army of the Republic, one to disfranchise anyone who had voted for Clement Vallandigham in 1863, and one to enfranchise adult women by removing the word *male* from the voting requirement. All were quickly rejected. With Davenport abstaining, Glover's measure carried on a strict party vote, sixty-three to twenty-nine.[51]

The Senate then attempted to remove the disfranchising clause, but the House stood adamant. Deadlock would probably have resulted except that the state constitution required that any amendment to that document had to have passed the General Assembly at least six months before the general election in which the voters would decide its fate. To qualify for submission in the October election, the legislature needed to act by April 8. With this deadline rapidly approaching, the Senate relented and approved the House version with the disfranchising clause. Ohio voters finally had the opportunity to decide if blacks would vote in the state.[52]

Quite obviously, twenty-two House Republicans had changed their votes between late February and early April. The most basic reason for the switch was the passage in early March of the Military Reconstruction Act, which required black enfranchisement in the South. Although some of the conservative Republicans argued that this provision was really meant to punish the South, and therefore, Ohio need not enfranchise blacks to avoid charges of hypocrisy, most party members concluded that the new Reconstruction policy left them little choice but to be as progressive as the South. The addition of the disfranchisement clause also persuaded some conservative Republicans, eight according to one report, to join the party majority.[53] These men apparently feared white backlash, especially from the working classes, if blacks in Ohio received the vote. They seem to have concluded that more Democrats than Republicans would be disfranchised by the clause, therefore minimizing the effect of white backlash. The disfranchisement clause was therefore not so much an attempt to punish deserters or turncoats as a maneuver to decrease the number of Democratic voters.[54]

The disfranchisement clause, however, immediately caused far more grief than the Republicans ever expected. Army records revealed over twenty-seven thousand deserters from Ohio, almost one-quarter of whom had left after Lee's surrender. These men had definitely not abandoned the Union in its time of need but were nevertheless classified as deserters. To remedy this situation and extricate the Republicans from a most inconvenient political snarl, the Ohio House asked Congress for help. The latter body bailed out Ohio Republicans in July 1867 when it passed the Ohio Deserters' Bill, which provided that no soldier or sailor who left his unit without authorization after April 19, 1865, should be considered a deserter. With the passage of that act, the Republicans breathed somewhat easier, although many Ohioans agreed with Governor Cox's analysis that the disfranchisement clause smacked of revenge and political opportunism without enhancing "public safety."[55]

The vast majority of Ohioans were happy that the black suffrage amendment was submitted to the electorate. Democrats typically could scarcely conceal their glee that the Republican wolf had finally taken off its sheep's clothing and admitted its love for blacks. One editor conveyed the general substance and tone of the Democratic reaction, sneering that the Republican party was so in need of votes that its "leaders cry out, 'help us, Sambo, or we sink.'" Democrats confidently expected that racial attitudes in Ohio would propel them to their first election triumph in five years.[56]

Conservative Republicans, many of whom opposed black enfranchisement for a variety of reasons ranging from prejudice to the desire for a literacy requirement to fear that the measure would hurt the party, could still feel satisfaction that the electorate would have the opportunity to settle the quarrelsome issue. If the amendment passed, they hoped racial issues would disappear from Ohio politics. If it failed, some of them would be pleased that the electorate had not been polluted by black voters. These Republicans could then insist that the people had spoken and that the party should not raise the matter again.

Some of the conservatives, however, considered the disqualification clause a terrible mistake that would cause serious problems for the party. For example, Governor Cox calculated that if the amendment passed the Republicans would gain about four hundred black voters and lose around twenty-four thousand whites, many of whom would leave the party in anger because of their opposition to the disqualification clause.[57]

Many Republicans worried about the political ramifications of endorsing the amendment in the party platform. They doubted the wisdom of tying such an explosive issue to the Republican banner and preferred to let the voters decide its fate solely on its merits.[58] This position of course reflected either their antipathy toward the proposal or their conviction that the public opposed it.

Many Republicans, though, indicate a willingness and even an eagerness to vote for the amendment. Some of them declared that the completion of Reconstruction and the establishment of long-range peace required black suffrage. A sizable number reasoned that the passage of the Military Reconstruction Act made ratification imperative to convince the South that the North intended to insist on its terms.[59] Some thought blacks should have the ballot because they had loyally supported the Union during the war. The editor of the *Bellefontaine Republican* used his belief in white supremacy as a reason to enfranchise blacks, paradoxically asserting that "the fact that a man is an inferior being is a *reason for giving him* the ballot."[60] Many held that backing the amendment was good policy for the party because its passage, which they considered virtually certain, would increase the number of Republican voters and silence the Democrats' incessant harping about racial issues.[61] A large number of Republicans, though only a minority of Ohioans, agreed with Richard Smith, who announced proudly but with uncharacteristic naïveté that "the principle is right and it is bound to succeed." Another advocate of this position, though, gave stern and prescient warning that the "intrinsic justice of the measure will not commend it to all men."[62] He fully comprehended the difficulties ahead for proponents of the amendment.

During 1867 an entirely different group of issues intruded for the first time into the debate on Reconstruction. These were economic questions, most of which grew out of the financing of the Union war effort. They arose at this time largely because the American business cycle, which had peaked in May 1865, was sliding toward a trough it would reach in December 1867. The Democrats, ever vigilant for any issue that promised votes, naturally jumped on economic hard times as a ticket that could take them back into office. The existence of a huge war-created federal debt and of over $400 million in unredeemable United States notes, commonly called greenbacks, greatly complicated the postwar economic debate and gave Democrats other weapons with which to flail their political opponents.[63]

In late 1865 Secretary of the Treasury Hugh McCulloch attacked these problems by asking Congress to authorize the withdrawal of the greenbacks from circulation. In April 1866 Congress agreed. Almost immediately McCulloch implemented the act, but the worsening of the postwar recession hampered his efforts and greatly increased the resistance to further contraction of the money supply. Americans increasingly blamed the hard times on McCulloch's policy.[64]

By 1867, even though twenty-seven of twenty-eight party members in the House had voted for McCulloch's plan, many Democrats realized the political possibilities of exploiting the current economic difficulties. They focused attention on four related issues: contraction, the medium of repayment of the principal of the war debt, federal taxation on the interest income from government bonds, and retention of the national banking system. Washington McLean, Democratic editor of the *Cincinnati Daily Enquirer*, led the attack, at least in part because he sought an issue that would increase his power within the party.

Noting that Congress had stipulated that the interest on much of the federal debt must be paid in gold but had made no such pronouncement concerning the repayment of the principal, McLean developed a plan that linked currency contraction and the repayment of the debt. His plan specifically pertained to the bonds commonly called 5-20s, because they were redeemable in five years and payable in twenty. Over $600 million worth of these bonds were outstanding in June 1865. In early 1867, realizing that many Ohioans and others resented that the war bonds had been purchased with depreciated greenbacks but that the government might now be obliged to repay the principal in gold, he advocated the payment of the Civil War debt with greenbacks. To do so, the government would have to curtail contraction severely or stop it altogether, keeping the United States notes in circulation. Rebuffed at the Democratic State Convention, McLean persevered and won an increasing number of adherents to his plan. He also gained the support of George Hunt Pendleton, the 1864 Democratic vice-presidential nominee and one of the most influential and able party members in Ohio. In fact, Pendleton liked McLean's idea so much that he took it for his own and refined it into the Pendleton Plan, also known as the "Ohio Idea."

During 1867 Pendleton spread his economic ideas across the state. He urged the redemption of the 5-20s with greenbacks, which, because the original act authorizing their issue contained no mention of the medium of repayment, was certainly not illegal. This plan would also facilitate the replacement of national bank notes with greenbacks. (The bank notes had never been popular with Jacksonian Democrats, who opposed both the national banking system and the national bank notes.) This pleasant result would occur because as the war bonds were retired they could no longer be used to back the issuance of the national bank notes, which would then have to removed from circulation. Thus, over a period of time the United States notes would completely replace the national bank currency. This procedure not only appealed to those who considered the entire national banking system the domain of the privileged few but also promised to reduce federal expenditures because the government would no longer need to pay the interest on the bonds that backed the national bank notes. To Pendleton and his followers the exchange of an interest-free debt, the greenbacks, for an interest-bearing one, the 5-20 bonds, seemed completely reasonable. Advocates of these ideas produced the Democratic slogan "The same currency for the plowholder and the bondholder."

The Pendleton Plan also attracted those who blamed contraction for their economic difficulties, because the uses Pendleton envisioned for the greenbacks necessitated that large amounts remain in circulation. More greenbacks in circulation promised to end the downward price spiral that many believed was causing their distress.[65]

The widespread acceptance of these financial doctrines dismayed many Republican strategists and caused much confusion about what position the party ought to take. Party leaders' anxiety was greatly increased by the lack of agreement in their own party on economic issues. For example, one Republican noted that most Republicans in his county actually favored keeping the greenbacks in circulation and warned that if McCulloch persisted in contracting the currency, many in Ohio would support outright repudiation of the federal debt. He feared that the Republicans might be condemned as "advocates and supporters of a policy that enriches the few at the Expense of the many."[66] Most Republicans, however, seem to have rallied behind payment of both principal and interest on the government bonds in gold and to have accepted contraction as a necessary step toward the resumption of specie payments.[67]

The Democrats accepted the challenge and charged forward, blasting the "bloated bondholders" with all the rhetoric they could muster. Not surprisingly, Washington McLean led the assault. During July, August, and September he printed nearly daily editorials praising Pendleton's plan and attacking contraction and the injustice of paying gold for bonds bought with cheap greenbacks. Other Democrats followed his example.[68]

Blessed with several potent issues, the Democrats jumped to the political offensive and maintained it throughout the fall campaign. They struck hard and incessantly on three politically promising matters, the proposed Ohio suffrage amendment, the congressional Reconstruction program, and the Pendleton Plan.

On the black suffrage question the Democrats followed their well-established pattern of appealing to racial fears and prejudice. Voters had an easy choice of declaring themselves "either white men or mongrels. Don't dodge! Be white or black; caucasian or mulatto!" Leading Democrats repeated the well-worn charges that the Republican party sponsored miscegenation and desired "in its inner heart that Ohio shall become a negro colony, controlled by Negro votes."[69] The Democrats dramatically warned that blacks would flood into Ohio if the suffrage amendment passed, and this influx would ruin the state because blacks had an "inherent" inability to vote intelligently. Furthermore, the state would face widespread white unemployment because blacks would drive wages down so low that no self-respecting white man could support his family. The ultimate result would be racial warfare in the Buckeye State. The message could not have been presented more clearly. To keep Ohio a white man's country, stave off black social and economic equality, and prevent a bloody struggle between the races, the "damned darkey" must be kept in the South where he belonged. Only Democratic and antiamendment votes could accomplish these objectives.[70]

Democratic accusations that congressional Reconstruction had forced military despotism on innocent, unoffending southerners reached a deafening peak as the campaign moved toward its climax. The Democrats not only charged the Radicals with running roughshod over the rights of white southerners but also blamed all the racial violence in the South, which nearly all northerners agreed was increasing, on the freedmen and their Radical allies. Democrats skillfully argued that the immoral and unconstitutional military Reconstruction program was also burying northerners under an ever-increasing and unbearable public debt. According to one analysis, "The enormous debt under which the people are now groaning, is the legitimate child of the Black Republican," who had created it to free the slaves and now added to it daily in an insane drive to force social and political equality on the country. The Democrats struck telling blows by connecting the greenback questions with the high cost of the congressional refusal to readmit southerners and then contrasting this sad situation with Ohioans' longing for peace and quiet. Democrats presented an appealing message that promised immediate restoration of southerners and an end to sectional strife.[71]

For the first time since 1862 many Ohio voters, perhaps a majority, seriously considered the Democratic message. As impatience over continued Reconstruction increased in the North, Congress had embarked upon a new plan that might delay reunion indefinitely. It also exceeded Ohioans' original Reconstruction terms. By promising immediate reunion without the haunting specter of black suffrage, the Democrats tapped a large source of support. The intrusion of the economic recession and the issues related to the payment of the federal debt gave the Democrats more reasons to appreciate being the "outs." They could capitalize on voter discontent and frustration by promising attractive alternatives to Republican policies. They spared no effort in portraying themselves as the party with the answers.

Beset with serious problems, Ohio Republicans attempted to rally their supporters. In what had become an annual ritual, many party members called the 1867 election the most critical since 1863, when Vallandigham ran for governor on a peace platform. In early May the Republican state executive and central committees announced their intention to focus the campaign on Reconstruction issues, the proposed amendment, and the disloyalty of the Democratic party. In a vague but vivid example of waving the bloody shirt, the Republican leadership charged that "our enemies are the same [as during the war] and their principles have undergone no change. We cannot forget the dark record of their transgressions, nor permit them to carry their designs into execution by a victory at the ballot box." [72]

At the state convention in June the party wrote a platform that directly addressed only one of the major issues facing the people, hedged on another, and ignored a third. One plank endorsed congressional Reconstruction and urged passage of whatever additional measures might be necessary to guarantee a secure future. The party's stance on the suffrage amendment reflected how much the situation had changed over the past year. Because the "whole people" and not just a "privileged class" should run a democracy and because "the spirit and tendency of Modern Civilization" suggested the time had come, the Republicans stood "on the simple and broad platform of impartial manhood suffrage, as embodied in the proposed amendment to the state constitution, appealing to and confiding in the intelligence, justice and patriotism of the people of Ohio, to approve it at the ballot box." Despite suggesting that the electorate vote for the amendment, however, the Republicans refused to endorse the whole proposal explicitly. The problem was the disfranchisement clause, which the party intentionally ignored in the platform. Apparently the Republicans considered it safer to endorse black voting in Ohio than to support the disfranchisement of white voters. More likely, the party consciously avoided the disfranchisement clause in order to allow party members who opposed black suffrage to vote against the amendment on the grounds that it disfranchised whites. Certainly some Republicans feared that the amendment would drag the party down to defeat, but they also could not consistently support congressional Reconstruction if they denied blacks the right to vote in Ohio. They therefore created a fiction that "good" Republicans could oppose the amendment but only because they could not sanction the disfranchisement clause.[73]

The Republican platform made no mention whatsoever of the economic questions facing the nation. Recognizing the deep divisions within the party on economic issues and concerned about losing votes over the suffrage amendment, the Republicans realized they did not need to drive more voters into the opposition with an inflexible stance on a difficult problem. Silence forced no one to advocate a party position he personally opposed.[74]

Reconstruction questions also influenced the nomination of a Republican candidate for governor. Jacob Cox disapproved of the party's decision to go beyond the Fourteenth Amendment as final terms for reunion and, consequently, announced in January 1867 his decision not to run for reelection.[75] His withdrawal opened the field to a host of candidates, among them James Garfield, Robert Schenck, Donn Piatt, Aaron F. Perry, Benjamin Cowen, Samuel Galloway, Columbus Delano, and Rutherford B. Hayes.[76] In an effort to pick the candidate most attractive to the voters, the party set some exacting criteria that were dominated by Reconstruction-related issues. The nominee should be a proponent of the state amendment, have a record of support for Congress in its struggles with Johnson, have a good military record, and have a strong following in southern Ohio, where the suffrage amendment was expected to have a difficult time. These requirements hurt some candidates, for example, Congressman Columbus Delano, who in March 1867 had checked the extent of his support and quickly learned that some key Republicans considered him too conservative on Reconstruction issues and too sympathetic toward President Johnson. His candidacy never really got going.[77] Rutherford B. Hayes, a congressman from Cincinnati, best fit these requirements and he won a second-ballot nomination.[78]

During the campaign most Republicans presented the suffrage amendment and Reconstruction as the two major issues before the voters. Party editors and speakers generally worked diligently to get the amendment approved, developing wide-ranging lists of reasons why the voters should ratify the proposal. Following the lead of gubernatorial candidate Hayes, who argued that the federal government ought to be not a white man's government but a government of free men, most party leaders urged approval of the amendment as a matter of principle. Voting, these Republicans insisted, was a fundamental civil right that all free Americans should enjoy. At the same time Hayes and others drew careful distinctions between political rights and social and economic equality.[79]

The editor of the *Springfield Daily Republic* presented a reason to vote for the amendment that better catered to Ohioans' attitudes. He bluntly asked his readers, "Do you want to get the negro out of politics? The adoption of the Constitutional Amendment will effect that object completely and forever. And nothing else will."[80] This man and many other Ohio Republicans expected, or at least hoped, that approval of the amendment would remove all racial questions from state politics. Although few Republicans put the matter so bluntly, most surely appreciated the political attraction of this position. Certainly *Cincinnati Daily Gazette* editor Richard Smith, who backed the amendment on principle, was bowing to public attitudes when he announced, "We will, therefore, merely remark that impartial suffrage is bound to come, and we may as well drive the negro out of politics now as at any future time."[81]

Many Republicans apparently believed that ending a public discussion of racial issues was the chief benefit the party would gain from ratification. They hoped to deprive the Democrats of their strongest campaign issue. Smith expressed the commonly held idea that once armed with the ballot, blacks could take care of all their other needs. Approval of the amendment would

> annihilate the Copperheads, North and South, beyond redemption. My doctrine is *choke this party to death with wool.* . . .
>
> Give the negro the right to vote and he will pass out of politics; the ballot will protect him and the Democratic party will die. It has lived on negro agitation for thirty-five years and it cannot live without it. The time has come when Republicans should see that this Democratic food is taken away. If Democrats fear negro equality as a consequence of impartial suffrage all they have to do is to join the Union party and they will be protected. Union men do not fear it; because it is not to be feared, except by the party that has been mingling with negroes for fifty years and corrupting the blood of the colored race. Impartial suffrage will put a stop to this business, and we shall have an end of social equality.[82]

Republicans bristled at Democratic taunts that the only purpose of the amendment was to increase the number of Republican voters. While vigorously denying such accusations, Richard Smith insisted that the addition of black voters in Ohio would "make no political disturbance" because so few blacks lived in the state. Still, the party was taking an enormous risk, and Smith tacitly admitted the wish that Republicans could gain more votes. "Were our opponents in our places," he charged, "they would enfranchise the mules if they would vote the Democratic ticket."[83]

While Republicans denied that politics motivated their advocacy of the amendment, they sought to calm voter anxiety that ratification would lead to black social equality. They told Ohioans that suffrage was a political right that had "nothing to do with social position or relations," and party leaders insisted that the vote and basic civil rights were the only rights blacks needed and deserved. Ratification of the amendment would not lead, they promised, to further rises in blacks' status.[84]

As election day approached several Republican papers, perhaps reflecting their growing desperation, printed long lists of reasons to support the proposal. One paper for example presented no less than sixteen points in support of ratification. In addition to those already mentioned, editors noted that adherence to the Golden Rule required black enfranchisement, that blacks in Ohio were taxpayers and Civil War veterans. Some insisted that Ohioans must accept black suffrage if they intended to force it on the South. One Republican cast aside all caution, asserting that blacks would be better voters than the lowest class of whites, a group he equated with the Democrats.[85]

Some Republicans, including two influential editors, Murat Halstead of the *Cincinnati Daily Commercial* and James Comly of the *Ohio State Journal,* the official state Republican paper, had never wholeheartedly backed the amendment, and late in the campaign they virtually abandoned it. Others completely ignored suffrage extension and chose to stress other issues.[86]

In their handling of the second major issue, Reconstruction, Republicans tended to twist the question into a discussion of the alleged disloyalty of all Democrats. The Republicans created a stereotypical Democrat, a man who had allowed secession, become a Copperhead during the war, and now would completely sell out the nation's need for security by allowing southerners back into the Union before they had given sufficient proof of loyalty. This Republican fiction was, of course, as inaccurate as the democratic charge that all Republicans were radicals, but as the campaign progressed and Republican prognosticators began to sense a potential disaster, party spokesmen relied increasingly on the faithful bloody shirt as the best way to convince voters that only the Republicans could deal with the continuing problem of Reconstruction. They denounced the Democrats as the party of disunion, warning soldiers that the issues of 1867 were exactly the same as those of 1863 and urging them to "vote as you shot."[87]

When Republicans discussed congressional Reconstruction, they often portrayed it as the struggle of a courageous Congress, fighting valiantly against a rebel-sympathizing president to save the country from unrepentant rebels. They hoped to convince the voters that the election would determine the fate of the nation.[88] In reality, the Republicans could not engage in an ideological defense of Military Reconstruction because many of the more conservative party members only tolerated rather than enthusiastically supported the program. To discuss the policy solely on its merits would have threatened party unity, already strained by the suffrage amendment and the economic issues.

Some Republicans had no problems attacking the Pendleton Plan and did so with gusto, relying heavily on pious pronouncements about how American national honor required payment of the war debt in gold and about the immorality of unbacked currency.[89] Here again, though, the Republicans were not only on the defensive but also divided. A fairly sizable portion of the party agreed with the Democrats and chose silence as the best way to deal with financial questions.

Although some Republicans publicly declared that the election would go well, most harbored grave concerns for their party. Perhaps the most extreme example was provided by editor James Comly, who cried, almost hysterically, "Bring in the aged and feeble. Send buggies for them. We need *every Union vote.*"[90] The Republican optimism of late 1866 had evaporated.

As the election returns became available, Ohioans rapidly realized that the Democrats had made significant gains since 1866. For three days the result of the gubernatorial race remained in doubt, before the official returns indicated that Hayes had defeated Allen Thurman by only 2,983 votes out of the 484,000 cast. That was the best news the Republicans had. The Democrats had captured majorities of fifty-six to forty-nine in the state House of Representatives and eighteen to seventeen in the Senate, thus giving them the bonus of being able to elect Senator Wade's successor. Furthermore, the voters had resoundingly rejected the proposed constitutional amendment.[91]

An analysis of the election results clarifies just how much the

Republicans had lost since 1865. In the first statewide election after the war Jacob Cox had won 53.57 percent of the total vote and carried fifty-six of eighty-eight counties. In 1866 Republican congressional candidates secured 54.23 percent of the vote and carried fifty-three counties, winning sixteen of nineteen Ohio congressional districts. Rutherford Hayes, however, won only forty-three counties and 50.31 percent of the vote, the lowest percentage a Republican gubernatorial candidate had received since 1857. In an election in which the total votes cast increased by nearly sixteen thousand compared to the previous year's turnout, Hayes got about eleven thousand fewer votes than the 1866 Republican congressional candidates. Either many Republicans chose not to vote, thousands of Republicans voted for Democrats, or huge numbers of Democrats who had not voted in 1866 did vote in 1867. Almost certainly all three phenomena occurred. Not only had the Republicans secured substantially fewer votes in 1867 than in previous postwar elections, their losses had been fairly uniform throughout the state. The party's share of the vote fell in eighty-six of the eighty-eight counties.[92]

The vote on the constitutional amendment further distressed the Republicans. The proposal garnered just under 217,000 votes or slightly less than 46 percent of the total. One might marvel that over two hundred thousand white males had indicated a willingness to allow blacks to vote in Ohio. Considering that a majority of Ohioans had never demanded that the enfranchisement of northern blacks be part of Reconstruction, that is a substantial statement in favor of racial justice. However, these numbers do not quite reflect the general hostility toward the amendment. The total vote on the amendment fell nearly twelve thousand short of the total vote of the gubernatorial candidates. Moreover, Hayes got twenty-seven thousand more votes than the proposed constitutional change. Assuming, as seems to be quite logical, that the twelve thousand men who did not vote on the amendment had all voted for Hayes, an additional fifteen thousand Republicans would have cast ballots against it. Considering that the antisuffrage total exceeded the vote for Thurman by 14,800 and assuming that virtually every Democrat (probably about as safe an assumption as one could ever make) voted against the amendment, it would be fair to conclude that about fifteen thousand Republicans did indeed vote against the measure. Furthermore, the 1867 Republican ticket ran nearly eleven thousand ballots behind its 1866 counterpart, even though the total vote in 1867 increased by nearly sixteen thousand. The suggestion is strong that thousands of Republicans simply stayed away from the polls rather than vote against the amendment. The no-shows nearly cost their party the governor's chair and did result in the loss of the legislature and consequently a seat in the United States Senate. Adding to these statistics a fairly sizable, though indeterminate number of Republicans who probably opposed the amendment but voted for it solely out of party loyalty, leads to a conclusion that no more than 40 percent of those who participated in the 1867 election genuinely endorsed black suffrage in Ohio.[93]

Viewed from almost any perspective, the election severely disappointed the Republicans, especially the Radicals, who had pushed for more stringent Reconstruction requirements than the Fourteenth Amendment and were responsible for submitting the proposed Ohio constitutional amendment to the voters. As had happened in several northern states, the electorate in Ohio had given the Republicans a clear rebuke for allowing the Radicals to assert too much power in early 1867. Voters throughout the North, including Ohio, gave ample proof that they would not endorse attempts to use Reconstruction to transform southern society on the northern model. After the election, Republican moderates moved quickly and successfully to regain ascendancy within the party.[94]

Despite the solid rejection of the amendment, a fair number of Republicans continued to favor black suffrage in Ohio. These men either denied that they had caused defeat or insisted that the party must stand on the principle of justice even if the voters rejected its doctrines. They chastised the voters for failing to do their duty to mankind. The repudiation of the amendment was a "reproach and a shame—a blot upon their claims to intelligence, and a serious reflection upon their pretentions to justice." Senator John Sherman concluded that the "chief trouble, no doubt, is the suffrage question. It is clearly right that suffrage should be impartial without regard to color. It is easy to convince people so, but harder to make them feel it—and vote it. We will have to carry it because it is right but it will be a burden in every election." The result forced Ohioans who still advocated suffrage extension to consider postponing their goal. They could either wait for public attitudes to change and then press for another statewide vote or push for federal action that woud transcend state laws. The latter option became increasingly attractive during the following months.[95]

Many moderate and conservative Republicans who had felt obligated by party loyalty to support the amendment during the campaign quickly attacked their Radical colleagues after its defeat. Blessed with excellent hindsight they insisted they had known all along that the amendment would fail and blamed party members from the Western Reserve for the debacle. One editor bluntly rejected the argument that principle demanded the immediate extension of suffrage to blacks in Ohio. "Of course negro suffrage is right," he wrote, "so is temperance in the abstract: so is going to church and vaccination. . . . There is a fitness of times and seasons in all things, and the most unfit time to force the Amendment before the people of Ohio was now." A central Ohio Republican, who also vigorously denounced those responsible for submitting the amendment to the voters, gave clear evidence of his position. "We are sorry that the Amendment did not carry," he stated, "although we are not greatly disappointed at the result. We were anxious to get the everlasting 'nigger' out of politics. He had been a disturbing element long enough."[96] Even radicals such as Senator Benjamin Wade understood how much hostility the amendment encountered and how it hurt Republican candidates, writing "We went in on principle, and got whipped." Other Republicans agreed that the Democrats had skillfully played on the electorate's racial fears and prejudice and had been rewarded for their efforts. In short, nearly all Ohio Republicans saw clearly that racial attitudes in the state simply prohibited the voluntary acceptance of political equality for blacks in Ohio.[97]

Despite the rancor among Republicans over their weak showing in 1867, the voters' verdict tended to unite the party. Members soon quit blaming each other for the defeats and agreed to keep racial questions out of future campaigns as much as possible; it was a clear victory for the conservatives and moderates. At the same time Ohio Republicans reached a significant conclusion on military Reconstruction. While other issues, particularly financial questions, greatly complicated analysis of the election results, nearly all Ohioans acknowledged that the voters had given at best grudging acceptance to military Reconstruction. Ohioans had not been convinced that black voting was essential in the South. Nonetheless, the party had little choice but to stick with military Reconstruction in the hope that it would somehow bring a quick and secure end to Reconstruction. Certainly the election made it clear that Ohioans and other northerners would not tolerate making further demands of southerners. That Republicans recognized the voters' attitudes was obvious in the presidential politicking that occurred immediately following the election.

The Republicans had concluded that above all else they needed an 1868 presidential candidate who could reverse the trend of 1867. By mid-October a large number of Ohio Republicans had endorsed Ulysses S. Grant for president, even though they knew little about his political views. Two main factors account for their decision. The 1867 election seemed to verify that a Radical Republican candidate, such as Salmon Chase or Benjamin Wade, the two most frequently mentioned possibilities, would not only be defeated in the general election but would drag other Republican candidates down to defeat with him. Grant may have been an unknown quantity, but he certainly was no Radical.[98] Furthermore, since the death of Lincoln, Grant had basked in the popularity of being the foremost surviving Union war hero.

Within a week of the 1867 election James Hall, the senior Republican in the Ohio Senate, asked Ohio Secretary of State William Henry Smith to help him arrange an endorsement by the Ohio General Assembly of Grant for president. Hall hoped this action would unify the party and guarantee success in 1868. In fact, Grant seemed infinitely electable and promised to improve the chances of Republican candidates in local and state elections and to retain strong majorities in Congress. The boom for Grant that developed throughout Ohio and the North boosted Republican spirits; it also reflected the decline of the Radicals' influence.[99]

The pro-Grant strategy was largely based on analyses of the election, which had concluded that the suffrage amendment had caused the outcome. Certainly, it had played a significant role in the election results, but many other issues, not all related to Reconstruction, helped to account for the resurgence of the Democrats. Their skillful manipulation of economic issues undoubtedly attracted many votes. In increasingly difficult economic times, many Ohioans must have responded positively to Democratic charges that high taxes resulted directly from the Republican's costly Reconstruction policies and to their promises to reduce taxes if elected.[100] McCulloch's continued contraction of the currency and the Democrats' advocacy of the Pendleton Plan also worked to their advantage. With more than a little condescension, William Henry Smith explained the role of economic issues, "We had to meet before ignorant people, the plausible theory of the Democratic speakers, for disposing of the National Debt, and saving taxation. There is nothing that pleases the laboring classes so much as to hear banks and rich people denounced, no matter whether their own interests are also involved. Promise a millennium of wealth and plenty and their imagination will make it presently real."[101] As much as Smith might sneer, each member of those "laboring classes" had a vote precisely as valuable as his and in 1867 probably used it to defeat Republican candidates.

For the first time since the war had ended Ohioans had gone through an election campaign not solely dominated by Reconstruction issues. In no sense was the 1867 election a referendum on the Military Reconstruction Acts, but Reconstruction-related issues did assume the largest role in the campaign. The most obvious factor in the Republican losses was that they had lost control of the issues. As long as they had been able to keep voters' attention focused on Reconstruction in the South, they had done very well. In 1867, however, partly because of their own decisions and partly because of growing weariness with Reconstruction, the Republicans saw the initiative slip away from them. The Democrats had taken the offensive and exploited the issues well. To win back the support of the voters in 1868, the Republicans would not only need a strong presidential candidate, they would also need to refocus voters' attention on the South. Nothing was certain, for Ohioans had shown clearly that their patience with Reconstruction had been nearly exhausted. Republicans faced a difficult future at best.

6

SUCCESS IN SIGHT?

Reconstruction upon a loyal basis is a success and though the Democracy and the rebels may gnash their teeth, the great majority of the people of the country will rejoice that the vexed question of reconstruction will soon be among the things of the past.

—*Marion Independent*, 1868

Republicans in Ohio had struggled through an extremely difficult and disappointing year in 1867, particularly in view of the high hopes generated by the 1866 election. As the Republicans meditated on the causes and consequences of the recent debacle during the winter of 1867-1868, attention focused on how to avoid a repeat performance in 1868. A national election disaster would have far greater significance than the state elections, and it must be avoided at all costs. In the heated atmosphere of the Reconstruction era Republicans might quarrel among themselves over policies and spoils, but they almost unanimously agreed that the nation could be saved from another and far more damaging civil war only if they remained in control of the federal government. To do so, they had to learn the bitter lessons of 1867.

Even before the new year began Ohio Republicans provided clear evidence that they had indeed learned much from their defeat and recognized that they needed new strategies if they were to keep the Democrats from regaining control of the federal government. Their behavior during the many critical events of 1868 reflected the Republicans' general conclusion that the congressional Reconstruction program would remain the basic policy in dealing with both white and black southerners. Reconstruction was rapidly becoming a settled issue in their minds, for the party realized that Ohioans' attention was drifting to other, particularly economic, issues.[1] Before Reconstruction matters could be safely ignored, however, Ohio Republicans had to assure themselves that the gains made during the war and solidified by federal legislation after it would not be lost. By the end of 1868 most Ohio Republicans concluded that the necessary assurances had been made and that Reconstruction could recede from the national spotlight.

Within days after the elections of 1867 Ohio Republicans began to consider ways to overcome one of the party's most critical problems, its radical image, which had been greatly amplified by the voters' perception that it had endorsed black enfranchisement. Anxiety over party image did not equate with a desire to retreat on the fundamentals of Reconstruction, but it did mean that Congress need not, indeed could not, demand more from the South. For example, in late November Edwin Cowles of the *Cleveland Leader* insisted that Reconstruction was "progressing admirably now" and concluded that therefore Congress need pass no further legislation on the matter. During the same week James Comly, editor of the *Ohio State Journal*, reprinted several editorials from weekly newspapers in Ohio in which the writers maintained that Congress must adhere to the principles that underlay the Military Reconstruction Acts but not go beyond them.[2]

Nonetheless, a sizable number of Republicans worried that Congress might push for more requirements and that these would inevitably lead to Democratic majorities throughout the North. For example, Representative James Garfield, who had definitely wearied of Reconstruction, believed that the Republicans must put more emphasis on other issues and cease its efforts to remake southern society. Otherwise, the Democrats would surely overwhelm them in 1868.[3]

By January 1868 these fears had increased as Congress debated several new Reconstruction bills. One Ohio Republican was provoked to write, "The future is to me dark. I confess I am satisfied that the people are turning against us more and more; and I am prepared to wake up ere long and find our enemies in power." Friedrich Hassaurek, a German immigrant who had considerable power in the Republican party, confronted the problem directly. "We cannot be blind," he warned Senator John Sherman, "to the fact that a reaction has set in. . . . We are losing ground daily. Men who have voted with us for many years, are going over to the opposition. The train-bands and camp followers who scent the coming storm, are leaving us by the hundreds, and, if the brakes are not put on in time, not even Gen. Grant's great popularity will be able to save us next October and November."[4]

Hassaurek had enunciated realities that disturbed many Republicans throughout the North, but he also had mentioned the most obvious way to overcome the party's damaging image. Immediately after the elections of 1867, moderate and conservative Republicans began urging the nomination of Ulysses S. Grant for president. During the winter months pressure and sentiment for his nomination increased dramatically, with the greatest percentage of it logically coming from moderate and conservative Republicans who were extremely concerned that the party appear more conservative than it had in 1867.[5]

By late winter even those Ohio Republicans who had reservations about Grant had generally accepted the inevitability of his nomination. For example, Lyman Hall, who knew his congressman, James Garfield, did not favor Grant, nonetheless informed him that the "masses" demanded the general even without any expression of political views. The report did not shock Garfield, who about two weeks earlier had concluded that "the Presidential outlook is anything but pleasing. The current for Grant seems irresistable, and if it be not checked or controlled, it will result in nominating him, without platform or pledge. Indeed some of our friends are so mad as to advocate precisely that course. I hope that some movement will compel the party to make a solid platform for the nominee."[6]

The momentum for Grant continued to mount until his nomination at Chicago in May, which permitted moderate and conservative Republicans to assert with some justification that they were regaining control of the party. During the same months, however, the move to impeach Andrew Johnson reemerged with potentially dangerous implications for party unity and for attempts to convince the electorate that the Radicals were no longer in command. Johnson had survived several previous impeachment attempts, usually led by Congressman James Ashley of Ohio.Then, in August 1867, when he suspended Secretary of War Stanton, discussion of impeachment resumed throughout the country.

In Ohio, Republicans seem to have been genuinely concerned that if Johnson were allowed to appoint a pliant secretary of war, he could defeat any congressional Reconstruction program, not only endangering the nation's future but threatening the supremacy of the Republican party. Johnson's removal increasingly came to be viewed as a "short cut to national peace." Even some of those who had previously been unconvinced of its necessity, began to speak in favor of impeachment. For example, Burke Hinsdale represented many Republicans in Ohio when he reported, "Johnson is rampant again. Stanton is out of office and Holt and Sheridan will probably go. Hitherto I have been opposed to impeachment, but I am beginning to think Johnson must be put out of the way."[7]

Johnson had even tried the patience of some from Ohio who despised congressional Reconstruction. Thomas Ewing, Sr., whom Johnson would shortly consider appointing permanent secretary of war and who had consistently backed the president against Congress, expressed exasperation over Johnson's actions. Ewing believed that the "public will become satisfied that Johnson is a persecuted man"; nevertheless, he could not completely suppress his frustration:

> Still he deserves nothing from his friends, or from those who would wish to protect him from wrong. He has a strong sense of right, and a stubborn determination to do it, but his action, when he acts, is never in the right time. It is spasmodic. For example, he knew for more than a year that Stanton was false to him and in daily conference with those who sought to destroy him but he kept him in position against the earnest advice of all his friends, and now after he has done the mischief, and after the power is taken from him to remove he goes through the form of removing him.[8]

In Washington the changing public opinion found expression in the House Judiciary Committee, which, shortly after Congress reconvened in November 1867, voted in favor of impeaching Johnson. Despite this action and Johnson's threatening annual report to Congress, which was released in early December, the full House, led in part by Ohioans Garfield, Spalding, and Bingham, rejected the committee's recommendation. Although clearly enraged by his behavior and startled by the rhetoric in the annual message, most House Republicans, including twelve of the seventeen from Ohio, were not yet convinced that Johnson had committed an impeachable offense, and thus they voted against impeachment.[9]

The House vote seems to have accurately reflected the opinions of Republicans in Ohio. Edwin Cowles, editor of the influential and Radical Republican *Cleveland Leader*, approvingly reported that "the impeachment movement has at last received its quietus." Aware that only a few months before many in Ohio had leaned toward impeachment but had since reconsidered, Cowles asserted with some exaggeration that Republicans in the state favored leaving Johnson alone by a margin of four or five to one and that only Richard Smith of the *Cincinnati Daily Gazette* continued to press for Johnson's removal. Cowles considered Johnson "a bad man, as a mean man, as a weak man, an incapable officer, a passionate and partisan ruler, and altogether the poorest and worst President that we have ever had," but not deserving of removal from office.[10]

James Comly, editor of the *Ohio State Journal*, generally agreed with his colleague from Cleveland. Comly also chided Smith and reprinted several editorials from Republican weeklies in Ohio that urged an end to any talk of impeachment.[11] Even Burke Hinsdale, who just weeks earlier had endorsed Johnson's removal, noticed that he was in the minority and in early December informed Garfield that "all the best minds" in Garfield's district, a Radical Republican stronghold, opposed impeachment. Certainly the key factor for all these Republicans was the Judiciary Committee's inability to establish that Johnson's obstruction had violated any law.[12] Apparently, too, some Ohio Republicans had tired of the House members' almost incessant discussion of the impeachment "of one who is hardly worth their attention." They believed the constant wrangling hurt the party and distracted congressional attention from more important issues, especially economic questions.[13]

Johnson seems to have interpreted his escape from impeachment as a sign of congressional weakness, for he continued to do his best to hamstring the execution of the Reconstruction laws. By the end of 1867 his actions again had a significant number of Ohioans, including some who until a few weeks earlier had opposed his removal, thinking of impeachment. One of those who was reassessing his opinion was Edwin Cowles, who charged that Johnson's removals of Generals E.O.C. Ord and John Pope, district commanders in the South, constituted misuse of the "lease on life and power" the House had granted him by defeating the impeachment resolution.[14]

The renewed pressure for impeachment greatly increased the tension within the Republican party between those who supported Johnson's removal without a specific violation of law and those who insisted that removal, however desirable, could not occur unless Johnson broke some law. For most of the first two months of 1868 party members snarled at each other, hurling accusations of cowardice and lack of respect for the law. At the same time the northern public's patience with what had come to seem the interminable Reconstruction crisis was nearing exhaustion. The reaction against the Republicans, so painfully clear in the 1867 elections, seemed to be gaining momentum. Thus, Republicans in Ohio and throughout the North found themselves in serious danger of being swept aside by a tidal wave of discontent. In late February, as he frequently had in the past, Johnson rescued them.[15]

On February 21 Johnson ordered the removal of Secretary of War Edwin Stanton and appointed General Lorenzo Thomas to that office on an interim basis. Because Congress was in session Johnson's action violated the Tenure of Office Act. It also restored Republican unity, particularly in Congress, where the majority party in the House of Representatives responded immediately. After less than two days' debate, the House impeached Johnson on February 24 by a strict party vote.[16]

The events in Washington also triggered a remarkable shift in Ohioans' attitudes. For nearly three years Ohioans of all political views had been frustrated in their hopes for a secure reunion and a peaceful future. Increasingly those who supported congressional Reconstruction blamed Johnson and his obstructionism for protracting the national crisis. When he committed what many, probably the vast majority, considered an illegal act, thus raising the definite possibility that the one major obstacle to successful reunion could and would be swept aside, their pent-up anger burst into the open.

Edwin Cowles typified these Republicans. In December 1867 the Cleveland editor had rejected the clamor for Johnson's impeachment because he believed the president had taken no illegal actions. The events of February led to a complete reversal of opinion. Two days before the House voted to impeach, Cowles called for Johnson's removal "if the President shall continue in his mad course of usurpation." Then, on the very day of the House vote, the editor announced that Johnson had knowingly and willingly violated a federal statute and, completely dismissing the president's claim that he had intended to test the constitutionality of the Tenure of Office Act, asserted that he had "no defence." Cowles reported that demands for Johnson's removal had come from every corner of the country. In short, Johnson had long since deserved to be impeached, and now he had finally committed a crime that would lead to the cherished result.[17]

James Comly, the editor of the *Ohio State Journal*, though more moderate than Cowles, experienced a similar transformation. In November 1867 he sympathized with congressional anger about Johnson's attempts to thwart the will of Congress on Reconstruction matters but still opposed an attempt to remove Johnson. Three weeks later Comly concluded in an editorial that the Tenure of Office Act, "if not unconstitutional, is practically absurd."[18] Yet, when the president attempted to remove Stanton while Congress was in session, Comly sang a different tune. In an editorial titled "Impeachment Impending" he argued that the sole issue was the constitutionality of the Tenure of Office Act. He insisted the Supreme Court would find the law constitutional and that "the immediate impeachment of Andrew Johnson will follow as certain as the day the night." Comly further asserted that "with united voices and willing hearts the people will sustain" Johnson's removal, which he expected to occur "perhaps before the close of the week." The editor concluded with almost an audible sigh of relief: "We are rejoiced that, at last, through the obstinacy and audacity of this bad man, a faithful Congress will be able to rid a patient and long-suffering people of an odious and detestable ruler."[19]

The editorial suggested a change of heart more apparent than real. Like many northerners Comly had long believed the removal of Johnson would promote the national interest, but he and many of them feared a premature attempt to impeach the president might backfire on Congress, creating sympathy for Johnson and, more important, political capital for the Democrats. So they waited, hoping Johnson would make some colossal blunder that would lead to his certain impeachment and removal. In February 1868 Johnson appeared to have finally made the fatal mistake, and they were ready.

Congressional supporters in Ohio quickly reached similar conclusions. They tended to agree that the removal of Stanton sealed Johnson's fate. The House of Representatives, in the words of one such Ohioan, had to choose: either "submit to this one man or impeach him." His conclusion that "the people will sustain Congress in the course it has taken" seems to have correctly gauged the position of nearly all Republicans in Ohio.[20] Of the leading Republicans, only Murat Halstead, the editor of the *Cincinnati Daily Commercial*, bucked the trend. He reported Johnson's impeachment with little enthusiasm and commented sarcastically, "We hope the excitable gentlemen who have been recommending impeachment as a remedy for all the ills of the body-politic feel more comfortable." The Cincinnatian warned his readers that Johnson's trial must be a judicial proceeding and admonished them that "popular demonstrations are not, therefore, becoming, and the judicious will avoid them."[21]

Ohio Republican advocates of impeachment initially based their position on Stanton's removal and Thomas's appointment, what one called Johnson's "aggressive obstinancy of this law." They also ridiculed Johnson's contention that he intended only to test the constitutionality of the Tenure of Office Act.[22] Then, having endorsed Johnson's removal, many of these Ohioans produced long lists of his alleged transgressions to justify their position.

Much of their anger was generated by their belief that Johnson had abused his presidential powers and usurped congressional powers, particularly through his activities related to the execution of the Military Reconstruction Acts. Republicans charged Johnson with trying to put himself above the law by refusing to enforce congressional enactments, arbitrary use of the veto, and efforts to use the appointment and pardon powers to circumvent federal policies.[23]

Johnson's foes fully realized that these actions by themselves were not impeachable offenses, but combined with the violation of the Tenure of Office Act, they led to one conclusion: for the good of the nation the Senate must take the "only path to peace" and remove Johnson from office.[24]

For many in Ohio, as well as the rest of the nation, Johnson's fate involved another matter. Benjamin Wade, president pro tem of the Senate, would become president of the United States if Johnson were removed. The possibility of Wade in the White House thrilled some but probably frightened more. Wade had not only been an outspoken advocate of black rights and strong Reconstruction measures, he had also endorsed greater rights for the working class and women's suffrage. As early as the late summer 1867 conservative Republican Murat Halstead foresaw a troubling scenario that would lead to Wade's elevation and concluded, "after Andrew Johnson, a more unsuitable person for President than Mr. Wade would be hard to discover."[25] Many mid-nineteenth-century Americans thought a man with Wade's views could not be trusted with leadership of the country.

Nonetheless, Wade had supporters in Ohio who relished the possibility of a Wade presidency.[26] Even Wade's most enthusiastic friends realized the awkward, perhaps untenable, position he would be in if he had to cast the deciding vote on Johnson's removal. One suggested that he resign as president pro tem, and then he could vote for conviction. Others indicated that he had every right, and indeed the responsibility to his Ohio constituents, to retain his position and vote, regardless of the consequences.[27] All these factors had somewhat greater significance because unless he became president, Wade faced the end of his political career when his Senate term ended in March 1869 because the Democrats had gained control of the Ohio legislature and would certainly not reelect him.

Nevertheless, Wade's position probably had little, if any, effect on Johnson's fate. Those who wanted Wade to become president almost certainly would have sought Johnson's removal regardless of who might become his successor. Perhaps some of those who were unsure about Johnson might have decided that he was preferable to Wade and the prospect of his presidency might thus have pushed them toward voting to acquit. Wade may very well have made some conservative Republicans far more uneasy than Johnson did, particularly because the Republicans would have been politically responsible for Wade's behavior, unlike Johnson's. Nevertheless, there is virtually no direct evidence to indicate that concern over Wade determined the ultimate Senate decision.[28]

Ohioans who endorsed the president's removal favored a speedy Senate trial. These people insisted that the majority of Ohioans had become outraged enough to demand his conviction, but they were concerned that the anger might subside if the Senate dawdled. Some congressmen shared this fear, and they became frustrated as the Senate trial continued day after day while public passion quieted. James Garfield wrote with obvious irritation: "Our Impeachment will prove its immortal vigor, if it survive the deluge of words which have been poured upon it. The windows of 'gab' have been opened and still the floods descend. I verily believe that if the choice were given to some of our fiercest impeachers to speak and lose the case—or to keep silent and win it—they would instantly decide to read a six hour speech to an unwilling audience."[29] In fact, some Ohioans undoubtedly retreated into indifference as the trial continued and the excitement of February became an increasingly distant memory. One Republican, for example, warned Garfield in mid-May that "there has been more excitement in Washington within a week than in the whole nation beside."[30] Still, though their ardor may have lessened, a large number of Ohioans, perhaps even a slight majority, longed for Johnson's removal.

Before and during the Senate trial, rumors that Johnson would attempt some type of military action to overthrow Congress circulated widely. Many Ohio Republicans, deeply committed to a secure future with renewed sectional harmony, found the rumors both frightening and believable. In February, for example, under the bold headline "Trouble Ahead," James Comly wrote: "We have unmistakable indications that the attempted *coup* of Andrew Johnson is in pursuance of a programme constructed by Democratic leaders, with a deliberate purpose of forcing a conflict." The Columbus editor never printed his evidence, but he did not hesitate to spread rumors, which some of his readers presumably accepted as truth. Some Ohio Republicans proposed solving the potential problem by suspending Johnson from his position for the duration of the trial, thus removing his opportunity and ability to foment a revolt. Others realized the illegality and political folly of suspending a president before his fate had been decided.[31]

The possibility of violence may have been real. Certainly one of Johnson's supporters in Ohio insisted that "many think it better that the constitution *breakers* [congressional Republicans], the men who are breaking down all our walls of freedom—be driven by *force* from their seats—sooner than to see the*Union perish*. Thousands are ready to go, on the president's call, and drive the *usurpers*, out of our national halls."[32] Whatever view Ohians held on the threat of renewed violence, that the matter was discussed at all reflected the anxiety and uncertainty of the early months of 1868.

Johnson, of course, had his defenders in Ohio. The list included extremely conservative Republicans, such as Thomas Ewing, Sr., who believed their party had deserted them. In late February, Ewing vociferously denounced the impeachment attempts, insisting, "There is no doubt the President had a right to do all he has done." Nevertheless, Ewing reflected how much Johnson had tried his patience, when he commented that Johnson had "precisely the same right" to remove Stanton and appoint Thomas "that he would have to face a herd of wild bulls and shake a scarlet cloak at them, and just the same amount of presidential wisdom were exhibited in one case as in the other."[33] Quite plainly Johnson had become a thorn in the side not only of most Republicans but even of the handful of Republicans who still endorsed his policies.

Although some Democrats apparently would have been relieved to have Johnson out of office, especially because he had made known his desire to receive the 1868 Democratic presidential nomination and they definitely did not want to be burdened with him, perhaps a majority of them in Ohio defended the president. Democratic editors vied for the honor of heaping the most vituperation on congressional Republicans, roundly denouncing the Senate proceedings as "the greatest farce of a trial ever known," "a mockery of justice," and "a scene transplanted from the French Revolution." Other Democrats conveyed their support directly to the president.[34]

After testing the nation's patience for weeks, the Senate finally voted on Johnson's fate in mid-May. Seven Republicans joined the Democrats to defeat by a single vote the attempt to remove him. The verdict enraged most Ohio Republicans, and many directed their bitterness at the "seven recreants," whom they accused of selfishness, ambition, jealousy, and flight from reason. Several journalists, one of whom titled an editorial "Senators Out for Gold," charged that Johnson or his friends had purchased his acquittal.[35] Some Republicans, including James Garfield, blamed the failure to remove Johnson on Chief Justice Salmon Chase, charging that he had conducted the trial in a pro-Johnson manner to further his own political ambitions. Garfield confided to a fellow Ohioan that "it is the hardest thing I ever have to do to withdraw confidence and love from a man whom I have once given them, but the conduct of Mr. Chase during the trial has been outrageous. Three senators, at least, were taken in hand by him privately and all the weight of his office and his indulgence were brought to bear to save Johnson." Although Chase certainly was guilty of flirting with anyone who suggested he could engineer Chase's election to the White House, accusations such as Garfield's have never been proved.[36]

After their spasm of anger a large number of Ohio Republicans realized that Johnson's acquittal was not the end of the world, or as one put it, "Impeachment is beaten. We all deeply regret it. But . . . we begin to perceive that the heavens haven't fallen yet." Some agreed with Murat Halstead, who had always contended that the Tenure of Office Act was unconstitutional and doubted that its provisions protected Stanton, a holdover from the Lincoln cabinet. With much of the impeachment case resting on this shaky foundation, some Republicans favored Johnson's removal more out of a sense of party loyalty than a conviction that it was merited by his actions in firing Stanton.[37] Moreover, for many of the reasons mentioned previously, some Ohio Republicans had genuinely feared the elevation of Benjamin Wade to the presidency. To many of them, a thoroughly rebuked Johnson, who presumably would now behave, seemed a decidedly better alternative. Thus a significant portion of Ohio Republicans shrugged and concluded that the impeachment furor had produced a satisfactory result. Having survived by a whisker-thin margin, the president would surely change his ways, and even if he did not, what more damage could he do in his remaining few months in office?[38] Republicans in Ohio and elsewhere turned their attention to the national convention, which met less than a week after Johnson's acquittal. Many impeachment advocates contented themselves with the pleasant thought of nominating the great Union war hero and placing him in the White House.

When the Republicans gathered in Chicago on May 20 and 21, the party faithful in Ohio had been cheered not only by the end of the agitation over impeachment but also by the change in party fortunes that seemed to have occurred in spring 1868. Election results in several local races indicated that when relieved of the burden of black suffrage, the Republicans remained the dominant political force in the state. The most outstanding example of the Republican resurgence happened in January 1868 when Republican John Beatty was elected to represent Ohio's eighth congressional district, replacing a Republican who had been murdered. Although he won by only a slight margin, the Republicans readily interpreted Beatty's victory as a sign that the tide had turned again in their favor.[39] Thus, those Ohio Republicans who traveled to Chicago in May thought they had many reasons to look forward with optimism to the fall campaigns.

In addition to nominating Grant, the convention drafted a platform that revealed a clear understanding of the party's basic problem during the 1867 elections. With the moderates once again firmly in control of the decision-making apparatus, the party beat a hasty retreat from its earlier, advanced position on black suffrage. The platform proudly proclaimed the success of congressional Reconstruction with its requirement of black suffrage in the former Confederacy but then unblushingly announced that "the question of suffrage in all the loyal States properly belongs to the people of those states."[40]

The blatant injustice to northern blacks and the transparent attempt to force on southern whites what they refused to demand of themselves and their neighbors bothered only a few Republicans in Ohio and the rest of the North.[41] At the Ohio Republican State Convention, held on March 4, the party had anticipated the national stance by unanimously approving a platform that avoided all reference to the suffrage issue. Party editors flooded the state with praise for the wisdom of this omission. One who had actively supported the suffrage amendment in 1867, easily shifted gears and, forgetting about those Americans who still lacked the vote, now applauded the document as "a platform for all the people."[42] It would, of course, be unfair to suggest that he underwent this conversion alone. The sad fact is that he typified most of his party colleagues, who could hardly have made more clear their recognition that the party that endorsed black enfranchisement in Ohio was courting political disaster.

The same sense of political realism was behind the national party plank on suffrage. Remembering that the basic purpose of a platform was to help win an election, the editor of the *Ohio Repository* concluded that it "is radical enough for the purpose intended." Even some Radicals understood the temper of the times and molded their positions accordingly. On May 12 Edwin Cowles, for example, had suggested a three-plank platform that included "equal suffrage," although he did not indicate precisely where it should apply. Nevertheless, upon receiving the actual platform he gushed, "Both in what it says and in what it omits to say, it fully and fairly represents the good sense, the discretion, and the statesmanship of the Republican party." Considering that Cowles had publicly advocated black suffrage in the South since 1865 and in Ohio since late 1866, his statement starkly reveals how practical a Radical could become when he knew that pushing on the suffrage issue would defeat the party and threaten the gains so far secured by congressional Reconstruction. Certainly winning elections and protecting their perception of the national interest mattered far more to Cowles and the overwhelming majority of Ohio Republicans.[43]

Shortly after the Republican convention adjourned, Congress reconvened and quickly took steps to readmit the South. By late June

1868 it had restored the states of Arkansas, North Carolina, South Carolina, Louisiana, Georgia, Alabama, and Florida, leaving only Texas, Virginia, and Mississippi still awaiting readmission to the Union. Congress insisted that each of these states had proved its loyalty by following the requirements of military Reconstruction and that in each the loyal element now securely held political control. Surely the vast majority of politically aware Americans also understood that Congress had another motive. Each of the restored southern states, with the virtual guarantee of solid support for the Republican party from the enfranchised blacks, would likely cast electoral votes for Grant.[44]

In Ohio most supporters of congressional Reconstruction believed that the return of the southern states proved that the policy was working and, in fact, was on the verge of success. These Ohioans had long demanded that before reunification could occur, the South must provide unmistakable evidence that it would never again threaten sectional strife. As the southerners ratified the Fourteenth Amendment, this goal now appeared close to realization. The relief and joy these Ohioans felt burst forth. "Reconstruction upon a loyal basis is a success," cheerily reported one journalist, "and though the Democracy and the rebels may gnash their teeth, the great majority of the people of the country will rejoice that the vexed question of Reconstruction will soon be among the things of the past." Another predicted that Reconstruction would be completed "before the leaves fall from the trees this fall."[45]

Ohioans had longed for such a result for years, and many considered the election of Grant the only additional step required to end the Reconstruction crisis forever. One Ohioan underscored the connection between successful restoration and the coming election, writing, "I want to elect next Pres. and then I shall consider the war a success and the country safe." These Ohioans, like many other Americans, looked forward to the end of Reconstruction in part because the terms that southerners had accepted nearly duplicated those Ohio Republicans had demanded in 1865, with the significant addition of black suffrage, which was added to ensure loyal control of the restored South.[46]

To believe that southerners had indeed become loyal once more and that political and racial affairs in the South would proceed acceptably after reunion required much faith, but most Ohioans wanted desperately to believe precisely that. Despite ample and widely known evidence that loyal southern whites and the freedmen lived in a dangerous environment, many Ohio Republicans were able to convince themselves that that once the South had agreed to the terms of congressional Reconstruction, everything would work out with only minor difficulty. Of course, the ascendancy of southern Republican parties calmed many of their lingering doubts. In the summer of 1868 these Ohioans had good reasons to think Reconstruction would succeed if Republicans remained in control of the federal government after the 1868 elections. The nation was in the process of peaceful reunification, and the class that had dominated the antebellum South was at least temporarily deprived of political power. The blacks had been freed, but white supremacy remained safely intact throughout the North.

Ohio Republicans prepared to rely during the approaching campaign on two main issues: Grant's popularity and Congress's apparent success reuniting the country; meanwhile Democrats in the Buckeye State had developed an aggressive election strategy of their own. Heartened by their strong showing in 1867, they held their state convention in early January 1868 and identified three issues they hoped to exploit. The Democrats denounced congressional Reconstruction for placing southern whites under the domination of the freedmen, which would "inevitably lead to the Africanization of the South." With almost audible cries of anguish they railed against the imposition of black suffrage on the South. The party also indicated it would again rely heavily on the trusty charge of "black Republicanism." Third, the Democrats had every intention of attempting to make a major issue out of the financial questions facing the country. A postwar recession had been exacerbated by currency contraction, leading to widespread distress and discontent with the federal policies related to bond repayment and a return to the gold standard. Hoping to capitalize on the public's anxiety and dismay, Ohio Democrats declared themselves in favor of the payment of the 5-20 United States bonds in greenbacks and the taxation of interest on government bonds. Spurred by the exertions of Washington McLean, editor of the *Cincinnati Daily Enquirer*, the convention endorsed George Pendleton for president and prepared to press his monetary views at the national convention in July.[47]

When Democrats met in July for their national convention a serious split arose between the eastern and western delegates over financial issues. In their handling of these divisive matters, the delegates confused an already difficult situation, much as they had in 1864, when they teamed a general, George McClellan, for president with Peace Democrat George Pendleton for vice-president and then wrote a peace platform.

In 1868, despite McLean's energetic activities, Ohio's favorite son lost the presidential nomination to Horatio Seymour of New York, the darling of the financially conservative, hard-money eastern Democratic establishment. Between January and July, McLean had managed to orchestrate a significant boom for Pendleton, basically turning the *Cincinnati Daily Enquirer* into the unofficial Pendleton organ. During those months discussions of the taxation of government bonds, currency contraction, and greenbacks so dominated that paper that editorials about the political aspects of Reconstruction virtually disappeared. McLean even organized a "Pendleton Escort" in hopes of influencing the delegates with the public support of his candidate. The editor lost the contest for the presidential nomination but not the struggle over the platform.[48]

Almost as if it intended to destroy its candidate's credibility, the party wrote a platform that advocated payment of the federal debt in greenbacks and taxation of government bonds. These planks in no way reflected Seymour's views and certainly put him in an awkward position, even if they did appeal to Pendleton's disappointed western supporters. Seymour, however, heartily agreed with other planks that demanded immediate restoration of the South, universal amnesty for former Confederates, state control of suffrage requirements, and economy in government and that denounced the corruption, usurpation, and Reconstruction program of the Republican party. The final accomplishment of the convention, the unanimous selection of former Union general Frank Blair, Jr., for vice-president, would later prove highly significant.[49]

When the campaign began, Ohio Democrats generally accepted the preeminence of the Reconstruction issue, which they tended to portray as a simple matter of illegal and unconstitutional actions by Congress. They attacked the entire military Reconstruction program but saved their bitterest venom for the enfranchisement of the freedmen, which was attacked as a gross injustice and a complete usurpation of states' rights by Congress. Party leaders usually linked criticism of Reconstruction, which they labeled a failure, with racist appeals. Thus, for example, one newspaperman concluded that "abolition reconstruction means this and nothing more—negro supremacy in the South, and a barbarian balance of power in the whole country." Other Democrats demanded a return to "white freedom" and the restoration of the "Union as our fathers formed it." In addition they also brought out the old bugaboo of racial equality; McLean, for example, attempted to frighten the voters by asking if they were "ready to help change [the federal government] from a white to a black and tan mongrel government? " Again the Democrats insisted, with no logic except the hope of gaining more votes, that the Republicans had secret plans to foist racial equality on unsuspecting Americans.[50]

Democratic appeals to racism and pledges to keep blacks in their place, though surely not political liabilities, seem not to have moved the electorate as much as the Democrats had anticipated. Furthermore, as the election drew nearer most Ohioans of all political views could see that congressional Reconstruction was restoring the South to the Union. Whether they approved of the terms or not, the plain fact was that the nation seemed to be nearing reunion. Democratic charges of congressional usurpations made few inroads with voters, who seem to have decided that, even if military Reconstruction had stretched the constitutional limits of federal power, a peaceful and secure future made the price worthwhile. Sensing the tone of public attitudes many Democrats late in the campaign nearly abandoned Reconstruction issues in favor of financial matters.

They frequently charged that the Republicans had established an aristocracy of bondholders, who had purchased government bonds during the war with cheap paper money yet received interest and principal repayment in gold. The Democrats assailed that policy as basically unfair to the taxpayers and to those who lacked the wealth to have bought bonds. The injustice could be easily remedied by repaying the principal with greenbacks, a plan officially endorsed by Ohio Democrats. Most of them did not share the Republican concern about returning to the gold standard; instead, they advocated increasing the number of greenbacks in circulation. Although this position certainly deviated from good Jacksonian Democratic principles, most Ohio Democrats, many of whom surely would have called themselves Jacksonians, apparently believed more in expediency and winning elections than they did in following Old Hickory.[51]

The Democratic clamoring about economic issues had considerable effect on Ohio Republicans, who at their state convention had adopted some ideas quite similar to portions of the Pendleton Plan even before the national Democratic party had endorsed it. Specifically, the Republicans urged that the 5-20 bonds be "paid in the currency of the country which may be legal tender when the Government shall be prepared to redeem such bonds." Thus, they hoped to attract the votes of those who favored using greenbacks to pay off the bonds by raising the possibility that that could happen if the greenbacks were legal tender at the time of repayment. The Republican platform also expressed its approval of the congressional mandate to end contraction, passed in February 1868 as a hasty response to the public outcry. In addition, the Republicans endorsed the principle of equal taxation of government bonds, "precisely as other property."

For some Republicans these planks verged on heresy. James Garfield, for example, concluded that his colleagues had accepted "some financial doctrines that, if I understand them, I cannot and will not endorse. If my constituents approve them they cannot approve me." Garfield had already given ample evidence of his hard-money views when he had been one of a small group of western congressmen who refused to vote to stop contraction. That vote may have cost him the chairmanship of the House Ways and Means Committee, an appointment he dearly wanted. As Garfield stated, his views differed from the state party platform, but Republicans in his congressional district smoothed over the conflict by resolving that the national Republican platform, which denounced the use of greenbacks to pay the 5-20s, was "the expression of our own views."[53] The district convention delegates made no mention of the financial planks in the state platform, but they pointedly reminded Garfield that they would not tolerate free trade, which many hard-money men such as Garfield favored.[54] Garfield's experience was hardly unique; financial issues definitely divided the Republicans, and thus they hoped to avoid them as much as possible.

Several factors helped keep these financial issues from seriously damaging the Republican campaign. The national Republican platform took a much harder line on debt repayment, denouncing "all forms of repudiation as a National crime," thus strongly implying that the debt must be repaid in gold, not greenbacks. This plank greatly buoyed the spirits of hard-money Ohio Republicans, many of whom agreed with an editor from Gallipolis who wrote that the Chicago convention gave "us a platform that more completely than any other represents the views of the whole party."[55] Some of these Republicans fought successfully in their county and congressional district conventions to have the delegates endorse the national, not the state, platform, when the major difference between the documents was the stand on financial issues.[56] At least in part to placate the greenbackers, the national platform also contained a vague plank that seemed to advocate taxation of government bonds. Thus, the national platform helped maintain party unity by offering something for all sides in the financial controversies.

The Democratic campaign, however, did even more to promote Republican harmony. By virtually adopting the Pendleton Plan and attempting to make it the major campaign issue, the Democrats basically forced those voters who approved of greenbackism into the position of having to endorse the Democratic policies on Reconstruction if they wanted to vote for greenbacks. Many considered this position quite unacceptable, especially when they recalled the behavior of the Ohio General Assembly since the Democrats secured control of it after the 1867 elections. In January 1868, for example, by straight party votes in each house, the General Assembly adopted a resolution to rescind ratification of the Fourteenth Amendment. Although Congress ignored this act and similar ones taken by New Jersey and Oregon such examples of Democratic "principles" did much to lend credibility to Republican charges that if the Democrats secured a majority in Congress or elected a president, future peace would be jeopardized and the gains won in blood during the war and by Congress since then would be lost.[57] Most voters who were inclined to vote Republican thus seem to have refused to let their economic views transcend their concern for future security.

The improved condition of the Ohio economy made that choice easier for them, too. From a trough in December 1867 the situation, especially for farmers, improved so markedly during 1868 that one economic historian has concluded that the American farmer enjoyed greater prosperity in the late 1860s than any other time until World War I.[58] Although it may not have contributed all that much to the economic upturn, the cessation of contraction certainly removed a policy that many held responsible for their earlier financial difficulties.[59] Its disappearance as an issue could only help the Republicans.

Realizing that some Ohioans would determine their votes solely on financial issues, the Republicans countered the Democrats' strategy by waging an aggressive antigreenback campaign. Apparently views had changed since early March, for despite the statement in their platform that implied acceptance of the idea of repaying the war debt using greenbacks, Republicans labeled their opponents the party of the "repudiators" and reminded voters that the debt had been incurred in saving the Union. Only traitors who despised the nation, Republicans charged, could deny the need to pay the debt honorably, which by late summer meant in gold. As these accusations indicate, Republicans took advantage of every opportunity to link debt repayment with the war, reminding voters that it was Democratic treachery that had made the war necessary. In the end, the Republican campaign on financial issues, despite the state platform, became a mixture of orthodox conservatism, with waving both the bloody shirt and the flag.[60]

Despite the rhetoric from all sides on financial questions, Ohio Republicans successfully pressed Reconstruction as the most important issue in the election. The Republicans defended congressional Reconstruction not only as necessary but clearly on the way to successfully ending Reconstruction. They specifically asked voters to decide whether the loyal North had the right to determine the terms of restoration. Answering their own question in the affirmative, they then declared that Congress had merely done precisely that, following the terms favored by the northern public. Countering Democratic accusations that they were the party of continued disunion, the Republicans portrayed themselves as the party of peace, whose presidential nominee would "guide us safely into a harbor of rest and quiet."[61]

Grant certainly helped immeasurably to promote this theme when he wrote in his letter accepting the presidential nomination that the American people wanted and he would strive to provide "peace, quiet and protection everywhere." The general concluded that letter with a thought that was uppermost in voters' minds, "Let us have peace."[62] Fully aware that Ohioans desired precisely what Grant promised, Republicans in the state quickly made that phrase their campaign slogan.

The Republicans handled the Reconstruction issue with a brand of rhetoric that frequently degenerated into name calling. Often rather than praise Congress for its successes, party leaders denounced their opponents as the party of war and continually warned that a Democratic victory would result in renewed rebellion. The party's official call for a state convention, issued in early February had set the tone. "We must judge our opponents not by their present professions alone," it contended, "but by their past actions. The same influence which in 1861 precipitated the rebellion, and for four years waged a treasonable war, still rules its council and will shape its policy should it return to power."[63] Party editors grabbed that theme and incessantly increased the frequency of such attacks as the campaign progressed. For example, from the Western Reserve came the reminder, "The question to be decided is, shall the Union be restored on a basis of liberty, justice, peace and safety, or shall the nation again be plunged into the horror of civil war?" A Xenia editor ominously announced, "There is nothing plainer than that the triumph of the democratic party at the next election will mean revolution." From Ironton came the admonition, "Remember, that it is still against the persistent attempt of Traitors to destroy your government, that the Republican party is allied." A central Ohio Republican pulled all the charges together, imploring, "Soldiers, vote for your brave comrades. Vote the straight Union ticket. Vote as you shot—not *for* the Rebels and their friends, but *at* them."[64] Perhaps some Ohioans wrote off such pleas as irrational campaign rhetoric, but the frequency and content of the Republican accusations suggest either a desparate and hysterical party trying to avoid defeat or, much more probably, a party that believed its message—and that voters believed it, too.

As happened with almost startling regularity during Reconstruc-

Table 4
Number of Counties Carried by Congressional Candidates, 1864-1868

Year	Republicans	Democrats
1864	58	30
1866	53	35
1868	47	39 (2 ties)

SOURCES: *Annual Report of the Secretary of State of Ohio* (1866), 34-38; (1868), 45-49.

tion, the Republicans received assistance from an unexpected source, this time the Democratic vice-presidential nominee. Shortly before the Democratic national convention Francis P. Blair, Jr., soon to be the vice-presidential candidate, wrote a letter to Colonel James Brodhead of Missouri in which Blair insisted that a Democratic president could refuse to enforce military Reconstruction, thus restoring control of the South to "white people," and could "use the army to undo the wrongs in the South perpetrated by Congress." Almost no other action could have lent more credence to Republican charges that the Democrats could not be trusted with protecting the fruits of victory. Some Republicans shrewdly concluded that, because the letter had been written before the convention, Blair had intended to use it as a springboard to the vice-presidential nomination. They reached the obvious conclusion that the Democrats therefore accepted Blair's views, which were allegedly designed to cater to white southerners.

Ohio Republicans responded to this political gift with some of the strongest accusations of the entire postwar period. For example, Cowles of Cleveland wrote, "When this letter was published we deemed its author drunk or crazy, but events have proved that he knew much better than we the temper of the Democracy." Another Republican insisted, "The letter of Frank Blair means war—nothing else."[65]

Blair's "credentials" assumed even greater significance when Republicans resurrected the old tales about hereditary insanity in the Seymour family. The fantastic stories spread about Seymour not only did nothing to enhance his chances for success but also raised the frightening prospect of Frank Blair in the White House. Even voters who did not agree with every aspect of congressional Reconstruction would pause for more than a moment before voting for the Seymour-Blair ticket, a pair called by one Republican "a lunatic" and "a disreputable and drunken bummer."[66]

Table 5
Presidential Election Results in Ohio, 1856-1868

Year	Republicans	Democrats	Other
1856	52.32	47.68	
1860	52.34	42.32	5.32
1864	56.37	43.63	
1868	54.01	45.99	

SOURCE: *Annual Report of the Secretary of State of Ohio* (1868), 103-6, 109-10.

The advantages the Republicans enjoyed led to Republican majorities in the October elections. They captured thirteen of Ohio's nineteen congressional seats and all the state offices contested in 1868. In November, Grant won Ohio's electoral votes by winning over 54 percent of the votes cast in the state.

Those numbers seem to suggest a substantial Republican victory, but a closer analysis leads to a somewhat different conclusion. As Table 4 shows, Republican congressional candidates carried fewer Ohio counties in 1868 than in either 1866 or 1864. In 1868 they suffered a net loss of eleven counties, compared to the 1864 election. They also saw their percentage of the total vote drop for the second straight congressional election (see Table 2).

Grant may have secured a solid majority, but his percentage was lower than Lincoln's in 1864. From the birth of the Ohio Republican party through 1868, only in 1856 did the Democratic presidential candidate receive a higher share of the vote in Ohio than Seymour (see Table 5). Given Grant's popularity as a war hero, these were truly troubling numbers for Ohio Republicans. They indicated reliance on Reconstruction issues was approaching or had reached the point of diminishing returns. Voters apparently were also responding quite favorably to Democratic appeals on economic issues.

Nonetheless, the Republicans had won, largely because they had understood that Ohioans wanted "political settlement and repose." Not only did voters signify that Grant's victory would provide "the country with Peace and Prosperity," they believed his selection would "settle the Reconstruction question." For many Ohioans that was indeed the key point. Grant's election seemed to guarantee that the few remaining steps of Reconstruction would proceed quickly and peacefully and that for all practical purposes the nation's long turmoil would be over.[67]

The majority of Ohioans who had voted for Grant surely understood that the South had not returned to complete loyalty and that white and black southern Republicans were still frequently intimidated and abused. They tended to believe, however, that with Grant in the White House and Republicans controlling southern state legislatures, this situation would soon change for the better. In short, Grant's victory signaled the end of a political era dominated by Reconstruction. As far as a majority of politically active Ohioans were concerned, Reconstruction was approaching an acceptable conclusion. Perhaps it had not been a complete success, but neither had it been a failure. The Republican majority in Ohio certainly approved of the basic terms that were bringing about reunification.

EPILOGUE

After the 1868 elections Ohio Republicans concluded that the basic framework of Reconstruction, developed by Congress between 1866 and 1868, had been endorsed by the American people. Because that program had resulted in the readmission of most southern states, they also concluded that Reconstruction was no longer the most pressing national concern. While recognizing that all of the war-related problems had not been overcome, they were nevertheless basically satisfied with the results.

The 1868 elections had shown that even if Republicans could deflect voter attention from racial and economic issues in the future, Reconstruction was no longer a winning issue for the party. They had run an enormously popular presidential candidate and still commanded only a fairly slim majority. Therefore, Ohio Republican leaders believed that future success would require coherent policies on issues unrelated to Reconstruction. Before they could completely dismiss Reconstruction, however, they had to dispose of the troubling matter of black suffrage.

In 1868 the Republican party had done all it could to avoid identification with the enfranchisement of black Americans, but after Grant's success, party leaders in Congress sought and in late February 1869 secured passage of the Fifteenth Amendment. The proposal, as sent to the states for ratification, was a compromise that directly enfranchised no one but rather made it unlawful to deny the right to vote on the basis of race. The amendment did not even guarantee blacks the right to hold public office. Nonetheless, the Ohio General Assembly, with a Democratic majority elected in 1867, lost no time in rejecting the amendment.[1]

The defeat of the amendment did not exactly galvanize Ohio Republicans in a crusade to overturn the decision. At its 1869 state convention, though, the party did endorse ratification, thus making the matter a part of the 1869 campaign. Nonetheless, the issue of black suffrage did not dominate the election. Although some Republicans argued strenuously that voters would render a decision on the suffrage question, others insisted that, because enough states would ratify the amendment to allow it to become part of the Constitution without any further action in Ohio, it simply was not an issue in the 1869 campaign.[2] Republicans much preferred to discuss economic issues, particularly questions related to the greenbacks and the restoration of the gold standard, stressing their solid stand as defenders of the debt and ridiculing the Democrats as "apostle[s] of repudiation."[3] In short, most Republicans saw it as wise politics to downplay the suffrage issue and elevate economic questions.

Perhaps sensing that Ohio voters wanted to concentrate on questions that did not pertain to Reconstruction, the Democrats generally relied more on the issues of greenbacks and bond payment than on matters of race. Occasionally an editor would insist that the Republicans intended to force black suffrage on Ohio, but by previous standards racial diatribes and appeals to racial prejudice were notably lacking. This campaign was really rather bland compared to most of the other elections in the 1860s.[4]

The voters' verdict proved to be as lacking in conviction as the campaign. Ohioans sent eighteen Republicans and seventeen Democrats to the state Senate. Fifty-three Republicans and forty-nine Democrats won House seats. Independent-Reformers also won two Senate and ten House seats, thus holding the balance of power in each chamber. Some Republicans declared the results a party victory and, because the party had endorsed the Fifteenth Amendment, a mandate for its ratification.[5] But such pronouncements vastly overstated the clarity of the voters' decision.

When the General Assembly convened in January 1870 it elected Independent-Reformers to preside over both houses. Then it dealt with the amendment. By a strict party vote of nineteen to eighteen, with the two Reformers voting with the Republicans, the Senate ratified the amendment. On January 21, with the Reformers split four yes and six no, all Republicans for and all Democrats opposed, the House gave approval by a vote of fifty-seven to fifty-five.[6] The immediate struggle over black suffrage thus ended, but the question of why the state reversed its clear decision of 1867 remains.

The simplest answer is that it had not. In 1867 the electorate had a straightforward proposition upon which to act. No such opportunity occurred again. Ohio's subsequent actions—for example, the state did not bother to remove the word "white" from the voting qualification listed in the state constitution until the twentieth century—indicate that voters probably would have rejected the Fifteenth Amendment had it been presented as a referendum.[7]

Why then did the Republican members of the General Assembly

risk their political futures for the amendment? William Gillette has argued that Republicans supported the amendment in the expectation that it would enfranchise enough blacks in the North, including Ohio, to more than compensate for the number of whites who might desert the party.[8] LaWanda and John Cox and Glenn M. Linden have attacked Gillette's conclusions, contending that commitment to justice motivated many Republicans, even though they anticipated losing votes. Michael Les Benedict has suggested that Republicans passed the amendment because they feared that the South was slipping away from the party and believed that the amendment was necessary to secure Reconstruction in the South. Most recently, Eric Foner has stressed the conservatism of the amendment, which had greater popular support because it allowed various states, especially northern states, to continue to disfranchise specific groups of voters as long as race was not the basis of the disqualification. Foner, for example, cites Rhode Island's requirement that foreign-born citizens must own $134 worth of real estate to vote and Pennsylvania's requirement that all state taxes be paid.[9]

Surely all these interpretations help explain the behavior of Ohio Republicans. Some undoubtedly believed in the justice of black suffrage; others thought the amendment would secure more Republican votes in both the North and South. Foner hints at another factor that may have proven critical in Ohio: "Even as they inscribed black suffrage in the Constitution, many party spokesmen believed the troublesome 'Negro question' had at last been removed from national politics. . . . Northern public opinion turned to other questions."[10] As I have suggested, Ohioans of both parties had had their fill of Reconstruction crises. Republicans wanted desperately to put the whole episode behind them and insisted that Grant's election allowed them to do so. A fair number of Republicans believed that perhaps the only way to end the Democrats' constant harping about "nigger equality" was to enfranchise blacks and thus remove the entire matter of race from state politics. That strategy may not seem perfectly logical, but at least some Republicans believed it would work. For example, W.D. Bickham, editor of the *Dayton Daily Journal*, promised that if the amendment became law, "the negro, as a party question, will be definitely removed from politics." Others agreed with him, or at least hoped he was right.[11] Some Ohioans proclaimed the amendment the crowning step of Reconstruction; others just wanted to move on to what they had come to consider more important matters.

Beginning in 1865 Ohioans had struggled with postwar issues, and the majority, fundamentally the Republicans, had made clear its expectations for the future. In 1865 they had demanded that the South give proof of future loyalty before readmission, that the Confederate debt not be paid, that the freedmen control and benefit from their own labor, and that the antebellum leaders not be allowed to dominate postwar politics in the South.

Initially, President Johnson had seemed to agree with those terms, but by mid-1866 he had rejected at least some of them. In the process he lost his Republican support in Ohio. Congress quickly adopted as the core of the Fourteenth Amendment most of what Ohio Republicans believed necessary for complete and secure reunion. In the fall elections of 1866 Ohio voters enthusiastically endorsed that amendment as the final terms of Reconstruction.

Their expectation that the nation would quickly be reunited was almost immediately dispelled when southerners resoundingly rejected the amendment. Ohioans were rather ambivalent about the Reconstruction policy Congress adopted in response to southern actions. Nonetheless, in 1868, with public interest generally waning and new groups of southerners following the requirements of military Reconstruction, Ohio Republicans carried the state for Grant and proclaimed Reconstruction a qualified success.

Certainly these Ohioans realized that many difficulties remained to be solved. With Republicans still in control of Congress and Grant in the White House, however, the remaining problems were now deemed incapable of threatening the country. From the point of view of most Ohioans, therefore, Reconstruction had not failed; in fact, it promised to ensure a peaceful, prosperous national future.

NOTES

Abbreviations Used in the Notes

AJP Andrew Johnson Papers, Library of Congress
BFWP Benjamin F. Wade Papers, Library of Congress
JAGP James A. Garfield Papers, Library of Congress
JDCP Jacob Dolson Cox Papers, Oberlin College Library
JSP John Sherman Papers, Library of Congress
RBHP Rutherford B. Hayes Papers, Rutherford B. Hayes Presidential Center Library, Fremont, Ohio

Introduction

1. Foner, *Reconstruction: America's Unfinished Revolution, 1863-1877*, 603-4.
2. Maizlish, *The Triumph of Sectionalism: The Transformation of Ohio Politics, 1844-1856*, xi-xii.
3. *Manufactures of the United States in 1860; Compiled from the Original Returns of the Eighth Census, under the Direction of the Secretary of the Interior*, 257, 419, 488, 544.
4. Kennedy, comp., *Agriculture of the United States in 1860; Compiled from the Original Returns of the Eighth Census, under the Direction of the Secretary of the Interior*, vii, x, xxix, xlvii, lix, lxiv, lxviii, lxxviii, lxxxii, lxxxvi, cxxvi.

1. Looking for Solutions

1. S.A. Bronson to John Sherman, May 19, 1865, JSP.
2. *Cincinnati Daily Gazette*, April 15, 1865. Stanbery, an extremely conservative Republican, served as Johnson's chief counsel at the impeachment proceedings in 1868.
3. *Circleville Union*, April 14, 1865. For similar views see *Clinton Republican*, April 14, 1865; *Scioto Gazette*, April 11, 1865. For a more lenient Democratic attitude, see *Crisis*, April 12, 1865.
4. Plumb to James A. Garfield, June 3, 1865, JAGP.
5. *Dayton Daily Journal*, April 11, 1865.
6. Holt, *The Political Crisis of the 1850s*, 51, 151-54, 202-3, 257-58; Foner, *Free Soil, Free Labor, Free Men: The Ideology of the Republican Party before the Civil War*, 97-102; Gara, "Slavery and the Slave Power: A Crucial Distinction," in Robert P.

Swierenga, ed., *Beyond the Civil War Synthesis: Political Essays of the Civil War Era*, 295-308; Rush R. Sloane to John Sherman, April 17, 1865, JSP.

7. Quill, *Prelude to the Radicals: The North and Reconstruction during 1865*, 63-64; W.R. Brock, *An American Crisis: Congress and Reconstruction, 1865-1867*, 16-17.

8. Benedict, *A Compromise of Principle: Congressional Republicans and Reconstruction, 1863-1869*, 103, 120; McKitrick, *Andrew Johnson and Reconstruction*, 18.

9. Holiday Ames to Wife, April 23, 1865, in Filler, ed., "Waiting for the War's End: The Letter of an Ohio Soldier in Alabama after Learning of Lincoln's Death," *Ohio History* 74 (Winter 1965): 56.

10. *Dayton Daily Journal*, April 17, 1865.

11. *Cleveland Leader*, April 17, 1865; *Sandusky Daily Commercial Register*, April 17, 1865; Benjamin Summers Diary, April 16, 1865, Benjamin Summers Papers, Western Reserve Historical Society; A.L. Brewer to John Sherman, May 22, 1865, JSP. Many thousands of northerners believed in the existence of a vast wartime, prosouthern Democratic conspiracy called by various names including the Knights of the Golden Circle and the Sons of Liberty. For a lucid discussion of the extent of the antiwar sentiment in the North during the Civil War, see Frank L. Klement, *The Copperheads of the Middle West* (Chicago: Univ. of Chicago Press, 1960).

12. Rush R. Sloane to John Sherman, April 17, 1865, JSP; Sherman, *Recollections of Forty Years in the House, Senate, and Cabinet* 1:355; McKitrick, *Johnson and Reconstruction*, 18-20.

13. Senator Benjamin Wade was among those Radical Republicans who acknowledged that they did not know what policy Johnson would pursue but still insisted he would lead the nation wisely through the Reconstruction crisis. B.F. Wade to Lewis Campbell, May 6, 1865, Lewis Campbell Papers, Ohio Historical Society. For southern attitudes, see Perman, *Reunion without Compromise: The South and Reconstruction, 1865-1868*, 13-53.

14. *Cleveland Leader*, April 21, 1865; *Ohio State Journal*, April 17, 1865; *Cincinnati Daily Gazette*, April 17, 1865.

15. *Cincinnati Daily Commercial*, April 17, 1865. At his vice-presidential inauguration, Johnson had delivered a wild harangue that greatly embarrassed the party leadership. Most observers believed, quite correctly, that Johnson was drunk, and the stories flew across the nation that the new vice-president was an alcoholic. In fact, Johnson rarely imbibed and had drunk only one glass of brandy to steady himself against the ravages of typhoid, which had afflicted him about a week earlier. Some Ohioans, such as the editors of the *Springfield Daily News and Republic*, April 20, 1865, and the *Sandusky Daily Commercial Register*, April 21, 1865, quickly forgave Johnson this one minor transgression; others did not.

16. *Elyria Democrat*, April 19, 1865; *Summit County Beacon*, April 20, 1865. For similar views, see *Lancaster Gazette*, April 20, 1865; *Scioto Gazette*, April 25, 1865; *Sandusky Daily Commercial Register*, April 21, 1865; *Portage County Democrat*, April 19, 1865; *Dayton Daily Journal*, April 24, 1865.

17. Tobias Plants to Andrew Johnson, April 15, 1865, James Ashley to Johnson, April 15, 1865, AJP; Robert Schenck to W.D. Bickham, April 20, 1865, W.D. Bickham Papers, Dayton Public Library.

18. B.F. Wade to Lewis Campbell, May 6, 1865, Campbell Papers; Salmon Chase to Andrew Johnson, April 16, 1865, AJP; Aaron F. Perry to Jacob D. Cox, May 13, 1865, JDCP; William Johnson to Rutherford B. Hayes, April 22, 1865, RBHP.

19. *Marietta Times*, May 11, 1865; *Cincinnati Daily Enquirer*, April 19, 26, May 3, 10, 1865; *Crisis*, April 19, 26, 1865.

20. Perman, *Reunion without Compromise*, 68-109.

21. McKitrick, *Andrew Johnson and Reconstruction*, 17-18.

22. *Eaton Weekly Register*, June 8, 1865. For similar views on the need for future security, see *Cincinnati Daily Gazette*, April 10, 1865; Bellamy Storer to William Greene, May 31, 1865, William Greene Papers, Cincinnati Historical Society.

23. *Cincinnati Daily Gazette*, April 12, 1865; *Elyria Democrat*, July 26, 1865; Bingham, Speech, *Cadiz Republican*, Sept. 27, 1865.

24. One of President Johnson's Ohio correspondents combined the two questions of the Confederate debt and the disfranchisement of rebel leaders into one proposal, suggesting to the new chief executive that all persons who had any connection with that debt, including the holding of it, should be disfranchised for life. Such a policy would surely have deprived far more southerners of the ballot than the majority of Ohioans considered necessary. Samuel B. Jackson to Johnson, June 23, 1865, AJP.

25. *Cincinnati Daily Commercial*, May 11, 1865; *Scioto Gazette*, May 9, 1865; Rush R. Sloane to John Sherman, April 17, 1865, JSP.

26. *Cincinnati Daily Gazette*, April 12, 27, 1865; *Sandusky Daily Commercial Register*, April 19, 1865; *Eaton Weekly Register*, June 8, 1865; R. Plumb to James A. Garfield, June 3, 1865, JAGP.

27. *Scioto Gazette*, May 9, 1865; *Eaton Weekly Register*, June 8, 1865; *Cincinnati Daily Gazette*, June 19, 1865.

28. *Sandusky Daily Commercial Register*, April 19, 1865; *Ohio Repository*, April 12, 1865.

29. *Cincinnati Daily Enquirer*, April 21, May 17, June 30, 1865; *Crisis*, July 19, 1865.

30. *Cincinnati Daily Gazette*, April 14, June 15, 1865; *Jeffersonian Democrat*, June 2, 1865.

31. *Cincinnati Daily Gazette*, June 15, 1865; *Eaton Weekly Register*, June 8, 1865. See also *Springfield Daily News and Republic*, May 12, 1865; *Elyria Democrat*, July 26, 1865.

32. John Sherman, Speech at Circleville, Ohio, June 16, 1865, JSP; *New York Tribune*, June 14, 1865, quoted in Benedict, *Compromise of Principle*, 111.

33. Sherman, *Recollections of Forty Years* 1:363-64.

34. Ahern, "The Cox Plan of Reconstruction: A Case Study in Ideology and Race Relations," 300-308; Belz, "Origins of Negro Suffrage during the Civil War," 118, 120.

35. *Portage County Democrat*, June 7, 1865.

36. V. Jacque Voegeli studied the racial attitudes of whites in the Old Northwest during the Civil War in *Free but Not Equal: The Midwest and the Negro during the Civil War*. He concluded that "the chief reason that most midwestern Republicans did not support full equality was that they did not believe in it. Belief in white racial superiority survived almost intact both the anti-slavery crusade and the rhetoric of equal rights. . . . At the close of the war it was abundantly plain that the Midwest's attitude toward the negro race had changed in many ways, but that the white people of that region still were far from an acceptance of true equality. Four years of war had tempered the racism of the Midwest, but had not purged it. Upon this most fragile foundation rested the radicals' hope for future equality and racial amity. Small wonder that they would fail" (178, 182).

37. "The situation, April 3, 1865," Salmon P. Chase Papers, Cincinnati Historical Society. See also Joseph Hartley to Andrew Johnson, April 30, 1865, AJP; *Summit County Beacon*, June 22, 1865; *Cincinnati Daily Gazette*, June 15, 1865; John Sherman

to William T. Sherman, May 16, 1865, in Thorndike, ed., *The Sherman Letters: Correspondence between the General and Senator Sherman, 1837 to 1891*, 251; Belz, "Origins of Negro Suffrage," 118.

38. Bronson to Sherman, May 19, 1865, JSP. See also Charles Raymond to Sherman, June 15, 1865, ibid.

39. *Elyria Democrat*, June 21, 1865. See also *Portage County Democrat*, June 7, 1865; *Jeffersonian Democrat*, June 2, 1865; *Cincinnati Daily Gazette*, June 15, 1865.

40. In *North of Reconstruction: Ohio Politics, 1865-1870*, Felice Bonadio asserts that some Ohio Republicans advocated black suffrage in the South mainly to enhance their leverage in the intraparty squabbles in their home state. In particular, he singles out Edwin Cowles of the *Cleveland Leader* as a man who used the suffrage issue for personal or factional advantage (see 48-49, 82-83, 100). These men, however, appear to have believed in the justice of suffrage or to have thought that the nation's future peace required it. When they backtracked, as they surely did, they were influenced more by the political climate in Ohio and their conviction that for the good of the country Republicans must remain in control of the state and national governments than by intraparty rivalries.

41. J.P. Charles to William H. Lough, Jan. 15, 1865, William Lough Papers, Cincinnati Historical Society; *Sandusky Daily Commercial Register*, June 12, 1865.

42. *Elyria Democrat*, July 26, 1865.

43. Jacob D. Cox to James A. Garfield, July 21, 1865, JAGP; "Reminiscences of Andrew Hickenlooper," Andrew Hickenlooper Papers, Cincinnati Historical Society, 2:9.

44. *Cincinnati Daily Gazette*, Nov. 10, 1864.

45. *Circleville Union*, June 16, 1865; William T. Coggeshall Diary, April 12, 1865, William T. Coggeshall Papers, Ohio Historical Society; Jacob Cox to Aaron F. Perry, June 12, 1865, JDCP.

46. *Scioto Gazette*, July 4, 1865. This Republican paper presents a good case study of how Radical Republicanism was not a monolithic movement. Frequently the same people would be more radical on some issues than others. The *Scioto Gazette*, for example, wanted to disfranchise rebel leaders for life, a rather radical idea, but it opposed black suffrage. See the issue of May 9, 1865. That this example reflects the norm more than an exception gives some appreciation for the difficulty of trying to categorize people as radical, moderate, or conservative.

47. *Ohio Repository*, June 7, 1865.

48. Even some Republicans who sincerely advocated black suffrage acquiesced in the majority's decision not to grant it. See Aaron F. Perry to Jacob Cox, June 4, 1865, JDCP. For a good example of the confusion and doubts the issue caused in many Ohio minds, see David K. Este to William Greene, Aug. 14, 1865, Greene Papers.

49. *Cincinnati Daily Enquirer*, June 26, 1865; *Cleveland Plain Dealer*, June 13, 1865; *Holmes County Farmer*, June 1, 1865; *Crisis*, May 3, 1865.

50. For a discussion of the Democrats' use of the racial issue in prewar Ohio, see Maizlish, *Triumph of Sectionalism*, 220, 232.

51. *Cleveland Plain Dealer*, May 27, 1865.

52. *Cincinnati Daily Enquirer*, June 16, May 18, 1865.

53. *The War of the Rebellion: A Compilation of the Official Records of the Union and Confederate Armies*, ser. 1, 47:243-44.

54. *Cleveland Leader*, April 24, 1865; *Clinton Republican*, April 28, 1865. See also *Elyria Democrat*, April 26, 1865; *Jeffersonian Democrat*, April 28, 1865; *Norwalk Reflector*, May 2, 1865; R. Plumb to James A. Garfield, April 25, 1865, JAGP.

55. In Cincinnati the *Gazette* and *Commercial* waged a weeklong debate over the

agreement. The *Gazette* condemned Sherman and urged his removal from command. The *Commercial* refused to rebuke the general. See both papers from April 24 to April 29, 1865. For the Democratic response, see *Portsmouth Times*, April 29, 1865; *Cincinnati Daily Enquirer*, April 25, 26, 1865.

56. *Sandusky Daily Commercial Register*, April 24, 1865; *Scioto Gazette*, May 2, 1865. Thomas Ewing, Sr., a very conservative Ohioan, who would later support Johnson throughout his troubles with Congress, insisted that Sherman had made no mistakes and done exactly as he should have. See Ewing to *Cincinnati Daily Commercial*, May 8, 1865, Thomas Ewing Family Papers, Library of Congress. Although Ewing undoubtedly agreed with what General Sherman had done, perhaps the fact that the general was his son-in-law had some influence on his position. See also J.M. Connell to Thomas Ewing, Jr., May 29, 1865, ibid.

57. Julian, *Political Recollections, 1840-1872*, 257; *Cincinnati Daily Enquirer*, June 6, 1865.

58. *Ohio Repository*, April 19, 1865; *Scioto Gazette*, April 25, 1865.

59. Milton Sutliff to Andrew Johnson, May 28, 1865, AJP.

60. *Dictionary of American Biography* (New York: Charles Scribner's Sons, 1929), 3:461.

61. Lewis Campbell to Andrew Johnson, May 8, 1865, AJP.

62. Amnesty Proclamation, May 29, 1865, in Richardson, comp., *A Compilation of the Messages and Papers of the Presidents, 1789-1902* 6:310.

63. North Carolina Proclamation, May 29, 1865, ibid. Although many people believed that the proclamation would pertain only to North Carolina and that other states might be reconstructed differently, the North Carolina Proclamation became the prototype of identical messages sent to the provisional governors of Mississippi, Georgia, Texas, Alabama, South Carolina, and Florida on June 13, 17, 21, 30, and July 13, 1865, respectively. Edward McPherson, *The Political History of the United States of America during the Period of Reconstruction, April 15, 1865-July 15, 1870*, 12. Despite Johnson's protestations of his inability to do so, he did tamper with North Carolina voting laws by forbidding unpardoned rebels from participating under his Reconstruction plans. The president's prejudices blinded him to this contradiction of his own constitutional scruples.

64. *Toledo Blade*, May 30, 1865; *Scioto Gazette*, June 6, 1865; *Ohio State Journal*, May 31, 1865; *Cincinnati Daily Commercial*, May 30, June 1, 1865. For favorable reactions to the amnesty proclamation, see *Ohio State Journal*, May 31, 1865; *Cincinnati Daily Gazette*, May 30, 1865; *Ohio Repository*, May 31, 1865; *Cleveland Leader*, June 1, 1865; *Circleville Union*, June 2, 1865.

65. *Cincinnati Daily Gazette*, May 30, 1865; *Cleveland Leader*, June 1, 1865.

66. *Springfield Daily News and Republic*, May 30, 1865.

67. *Crisis*, June 7, 1865; *Circleville Democrat*, June 2, 1865; *Cadiz Sentinel*, June 7, 1865; *Cincinnati Daily Enquirer*, June 1, 1865. The reaction of Democratic editors in Ohio seems to contradict McKitrick's assertion that "the proclamations were received by the Democrats with unconcealed glee, and it was not long before their newspapers were giving the President fulsome assurances of support." *Johnson and Reconstruction*, 69. One must add, though, that Ohio Democrats did cheerfully approve the provision in the North Carolina Proclamation that denied suffrage to the freedmen.

68. *Lancaster Gazette*, June 8, 1865; *Cincinnati Daily Commercial*, June 1, 19, 1865; *Ohio Repository*, June 7, 1865; *Clinton Republican*, June 2, 1865.

69. *Cincinnati Daily Enquirer*, June 13, 1865, and June 1, 6, 10, 1865; *Cleveland Plain Dealer*, May 30, 1865. Only the cantankerous *Crisis* withheld its approval. It

announced, "We see nothing in the policy thus far shown by him to entitle him to the confidence or encomiums of the Democracy, or the real lovers of the country" (May 31, 1865).

70. *Portage County Democrat*, June 7, 1865; *Dayton Daily Journal*, June 12, July 6, 1865.

71. *Lancaster Gazette*, June 8, 1865, and *Cincinnati Daily Commercial*, June 1, 1865, asserted that Johnson had decided on his final policy. The *Scioto Gazette*, June 6, 1865, and *Dayton Daily Journal*, June 15, 1865, considered the president's plan an experiment. The Mississippi Proclamation of mid-June convinced the editor of the *Dayton Daily Journal* that Johnson had settled on a plan, but other Republicans continued to believe that the president's policy was amendable until his first annual message to Congress in early December 1865.

72. Hoadly to Smith, June 5, 1865, William Henry Smith Papers, Ohio Historical Society.

2. The Endorsement of Johnson's Policy

1. Lewis Campbell to Andrew Johnson, August 21, 1865, AJP.

2. McKitrick, *Johnson and Reconstruction*, 42-48.

3. Precisely the opposite situation, Democrats wallowing in the prestige of being the party of the "Lost Cause," obtained in the South for decades after the War.

4. McKitrick, *Johnson and Reconstruction*, 75.

5. Bonadio. *North of Reconstruction*, viii, 1-33.

6. Silbey, *A Respectable Minority: The Democratic Party in the Civil War Era, 1860-1868*, 177-90.

7. Gerber, *Black Ohio and the Color Line, 1860-1915*, 25-43; Voegeli, *Free but Not Equal*, 178, 182; Wood, *Black Scare: The Racist Response to Emancipation and Reconstruction*, 1-16.

8. Benedict, *Compromise of Principle*, 100-116.

9. Michael Les Benedict has argued quite cogently that the number of suffrage advocates increased in spring 1865. See *Compromise of Principle*, 100-106, 110-16. Nevertheless, the situation in Ohio seems to contradict his conclusion that "in the summer of 1865 nearly the entire Republican party was prepared to endorse black suffrage as an element of Reconstruction in the South, until President Johnson's opposition persuaded the more conservative to abandon the measure, not because they believed it wrong, but because they believed it impolitic." Ibid., 41, 43.

10. Coggeshall Diary, June 20, 1865.

11. A.F. Perry to Jacob Cox, June 4, 1865, JDCP. See also W.M. Dickson to Cox, May 31, 1865, ibid.

12. Cox to Aaron F. Perry, May 25, 1865, ibid.

13. *Ohio Repository*, June 7, 21, 1865; *Cincinnati Daily Commercial*, June 12, 1865; *Circleville Union*, June 16, 1865; "Reminiscences of Andrew Hickenlooper," Hickenlooper Papers, 2:9; Jacob Cox to A.F. Perry, May 25, 1865, JDCP; Lewis Campbell to Andrew Johnson, May 8, 1865, AJP; Coggeshall Diary, April 12, 1865.

14. Smith, ed., *History of the Republican Party in Ohio and Memoirs of Its Representative Supporters* 1:202; Porter, *Ohio Politics during the Civil War Period*, 204.

15. Porter, *Ohio Politics*, 205.

16. Henry Brackman to William Henry Smith, May 23, 1865, Smith Papers;

Springfield Daily News and Republic, June 2, 1865; *Dayton Daily Journal,* June 5, 1865.

17. Joering, "Jacob Dolson Cox, His Political Career, 1865-1872," 3-7; *Dictionary of American Biography* (New York: Charles Scribner's Sons, 1930), 4:476.

18. William Dickson to Jacob Cox, May 4, 1865, Aaron F. Perry to Cox, May 13, 29, 1865, Cox to Perry, May 25, 1865, JDCP; Eugene D. Schmiel, "The Oberlin Letter, the Post-Civil War Northern Voter, and the Freedman," 75-76.

19. Lewis Campbell, one of Johnson's key advisers in Ohio, glowingly reported to the president, "We hived the swarm of radicals and your policy was triumphantly approved." Campbell to Johnson, Aug. 21, 1865, AJP. See also *Gallipolis Dispatch,* June 23, 1865; *Cincinnati Daily Commercial,* June 23, 1865.

20. Coggeshall Diary, June 21, 1865; Porter, *Ohio Politics,* 206-7.

21. Smith, *History of the Republican Party,* 207; Porter, *Ohio Politics,* 207. For examples of the view that Johnson would amend his policy if the need arose, see *Cincinnati Daily Commercial,* June 1, 16, July 17, Aug. 17, 1865; *Dayton Daily Journal,* July 6, 1865; *Toledo Blade,* July 24, Aug. 5, 1865; William Dickson to Jacob Cox, May 31, 1865, JDCP.

22. *Ohio Repository,* July 12, 1865; Coggeshall Diary, June 20, 1865; Jacob Cox to James A. Garfield, July 21, 1865, JAGP.

23. Smith, *History of the Republican Party,* 207.

24. *Cleveland Leader,* June 23, 1865; *Jeffersonian Democrat,* June 30, 1865.

25. *Portage County Democrat,* June 28, 1865.

26. A.F. Perry to Jacob Cox, June 23, 1865, JDCP; *Dayton Daily Journal,* June 23, 1865; *Cincinnati Daily Commercial,* June 22, 23, 28, 29, 1865; *Ohio Repository,* July 28, 1865; *Clinton Republican,* June 30, 1865; Lewis Campbell to Andrew Johnson, Aug. 21, 1865, AJP.

27. *Summit County Beacon,* June 22, Aug. 24, 1865; Letter to the editor, *Scioto Gazette,* Aug. 29, 1865; *Springfield Daily News and Republic,* July 27, 1865; *Cincinnati Daily Gazette,* July 1, 12, Aug. 1, 3, 1865; James A. Garfield Speech at Ravenna, Ohio, July 4, 1865, in Hinsdale, ed., *The Works of James Abram Garfield* 1:86-87; Garfield to Jacob Cox, July 14, 1865, JDCP; D.C. Goodhart to Andrew Johnson, July 3, 1865, AJP.

28. *Portage County Democrat,* July 5, 1865.

29. *Portsmouth Times,* July 29, 1865.

30. Jacob Cox to William Dennison, July 9, 1865, JDCP; Cox to James A. Garfield, July 21, 1865, JAGP.

31. Fairchild and Plumb (Oberlin Committee) to Cox, July 24, 1865, JDCP.

32. Cox to Ellis, July 22, 1865, ibid.

33. Cox had earlier informed Postmaster Dennison that he would probably make a public statement sometime in August and thus had almost certainly begun drafting a speech on suffrage before the letter from the Oberlin Committee arrived. Cox to Dennison, July 9, 1865, ibid.

34. Cox to Fairchild and Plumb, July 25, 1865, JDCP.

35. At least one Ohio Republican thought Cox's position a "*taking idea*" that would greatly aid his campaign. D. Taylor to John Sherman, Sept. 4, 1865, JSP.

36. Garfield to Jacob Cox, July 26, 1865, JDCP.

37. Jacob Cox to Charles F. Cox, July 26, 1865, ibid.; Schmiel, "The Oberlin Letter," 80.

38. Ahern, "Cox Plan of Reconstruction," 299-302, 306-8.

39. Jacob Cox to James Garfield, July 30, 1865, JAGP; Cox to William Dennison,

July 30, 1865, Cox to Charles F. Cox, July 26, 1865, Cox to sister Redelia, Aug. 2, 1865, JDCP.

40. *Cincinnati Daily Commercial*, Aug. 1, 1865; *Dayton Daily Journal*, Aug. 2, 1865; *Lancaster Gazette*, Aug. 3, 1865; *Summit County Beacon*, Aug. 10, 1865; *Circleville Union*, Aug. 4, 1865; *Bucyrus Journal*, Aug. 5, 1865; *Morgan County Herald*, Aug. 11, 1865; C.S. Burnett to Jacob Cox, Aug. 4, 1865, Stephen Johnston to Cox, Aug. 2, 1865, JDCP.

41. *Scioto Gazette*, Aug. 8, 1865; *Ohio Repository*, Aug. 2, 1865; *Cadiz Republican*, Aug. 9, 1865; R.M. Corwine to John Sherman, July 28, 1865, JSP; A.J. Ricks to Jacob Cox, Aug. 5, 1865, A. Ball to Cox, Aug. 12, 1865, Dwight Bannister to Cox, Aug. 1, 1865, JDCP.

42. Lewis Campbell to Andrew Johnson, Aug. 21, 1865, AJP; A.F. Perry to Jacob Cox, July 28, 1865, JDCP. Even the radical Garfield wrote, "I was glad to see the Oberlin people snubbed for their intermeddling spirit, but I wish the Genl. had closed his letter when he finished dressing them down." Garfield to Robert Schenck, Aug. 19, 1865, Robert Schenck Papers, Miami University Library.

43. Garfield to Cox, Aug. 5, 1865, JDCP; Coggeshall Diary, July 28, 1865. See also D. Taylor to John Sherman, Sept. 4, 1865, JSP; Garfield to Robert Schenck, Aug. 5, 19, 1865. Schenck Papers.

44. *Jeffersonian Democrat*, Aug. 11, 1865; *Portage County Democrat*, Aug. 9, 1865; *Elyria Democrat*, Aug. 9, 1865; *Cincinnati Daily Gazette*, Aug. 1, 1865; *Springfield Daily News and Republic*, Aug. 2, 1865; Harmon Austin to James Garfield, Aug. 6, 1865, Samuel Plumb to Garfield, Aug. 7, 1865, JAGP.

45. *Toledo Blade*, Aug. 2, 1865; *Dayton Daily Journal*, Aug. 2, 1865; *Elyria Democrat*, Aug. 9, 1865; A.F. Perry to Jacob Cox, Aug. 1, 1865, William Dennison to Cox, Aug. 4, 5, 1865, C.S. Burnett to Cox, Aug. 4, 1865, Dwight Bannister to Cox, Aug. 1, 1865, JDCP.

46. *Cincinnati Daily Enquirer*, May 18, June 14, July 26, 1865; *Cleveland Plain Dealer*, June 5, 1865; *Crisis*, July 5, 1865; *Portsmouth Times*, March 18, 1865.

47. *Cleveland Plain Dealer*, June 13, 1865; *Holmes County Farmer*, June 1, 1865; *Cincinnati Daily Enquirer*, May 18, June 26, 1865.

48. *Crisis*, July 5, 1865; *Portsmouth Times*, June 3, July 1, 1865; *Cleveland Plain Dealer*, June 19, 20, 22, 1865; *Cincinnati Daily Enquirer*, June 26, 1865.

49. *Cincinnati Daily Enquirer*, Aug. 2, 1865; *Crisis*, Aug. 9, 16, 1865; *Cadiz Sentinel*, Aug. 9, 1865; *Marietta Times*, Aug. 10, 1865; *Cleveland Plain Dealer*, Aug. 2, 7, 1865.

50. *Cincinnati Daily Enquirer*, June 1, 6, 10, 13, 30, 1865. See also *Cleveland Plain Dealer*, May 25, July 6, 1865; *Holmes County Farmer*, June 29, 1865; *Gallipolis Dispatch*, June 23, 1865; James Mickens to Andrew Johnson, Sept. 3, 1865, James B. Steedman to Johnson, June 12, 1865, AJP; Silbey, *A Respectable Minority*, 178-81.

51. Porter, *Ohio Politics*, 213. For a discussion of this so-called Corry Democracy, see Heidish, "Alexander Long—Ultra Conservative Democrat," 146-56.

52. *Cleveland Plain Dealer*, July 1, 1865; *Holmes County Farmer*, June 29, 1865; George W. Morgan to Andrew Johnson, Sept. 4, 1865, AJP.

53. M.H. Munnell to Alexander Long, June 17, 1865, Alexander Long Papers, Cincinnati Historical Society; Porter, *Ohio Politics*, 213.

54. *Cincinnati Daily Enquirer*, Aug. 25, 1865.

55. *Cleveland Plain Dealer*, Aug. 25, 1865; Porter, *Ohio Politics*, 214-15.

56. *American Annual Cyclopaedia, 1865*, 685-86; *Crisis*, Aug. 30, 1865.

57. Many Democrats thought Johnson's program was too harsh on the South.

They especially disapproved of the exclusions from the general amnesty grant and insisted that the South required no reconstruction before readmission. *Cincinnati Daily Enquirer*, June 30, 1865.

58. Unionists quarreled among themselves over the loyalty issue. Some insisted that only southerners who had never supported secession or the Confederacy should be allowed to take an oath of loyalty. Others reasoned that future loyalty was the goal and would therefore permit those who had worked and fought for the Confederacy to take an oath of future allegiance. See Hyman, *The Era of the Oath: Northern Loyalty Tests during the Civil War and Reconstruction* (Philadelphia: University of Pennsylvania Press, 1954).

59. James Garfield to Jacob Cox, July 26, 1865, JDCP; Benjamin Fenn to Andrew Johnson, Sept. 11, 1865, AJP; *Cincinnati Daily Commercial*, Aug. 17, 1865; *Cincinnati Daily Gazette*, July 14, 1865.

60. George Hunt Pendleton and General George W. Morgan, Speeches at Chillicothe, Ohio, Oct. 4, 1865, in *Cincinnati Daily Enquirer*, Oct. 5, 1865, and see Sept. 16, 1865; *Cleveland Plain Dealer*, Oct. 6, 1865; *Marietta Times*, Aug. 3, Sept. 28, 1865; *Crisis*, July 12, 26, Sept. 20, Oct. 4, 1865; *Zanesville Weekly Signal*, Oct. 5, 1865.

61. John A. Bingham, Speech at Cadiz, Ohio, Sept. 15, 1865, in *Cadiz Republican*, Sept. 27, 1865. See also *Cincinnati Daily Gazette*, July 28, 1865; *Dayton Daily Journal*, Sept. 5, 13, 1865; *Ohio Repository*, Oct. 4, 1865; *Summit County Beacon*, Sept. 14, 1865; Schmiel, "The Career of Jacob Dolson Cox, 1828-1900: Soldier, Scholar, Statesman," 158.

62. *Ohio Repository*, July 12, 1865; *Cincinnati Daily Commercial*, Oct. 5, 1865; *Daily Zanesville Courier*, Aug. 12, Oct. 7, 1865; *Scioto Gazette*, Aug. 22, 29, Sept. 12, 1865; *Dayton Daily Journal*, Sept. 6, 1865; *Cincinnati Daily Commercial*, July 31, 1865; *Lancaster Gazette*, July 13, Aug. 18, Sept. 25, Oct. 4, 1865; James Garfield to Robert Schenck, Aug. 19, 1865, Schenck Papers.

63. *Cincinnati Daily Gazette*, Aug. 3, 1865; C.A. Trimble to John Sherman, Sept. 3, 1865, Joseph H. Geiger to Sherman, Oct. 15, 1865, JSP; *Summit County Beacon*, Aug. 24, 1865; Bingham Speech at Cadiz, Sept. 15, 1865; David K. Este to William Greene, Aug. 14, 1865, Greene Papers; *Springfield Daily News and Republic*, July 27, 1865.

64. These Union platforms appeared in *Elyria Democrat*, June 21, 1865; *Western Reserve Chronicle*, Aug. 30, 1865; *Jeffersonian Democrat*, Sept. 1, 1865; *Summit County Beacon*, June 10, Aug. 31, 1865; *Marietta Times*, Aug. 3, 1865; *Portsmouth Times*, Sept. 9, 1865; *Eaton Weekly Register*, June 22, 1865. The vote for governor can be found in *Annual Report of the Secretary of State to the Governor of the State of Ohio, including the Statistical Report to the General Assembly for the Year 1868*, 107-9.

65. The platforms appeared in *Ohio State Journal*, Aug. 2, 5, 1865; *Circleville Union*, Sept. 1, 1865; *Morgan County Herald*, Aug. 11, 1865; *Toledo Blade*, Aug. 4, 5, 22, 30, 1865; *Cincinnati Daily Gazette*, Sept. 13, 1865; *Cleveland Leader*, Aug. 21, 1865.

66. For these platforms, see *Springfield Daily News and Republic*, Aug. 26, 1865; *Bucyrus Journal*, June 17, 1865; *Ironton Register*, Aug. 24, 1865; *Marietta Register*, Aug. 10, 1865; *Daily Zanesville Courier*, Aug. 17, 1865; *Dayton Daily Journal*, Aug. 14, 1865; *Toledo Blade*, Aug. 24, 28, 1865; *Norwalk Reflector*, Aug. 22, 1865.

67. *Cincinnati Daily Commercial*, Sept. 14, 25, 1865; *Circleville Union*, Oct. 6, 1865; *Cincinnati Daily Gazette*, Sept. 20, 1865; James C. Hall to Robert Schenck, July 29, 1865, Schenck Papers; A.C. Sands to John Sherman, Sept. 22, 1865, JSP.

68. Benjamin Wade to Charles Sumner, July 29, 1865, BFWP; James Garfield to

Jacob Cox, July 26, 1865; JDCP; *Toledo Blade*, Aug. 5, 1865; *Western Reserve Chronicle*, Oct. 11, 1865.

69. Smith, *History of the Republican Party* 1:210-11; Porter, *Ohio Politics*, 219.

3. Johnson's Policy Rejected

1. *Cincinnati Daily Commercial*, Oct. 6, 12, Nov. 14, 1865; A.L. Brewer to John Sherman, Nov. 19, 1865, Simeon Nash to Sherman, Dec. 7, 26, 1865, JSP; Kleinpell, "James M. Comly, Journalist-Politician," 38.

2. Benjamin Wade to Charles Sumner, July 29, 1865, James Fraser to Wade, July 3, 1865, BFWP; Benjamin Fenn to Andrew Johnson, Sept. 11, 1865, Joseph K. Smith to Johnson, Sept. 1, 1865, AJP; *Western Reserve Chronicle*, Oct. 11, 1865.

3. *Cincinnati Daily Commercial*, Oct. 12, Nov. 14, 1865.

4. Simeon Nash to John Sherman, Dec. 26, 1865, JSP; *Cincinnati Daily Commercial*, Nov. 17, 1865; Wood, *Black Scare*, 105-6; Kenneth M. Stampp, *The Era of Reconstruction, 1865-1877*, 75-81.

5. James Garfield to Jacob Cox, Nov. 28, 1865, JDCP; R.P.L. Baber to John Sherman, Nov. 4, 1865, JSP; *Cincinnati Daily Commercial*, Oct. 26, 1865; *Morgan County Herald*, Oct. 20, 1865.

6. Richardson, comp., *Messages and Papers of the Presidents* 5:3551-60.

7. *Lancaster Gazette*, Dec. 7, 1865; *Toledo Blade*, Dec. 6, 1865; James A. Garfield to Burke Hinsdale, Dec. 11, 1865, in Hinsdale, ed., *Garfield-Hinsdale Letters: Correspondence between James Abram Garfield and Burke Aaron Hinsdale*, 76.

8. For strong endorsements of the annual message, see *Daily Zanesville Courier*, Dec. 6, 1865; *Ironton Register*, Dec. 14, 1865; *Cincinnati Daily Commercial*, Dec. 7, 1865; *Circleville Union*, Dec. 8, 1865; William Dennison to Jacob Cox, Nov. 29, 1865, Cox to Dennison, Dec. 12, 1865, JDCP. For examples of Republicans who generally approved the document but expressed relief that Johnson had pledged to work with Congress, see *Cincinnati Daily Gazette*, Dec. 6, 1865; *Dayton Daily Journal*, Dec. 6, 7, 1865; *Elyria Democrat*, Dec. 13, 1865. For examples of concern on the suffrage issue, see *Cleveland Leader*, Dec. 6, 1865; *Portage County Democrat*, Dec. 13, 1865. For favorable responses from the Democrats, see *Cleveland Plain Dealer*, Dec. 6, 1865; *Circleville Democrat*, Dec. 8, 1865.

9. *Scioto Gazette*, Jan. 16, 1866; M.A. Jacobi to John Sherman, Dec. 13, 1865, JSP.

10. *Dayton Daily Journal*, Jan. 30, 1866; *Scioto Gazette*, Jan. 16, 1866, Feb. 6, 1866; Jacob Cox to John Sherman, Jan. 27, 1866, JDCP; Richard Smith to James Garfield, Jan. 14, 1866, JAGP; E.B. Sadler to Sherman, Feb. 16, 1866, Warner Bateman to Sherman, Feb. 7, 1866, JSP.

11. *Cincinnati Daily Commercial*, Feb. 7, 1866; Richard Smith to James Garfield, Jan. 14, 1866, JAGP. See also *Daily Zanesville Courier*, Jan. 9, 1866; *Dayton Daily Journal*, Jan. 13, 18, 1866; C.A. Trimble to John Sherman, Dec. 21, 1865, JSP; Thomas Ewing, Sr., to William T. Sherman, Dec. 27, 1865, Ewing Family Papers; William F. Hunter to Andrew Johnson, Feb. 8, 1866, AJP.

12. *Congressional Globe*, 39th Cong., 1st sess., 132-33, 158-59. See also James Hubbell, Speech, ibid., 662.

13. James M. Ashley to Governor A.C. Gibbs, Jan. 16, 1866, A.C. Gibbs Papers, Oregon Historical Society.

14. *Congressional Globe*, 39th Cong. 1st sess., 667, 727-28, and app. 90-91. See also Rufus Spalding and William Hubbell, Speeches, ibid., 133, 662.

15. Ibid., 142-45; Samuel Shellabarger to James Comly, n.d., James Comly Papers, Ohio Historical Society; McKitrick, *Johnson and Reconstruction*, 113-15.

16. Rutherford B. Hayes to General M.F. Force, March 17, 1866, in Charles R. Williams, ed., *Diary and Letters of Rutherford B. Hayes* 3:20; James Garfield to Burke Hinsdale, Feb. 19, 1866, in Hinsdale, ed., *Garfield-Hinsdale Letters*, 80.

17. John Sherman to Warner Bateman, Feb. 10, 1866, Warner Bateman Papers, Western Reserve Historical Society.

18. Richard Smith to James A. Garfield, Jan. 14, 1866, JAGP; Jacob Cox to John Sherman, Jan. 27, 1866, William Dennison to Cox, Jan. 2, 1866, JDCP; Rutherford B. Hayes to Warner Bateman, Feb. 1, 1866, Bateman Papers; Rush R. Sloane to John Sherman, Feb. 17, 1866, JSP; *Dayton Daily Journal*, Jan. 15, 30, Feb. 14, 1866; *Cincinnati Daily Commercial*, Feb. 15, 1866; *Cleveland Leader*, Feb. 9, 1866; *Summit County Beacon*, Feb. 8, 1866.

19. McPherson, *Political History of the United States*, 72-74.

20. *Congressional Globe*, 39th Cong., 1st sess., 421, 688; *Cleveland Leader*, Feb. 8, 1866; McKitrick, *Johnson and Reconstruction*, 284.

21. Richardson, *Messages and Papers* 5:3596-603.

22. A.B. Buttles to John Sherman, Feb. 27, 1866, Rush R. Sloane to Sherman, Feb. 26, 1866, JSP; *Daily Zanesville Courier*, Feb. 21, 1866; *Toledo Blade*, Feb. 21, 1866; *Cincinnati Daily Commercial*, Feb. 20, 21, March 2, 1866; *Cleveland Herald*, Feb. 22, 23, 26, March 1, 1866; *Gallipolis Dispatch*, March 2, 1866.

23. *Ohio Repository*, Feb. 28, 1866. See also J.J. Janney to William Dennison, Feb. 28, 1866, J.J. Janney Papers, Ohio Historical Society; William T. Coggeshall to Jacob Cox, Feb. 22, 1866, Cox to Dennison, March 13, 1866, JDCP.

24. In addition to the newspaper evidence supporting the veto, Johnson received many congratulatory letters from Ohioans (all in AJP). See from Enoch Carson, Feb. 20, 1866, J.A. Stader, Feb. 22, 1866, R.B. Warden, Feb. 26, 1866, J.A. Patterson, March 4, 1866, George W. Houk, March 8, 1866, S.D. Norton, Feb. 28, 1866, John E. Hunt, March 1, 1866, Jonathan O'Neill, March 1866, Henry Bishop, Feb. 20, 1866, Joseph Cable, Feb. 23, 1866, J.L. Newsom, Feb. 21, 1866, John C. Riley, Feb. 23, 1866, T.W. Bartley, Feb. 24, 1866, and D.M. Sommerville, Feb. 24, 1866. The John Sherman Papers also contain evidence of the strong support Johnson received for the veto. See letters to Sherman from Joseph H. Geiger, Feb. 20, 21, 1866, Rush R. Sloane, Feb. 21, 1866, D.M. Fleming, Feb. 27, 1866, Warner Bateman, Feb. 21, 1866; and E.B. Sadler, Feb. 28, 1866. See also Coggeshall Diary, Feb. 25, 1866.

25. For some who believed that Johnson had irrevocably broken with the Union party, see *Cleveland Leader*, Feb. 22, 1866; *Buckeye State*, Feb. 22, 1866; *Springfield Daily News and Republic*, Feb. 20, 21, 1866; *Bucyrus Journal*, March 3, 1866; *Ironton Register*, March 1, 1866; Donn Piatt to Robert Schenck, Feb. 28, 1866, Schenck Papers; Samuel Shellabarger to James Comly, n.d., Comly Papers; R. Plumb to James A. Garfield, March 5, 1866, L.W. Hall to Garfield, Feb. 23, 1866, JAGP; J.A. Chase to John Sherman, Feb. 22, 1866, JSP.

26. *Portage County Democrat*, Feb. 28, 1866. See also *Scioto Gazette*, Feb. 27, 1866; *Marietta Register*, Feb. 22, 1866; *Morgan County Herald*, Feb. 23, 1866; *Dayton Daily Journal*, Feb. 21, 1866; *Western Reserve Chronicle*, Feb. 22, 1866; John Russell to Wife, Feb. 22, 1866, John Russell Papers, Ohio Historical Society; George B. Wright to Jacob Cox, March 1, 1866, JDCP; James Garfield to James Comly, Feb. 21, 1866, Comly Papers; Rutherford B. Hayes to Sardis Birchard, Feb. 28, 1866, in Williams, ed., *Diary and Letters* 3:18; A. Denny to John Sherman, Feb. 21, 23, 1866, E.B. Sadler to Sherman, Feb. 19, 1866, Warner Bateman to Sherman, Feb. 21, 1866, JSP. For examples of those

who were ready to follow Congress if Johnson continued to reject the will of the people, see D.C. Pinkerton to Sherman, March 1, 1866, Mahlon Chance to Sherman, March 1, 1866, JSP.

27. *Cincinnati Daily Enquirer*, Feb. 20, 21, 1866; *Zanesville Weekly Signal*, Feb. 22, 1866; *Dayton Empire*, Feb. 20, 1866; *Portsmouth Times*, Feb. 24, 1866; *Crisis*, Feb. 14, 21, 28, 1866; *Cleveland Plain Dealer*, Feb. 20, 22, 27, 1866; *Marietta Times*, Feb. 22, 1866.

28. Kenneth Stampp, for example, lumped this veto with the later one on the Civil Rights Bill and concluded that they "made the breach between Johnson and Congress all but final" (*The Era of Reconstruction*, 113). One difficulty is that Stampp and many others deal mainly with Congress, which was decidedly more hostile toward Johnson than most Ohioans. Fawn Brodie asserts that "Johnson could hardly have chosen a worse issue upon which to break with the Republican party," in *Thaddeus Steven, Scourge of the South*, 253. James M. McPherson leaves his readers with the impression that northerners sharply criticized the veto in *The Struggle for Equality: Abolitionists and the Negro in the Civil War and Reconstruction* (Princeton: Princeton University Press, 1964), 347-48. Another study argues that the veto, while causing considerable consternation among Radical Republicans, resulted in increased efforts to secure future party harmony. Benedict, *Compromise of Principle*, 158. McKitrick, *Johnson and Reconstruction*, 290-98, contends that although the veto angered the North, the possibility of peace between Johnson and Congress "remained considerable." For a study of reaction in Ohio that disagrees with that presented here, see Bonadio, *North of Reconstruction*, 60. With no apparent supporting evidence, Bonadio writes: "Few Republicans in Ohio remonstrated with [Johnson], for most were convinced that their worst suspicions were true; at best Johnson cared nothing for the party and at worst, he would destroy it or watch it collapse under the weight of its dissensions."

29. *Cincinnati Daily Commercial*, Feb. 23, 24, 1866; *Dayton Daily Journal*, Feb. 24, 26, 1866; *Cleveland Herald*, Feb. 26, 1866; *Toledo Blade*, Feb. 23, 1866; *Portage County Democrat*, Feb. 28, 1866; E.J. Tishener to Benjamin Wade, BFWP; W.B. Derrick to John Sherman, March 21, 1866, JSP.

30. L.W. Hall to James A. Garfield, Feb. 23, 1866, JAGP; Samuel Shellabarger to James Comly, n.d., Comly Papers; C. Waggoner to John Sherman, Feb. 28, 1866, Warner Bateman to Sherman, Feb. 21, 1866, JSP; W.T. Coggeshall to Jacob Cox, Feb. 22, 1866, JDCP; *Elyria Democrat*, Feb. 21, 1866; *Scioto Gazette*, Feb. 27, 1866.

31. John Sherman to Jacob Cox, Feb. 10, 1866, JDCP.

32. *Cincinnati Daily Commercial*, Feb. 27, 1866; *Scioto Gazette*, March 6, 1866.

33. Jacob Cox to General George Wright, quoted in *Cincinnati Daily Commercial*, Feb. 27, 1866.

34. *Dayton Daily Journal*, Feb. 28, 1866; *Bucyrus Journal*, March 3, 1866; *Portage County Democrat*, March 7, 1866; *Cincinnati Daily Commercial*, Feb. 27, 1866; *Scioto Gazette*, March 6, 1866. See also George Wright to Jacob Cox, March 1, 1866, JDCP.

35. Jacob Cox to Aaron F. Perry, March 10, 1866, JDCP; Coggeshall Diary, March 4, 1866.

36. John Sherman, Speech, Feb. 26, 1866, *Congressional Globe*, 39th Cong., 1st sess., app., 124-33.

37. C.L. Blakeslee to John Sherman, March 3, 1866, R.C. Parsons to Sherman, March 19, 1866, JSP. The one critic minced no words, "I did not like the synopsis and I like the speech less. It is good Lord good Devil with you; first on this side, then on that,

and being neither hot nor cold you will be spewed out by the people." John M. Pease to Sherman, March 14, 1866, JSP. The remainder of the favorable comments are in the Sherman Papers from Feb. 27, 1866, to March 29, 1866.

38. H.H. Leavitt to John Sherman, March 19, 1866, JSP; Stanley Matthews to Warner Bateman, March 6, 1866, Bateman Papers; Rutherford B. Hayes to S. Birchard, March 2, 4, 1866, in Williams, ed., *Diary and Letters* 3:19; Congressman Ralph P. Buckland, Speech, *Congressional Globe*, 39th Cong., 1st sess., 1625; *Summit County Beacon*, March 8, 1866; *Elyria Democrat*, March 7, 14, 21, 1866; *Geauga Democrat*, March 21, 1866.

39. E.B. Sadler to John Sherman, March 23, 1866, JSP; W.C. Howells to James Garfield, March 26, 1866, JAGP; Rutherford B. Hayes to Friedrich Hassaurek, April 8, 1866, RBHP.

40. Cox's conclusion was not entirely accurate. Ohio Republicans desired some guarantee of basic civil rights for the freedmen but not necessarily this bill. See Rutherford B. Hayes to Friedrich Hassaurek, April 8, 1866, RBHP; C.H. Beekman to John Sherman, March 16, 1866, Jesse Baldwin to Sherman, March 19, 1866, JSP.

41. Cox to Andrew Johnson, March 22, 1866, AJP.

42. Among the Republicans who considered the bill unconstitutional were the editors of the *Daily Zanesville Courier*, March 27, 1866; *Cincinnati Daily Commercial*, March 28, 30, 1866; *Toledo Blade*, March 28, 1866; *Lancaster Gazette*, April 5, 1866. See also Aaron F. Perry to Jacob Cox, March 26, 1866, JDCP. Republican congressmen Columbus Delano and John Bingham also had some doubts on this issue. See *Congressional Globe*, 39th Cong., 1st sess., app., 157-58; *Cincinnati Daily Commercial*, March 28, 1866.

43. *Daily Zanesville Courier*, March 28, 1866. See also Benjamin F. Hoffman to James A. Garfield, March 30, 1866, JAGP; E. Conklin to John Sherman, April 10, 1866, JSP; Rutherford B. Hayes to Mrs. Hayes, March 29, 1866, in Williams, ed., *Diary and Letters* 3:21.

44. *Scioto Gazette*, April 13, 1866; *Cleveland Leader*, March 29, 1866; *Cincinnati Daily Gazette*, March 28, 1866; *Western Reserve Chronicle*, April 4, 1866; *Buckeye State*, April 5, 1866; E. Conklin to John Sherman, April 10, 1866, JSP; B.F. Hoffman to James Garfield, March 30, 1866, JAGP; Robert Schenck to W.D. Bickham, April 24, 1866, Bickham Papers.

45. W.C. Howells to James A. Garfield, March 26, 1866, JAGP; Warner Bateman to John Sherman, March 30, 1866, JSP.

46. H.S. Burnett to John Sherman, April 7, 1866, JSP; J.H. Rhodes to James Garfield, April 8, 1866, JAGP. William Stedman perhaps expressed the shaken faith in Johnson best in a letter to John Sherman. "I *cannot* I *will not* believe that the Pres. is going to abrogate all he has said up to this time in favor of supporting & caring for the freedmen" (April 7, 1866, JSP).

47. Many Democratic journals cheered the veto and congratulated Johnson for protecting "the people" from the attempted "despotism" of Congress. *Cadiz Sentinel*, April 4, 11, 1866; *St. Clairsville Gazette*, April 5, 1866; *Gallipolis Dispatch*, April 13, 1866; *Circleville Democrat*, March 30, 1866; *Holmes County Farmer*, April 5, 1866.

48. For examples of those who remained optimistic, see Rutherford B. Hayes to Wife, April 8, 1866, Hayes to Mother, April 12, 1866, in Williams, ed., *Diary and Letters* 3:22, 22-23; E.B. Taylor to James Garfield, May 20, 1866, L.W. Hall to Garfield, April 12, 1866, JAGP. For examples of those who believed that Johnson had already departed from the Republican party, see W.C. Howells to Garfield, April 27, 1866, ibid.; Thomas Ewing, Jr., to Thomas Ewing, Sr., April 12, 1866, Ewing Family Papers; M.F. Force to John Sherman, May 26, 1866, Warner Bateman to Sherman, May 2, 1866, JSP.

49. *Cincinnati Daily Commercial*, Dec. 28, 1865, June 21, 1866; *Marietta Register*, May 17, 1866; *Dayton Daily Journal*, May 12, 1866; *Toledo Blade*, June 13, 1866.

50. Jacob Cox to John Sherman, Jan. 27, 1866, W.E. Gallup to Sherman, March 13, 1866, JSP.

51. J.M. Workman to John Sherman, April 1, 4, 1866, JSP.

52. M.B. Wright to John Sherman, Feb. 27, 1866, JSP; *Marietta Register*, May 17, 1866. See also *Cincinnati Daily Commercial*, Jan. 11, 24, Feb. 9, 1866; *Dayton Daily Journal*, Feb. 14, 1866; R.P.L. Baber to John Sherman, Jan. 27, 1866, J.H. Geiger to Sherman, Feb. 5, 1866, JSP; Samuel Shellabarger to James Comly, n.d., Comly Papers; Rutherford B. Hayes Diary, June 14, 1866, in Williams, ed. *Diary and Letters* 3:27; W.A. Platt to Sardis Birchard, March 31, 1866, Sardis Birchard Papers, Hayes Presidential Center; Kleinpell, "Comly," 42-43.

53. B.F. Hoffman to James Garfield, April 9, 1866, JAGP; Z. Street to John Sherman, March 30, 1866, R.P.L. Baber to Sherman, March 12, 1866, JSP; *Daily Zanesville Courier*, March 22, 1866; *Cincinnati Daily Commercial*, Dec. 30, 1865.

54. J.T. Catlin to James Garfield, June 1, 1866, JAGP; Charles Raymond to John Sherman, April 25, 1866, Warner Bateman to Sherman, May 2, 1866, JSP; *Morgan County Herald*, Feb. 23, 1866.

55. *Dayton Daily Journal*, May 12, 1866. See also *Cincinnati Daily Commercial*, June 21, 1866; John Sherman to Warner Bateman, Feb. 10, 1866, Bateman Papers.

56. Some Ohioans favored a permanent ban on officeholding for disloyal southern whites; others wanted a liability of fixed duration. See speeches of Congressmen Ephraim Eckley, James Garfield, Robert Schenck, Rufus Spalding, *Congressional Globe*, 39th Cong. 1st sess., 2534-36, 2462-63, 2470-71, 2509-10; William Coggeshall Diary, May 11, 1866; B.F. Hoffman to James Garfield, April 9, 1866, JAGP; R. Brinkerhoff to John Sherman, May 25, 1866, JSP. For examples of those who preferred the section as finally adopted, see Jacob Cox to Garfield, Jan. 1, May 4, June 22, 1866, JAGP; Wm. Penn Nixon to Sherman, June 6, 1866, JSP.

57. *Marietta Register*, June 14, 1866. See also J. Reed to James Garfield, June 18, 1866, Thomas J. McLain to Garfield, June 11, 1866, JAGP; Warner Bateman to John Sherman, June 6, 1866, W.T. Bascom to Sherman, June 4, 1866, JSP.

58. Senator Benjamin F. Wade for example believed that Congress had made a binding commitment to southerners, and he refused to consider further requirements of them until after they rejected the amendment.Trefousse, *Benjamin Franklin Wade: Radical Republican from Ohio*, 278-79. See also *Dayton Daily Journal*, July 21, 1866.

59. *Sandusky Daily Commercial Register*, Jan. 30, 1866. See also *Springfield Daily News and Republic*, June 13, 1866; *Dayton Daily Journal*, May 10, 1866; *Toledo Blade*, June 11, 13, 1866; *Cincinnati Daily Commercial*, June 17, 1866; *Marietta Register*, May 17, 1866; Rutherford B. Hayes to Warner Bateman, May 15, 1866, Bateman Papers; George Wright to Jacob Cox, March 1, 1866, JDCP.

60. Benedict, *Compromise of Principle*, 159-87; Horowitz, *The Great Impeacher*, 118-19; *Cincinnati Daily Commercial*, June 21,1866; *Toledo Blade*, June 13, 1866; Jacob Cox to William Dennison, May 19, 1866, A.F. Perry to Cox, June 22, 1866, JDCP; W.P. Richardson to John Sherman, June 18, 1866, JSP.

61. Jacob Cox to James Garfield, June 22, 1866, JAGP. See also W.P. Richardson to John Sherman, June 18, 1866, JSP.

62. Jacob Cox to Andrew Johnson, June 21, 1866, AJP; Cox to James Garfield, June 22, 1866, JAGP. For examples of those who believed that Johnson and Congress might still work together if Johnson endorsed the proposed amendment, see *Cincinnati Daily Commercial*, May 28, 1866; Warner Bateman to John Sherman, June 6, 1866, R.M. Corwine to Sherman, June 17, 1866, JSP.

63. *Congressional Globe*, 39th Cong., 1st sess., 3349; Hans L. Trefousse, *Impeachment of a President, Andrew Johnson, the Blacks, and Reconstruction*, 5-6, 8-9, 28- 29.

64. Jos. W. Dwyer to John Sherman, May 25, 1866, R.M. Corwine to Sherman, May 7, 1866, JSP. A Cincinnatian told Sherman that he expected Johnson to endorse the proposed amendment and then "all differences [would be] healed" (R. Brinkerhoff to Sherman, May 25, 1866, JSP).

65. Tom O. Edwards to John Sherman, April 26, 1866, JSP.

66. B.F. Hoffman to James A. Garfield, April 30, 1866, JAGP. See also John Russell to Warner Bateman, April 16, 1866, E.J. Hall to Bateman, May 1, 1866, Bateman Papers; Warner Bateman to John Sherman, May 2, 1866, W.H.P. Denny to Sherman, May 7, 1866, JSP.

67. *Eaton Weekly Register*, June 28, 1866; *Dayton Daily Journal*, June 23, 1866; *Ohio Repository*, July 18, 1866; *Norwalk Reflector*, July 3, 1866; *Cincinnati Daily Commercial*, June 27, 1866; Augustus Proctor to John Sherman, June 22, 1866, JSP.

68. McKitrick, *Johnson and Reconstruction*, 357.

69. Lewis Campbell to D.T. Patterson, Jan. 22, 1866, AJP. John Sherman, whose correspondents kept him extraordinarily well informed of events in Ohio, had learned of the movement toward party realignment at least as early as February. See Nathan Hollister to John Sherman, Feb. 19, 1866, JSP.

70. Lewis Campbell to D.T. Patterson, Jan. 22, 1866, AJP. See also Campbell to Andrew Johnson, Jan. 19, 1866, AJP, in which Campbell urged Johnson to rid himself of all Radical advisers.

71. George Hunt Pendleton to Andrew Johnson, Jan. 28, 1866, George W. Morgan to Johnson, Feb. 8, March 19, 1866, AJP. For further evidence of support coalescing around Johnson, see T.W. Bartley to Johnson, Feb. 24, 1866, Joseph Geiger to James R. Doolittle, Feb. 11, 1866, James Crutcher to Johnson, March 6, 1866; Henry S. Bishop to Johnson, April 5, 1866, C.F. Baldwin to Johnson, July 21, 1866, Joseph Newell to Johnson, July 17, 1866, AJP.

72. For samples of approval before the Freedmen's Bureau Bill veto, see *Cleveland Plain Dealer*, Jan. 16, Feb. 8, 1866; *Cincinnati Daily Enquirer*, Feb. 9, 1866. On the Civil Rights Bill and Johnson's veto of it, see *Crisis*, March 21, April 4, 11, 1866; *Portsmouth Times*, March 31, April 7, May 5, 1866; *Zanesville Weekly Signal*, March 29, 1866; *Cincinnati Daily Enquirer*, March 17, 28, 29, 31, April 7, 1866; *Cleveland Plain Dealer*, March 27, 28, 29, April 2, 1866. On Johnson and the proposed amendment, see *Cleveland Plain Dealer*, June 23, 1866; *Cincinnati Daily Enquirer*, June 25, 1866. For reluctant supporters, see W.H. Mitchell to J.A. Trimble, Jan. 22 1866; John A. Trimble Papers, Ohio Historical Society; Alexander Long to Alexander Boys, Jan. 21, 1866, Alexander Boys Papers, Ohio Historical Society.

73. R.P.L. Baber to James Doolittle, Feb. 28, March 29, 1866, James R. Doolittle Papers, State Historical Society of Wisconsin; R.P.L. Baber to Andrew Johnson, March 29, 1866, Baber to William Seward, March 30, 1866, Lewis Campbell to Johnson, June 22, 1866, AJP.

74. Campbell to Cox, March 6, 8, 12, 1866, Cox to Campbell, March 12, 1866, JDCP.

75. James C. Hall to John Sherman, May 24, 1866, Warner Bateman to Sherman, June 6, 25, 1866, James A. Biggs to Sherman, June 12, 1866, W.P. Richardson to Sherman, June 18, 1866, JSP.

76. Campbell to Cox, April 8, 1866, JDCP; C.L. Vallandigham to George W. Morgan, June 29, 1866, Clement L. Vallandigham Papers, Western Reserve Historical

Society. For examples of concern that the party unite behind the amendment before going to the voters, see Geo. B. Wright to John Sherman, June 4, 1866, W.T. Bascom to Sherman, June 4, 1866, Warner Bateman to Sherman, June 6, 1866, JSP. For examples of Republican concern about the activities of the pro-Johnson men at the convention and reports on how impotent they proved to be, see Norman L. Chaffee to James Garfield, May 25, 1866, Abner Kellogg to Garfield, June 25, 1866, JAGP; Robert Schenck to James Comly, May 22, 1866, Comly Papers. For editorial praise for the platform, see *Cleveland Leader*, June 21, 1866; *Lancaster Gazette*, June 21, 1866; *Eaton Weekly Register*, June 28, 1866; *Cincinnati Daily Commercial*, June 22, 1866; *Summit County Beacon*, June 28, 1866.

77. R.P.L. Baber to Andrew Johnson, June 28, 1866, Lewis Campbell to Johnson, June 22, 1866, James E. Cox to Johnson, July 17, 1866, AJP; Henry B. Payne to Campbell, July 19, 1866, Campbell Papers; Campbell to Isaac Strohm, September 7, 1866, Isaac Strohm Papers, Ohio Historical Society.

78. Congressman James Ashley, who had quarreled with many of Johnson's actions during spring 1866, finally concluded in early July that "Johnson may be regarded as having passed the Rubicon and, no doubt, will eventually cooperate with the opposition." Ashley to Gov. A.C. Gibbs, July 6, 1866, Gibbs Papers.

79. *Cincinnati Daily Commercial*, July 25, 1866, and see July 3, 1866; *Dayton Daily Journal*, July 13, 1866; *Marietta Register*, July 19, 1866; *Ohio Repository*, July 25, 1866.

80. *Scioto Gazette*, July 24, 1866. See also John Sherman to William T. Sherman, July 8, 1866, in Thorndike, ed., *The Sherman Letters*, 276-77; Tom O. Edwards to John Sherman, July 25, 1866, J.J. Janney to Sherman, July 19, 1866, JSP. Newspapers that repudiated Johnson over his endorsement of this movement or its convention in August included *Elyria Democrat*, July 1, 1866; *Circleville Union*, July 20, 1866; *Lancaster Gazette*, Aug. 30, 1866; *Delaware Gazette*, Aug. 24, 1866.

81. Bateman to Sherman, July 9, 1866, JSP. See also A.P. Denny to Sherman, July 15, 1866, W.H.P. Denny to Sherman, July 20, 1866, JSP; T.J. McLain to James Garfield, July 18, 1866, JAGP.

82. McKitrick. *Johnson and Reconstruction*, 395, 396, 397, 400-410; Cox and Cox, *Politics, Principle, and Prejudice, 1865-1866: Dilemma of Reconstruction America*, 220-23.

83. Dennison to J.J. Janney, July 19, 1866, Janney Papers. See also Janney to Dennison, July 16, 1866, ibid.; *Circleville Union*, July 20, 1866; Dennison to Jacob Cox, July 16, 1866, JDCP. In the letter to Cox, Dennison showed his awareness of the symbolic importance of his desertion of the president. "My resignation," he suggested, "seems to have almost—if not altogether completed the breach between the Prest & our friends. I felt this step of withdrawing might be important, etc., but felt it my duty to resign whatever the consequences." As late as May 10 Dennison had held hopes for "the speedy adjustment of all matters in the controversy between" Johnson and Congress. The president's actions since then had exploded that dream. Dennison to Cox, May 10, 1866, JDCP.

4. Standing Firm

1. Vallandigham to Allen G. Thurman, May 17, 1866, Allen G. Thurman Papers, Ohio Historical Society; Reginald McGrane, *William Allen: A Study in Western*

Democracy, 173; *Cincinnati Daily Enquirer*, Feb. 27, 1866; *Cleveland Plain Dealer*, May 25, 1866; Porter, *Ohio Politics*, 223-25.

2. W.P. Nixon to John Sherman, May 28, 1866, George B. Wright to Sherman, June 4, 1866, JSP; E.B. Sadler to Warner Bateman, May 29, 1866, Bateman Papers; *Dayton Daily Journal*, June 15, 1866; *Cincinnati Daily Commercial*, June 20, 1866.

3. Rush R. Sloane to Andrew Johnson, May 5, 1866, R.P.L. Baber to Johnson, June 28, 1866, Lewis Campbell to Johnson, June 22, 1866, AJP; Campbell to Jacob Cox, April 8, 1866, JDCP; John M. Connell to Thomas Ewing, Jr., June 14, 1866, Ewing Family Papers.

4. Norman L. Chaffee to James A. Garfield, May 25, 1866, M.C. Canfield to Garfield, June 4, 1866, JAGP; *Cadiz Republican*, May 16, 1866. While Congressman Robert Schenck reported that Johnson's supporters would unscrupulously attempt to pack the convention with the president's men, Lewis Campbell insisted that the Radicals had done precisely the same thing with delegates "from the ranks of your [Johnson's] enemies." Robert Schenck to James Comly, May 22, 1866, Comly Papers; Lewis Campbell to Andrew Johnson, June 22, 1866, AJP.

5. Jacob Cox to James A. Garfield, April 10, 1866, JAGP; *Ironton Register*, June 28, 1866; Kleinpell, "Comly," 49-50.

6. Porter, *Ohio Politics*, 226-27; *Cadiz Republican*, June 27, 1866; *Lancaster Gazette*, June 21, 1866; Coggeshall Diary, June 20, 1866; Smith, *History of the Republican Party* 1:227.

7. *Eaton Weekly Register*, June 28, 1866. For other examples of editorial approval of the platform, see *Ironton Register*, June 28, 1866; *Springfield Daily News and Republic*, June 22, 1866; *Cleveland Leader*, June 21, 1866; *Elyria Democrat*, June 27, 1866; *Circleville Union*, June 22, 1866; *Daily Zanesville Courier*, June 21, 1866.

8. Jacob D. Cox to Andrew Johnson, June 21, 1866, AJP.

9. Baber to Andrew Johnson, June 28, 1866, Campbell to Johnson, June 22, 1866, AJP.

10. Lewis Campbell to Andew Johnson, Jan. 19, 1866, AJP; R.P.L. Baber to Senator James R. Doolittle, March 29, 1866, James R. Doolittle Papers, State Historical Society of Wisconsin; Baber to William H. Seward, March 30, 1866, AJP.

11. C.N. Locke to John Sherman, May 28, 1866, Warner Bateman to Sherman, May 2, 1866, JSP; Lewis Campbell to Andrew Johnson, June 22, 1866, AJP; John M. Connell to Thomas Ewing, Jr., June 14, 1866, Ewing Family Papers; Henry B. Payne to Campbell, July 19, 1866, Campbell Papers; J.V. Offenbacher to J.J. Janney, Aug. 3, 1866, Janney Papers.

12. Lewis Campbell to Jacob Cox, March 19, 1866, JDCP; Henry B. Payne to Campbell, July 19, 1866, Campbell Papers.

13. Lewis D. Campbell to Thomas Ewing, Sr., July 14, 1866, Ewing Family Papers; Joseph H. Geiger to Andrew Johnson, Aug. 2, 1866, AJP.

14. George W. Morgan to Andrew Johnson, July 14, 1866, AJP. For Democratic approval of the committee's action, see *Cleveland Plain Dealer*, July 16, 25, 1866; *Crisis*, July 11, 18, 1866. For the opposite view, see *Cincinnati Daily Enquirer*, Aug. 6, 1866. For further discussion of the preparations for the meeting, see James E. Cox to Andrew Johnson, July 17, 1866, R.P.L. Baber to Johnson, June 28, 1866, AJP; Lewis Campbell to Thomas Ewing, Sr., July 14, 1866, Ewing Family Papers.

15. For Democratic reactions, see *Circleville Democrat*, Aug. 24, 1866; *Holmes County Farmer*, Aug. 23, 1866; (Delaware) *Weekly Herald*, Aug. 23, 1866. See also *Crisis*, Aug. 22, 1866; *Cadiz Sentinel*, Aug. 22, 1866; *Cleveland Plain Dealer*, Aug. 16, 17, 1866; *Portsmouth Times*, Aug. 18, 25, 1866; Thomas Ewing, Jr., to My darling Ellen,

Aug. 23, 1866, Ewing Family Papers; D.M. Fleming to Andrew Johnson, Aug. 20, 1866, AJP. For responses of Republicans, see *Bucyrus Journal*, Aug. 18, 1866; *Marietta Register*, Aug. 16, 1866; *Cincinnati Daily Commercial*, Aug. 6, 16, 17, 1866; *Eaton Weekly Register*, Aug. 16, 1866; *Springfield Daily News and Republic*, Aug. 17, 1866; *Cadiz Republican*, Aug. 22, 1866; *Dayton Daily Journal*, Aug. 1, 1866; *Daily Commercial Register*, Aug. 2, 1866; *Portage County Democrat*, June 8, 1866; Granville Moody to Andrew Johnson, July 12, 1866, AJP; A.B. Nettleton to James Comly, July 26, 1866, Comly Papers; A.F. Perry to Jacob Cox, Aug. 16, 1866, JDCP; B.F. Hoffman to James Garfield, Aug. 17, 1866, JAGP.

16. *Ohio Repository*, Aug. 15, 1866.

17. *Elyria Democrat*, July 11, 1866; *Cleveland Herald*, Aug. 21, 1866; *Lancaster Gazette*, Aug. 30, 1866; *Delaware Gazette*, Aug. 24, 1866.

18. McPherson, *Struggle for Equality*, 358-59; *Cincinnati Daily Commercial*, May 4, 5, 1866; *Daily Zanesville Courier*, May 7, 1866; *Eaton Weekly Register*, May 10, 1866. For a typical Democratic reaction to the Memphis riot, see *Cincinnati Daily Enquirer*, May 4, 5, 1866. Its report called the massacre "one of the fruits of the Republican policy in regard to the negro." Washington McLean, the editor, blamed the Republicans because they had made the blacks uppity, "discontented with [their] condition," and predicted that a race war would result from the "abolition agitation." See also *Circleville Democrat*, May 11, 1866.

19. Brodie, *Thaddeus Stevens*, 273-82; Edwards, "Radical Reconstruction and the New Orleans Riot of 1866," 48-64.

20. Nelson, "The North, the South, and the Republican Ideology: The Northeastern Republican Press, 131.

21. J.V. Offenbacher to J.J. Janney, Aug. 3, 1866, Janney Papers.

22. *Dayton Daily Journal*, July 31, Aug. 1, 1866; *Ohio Repository*, Sept. 5, 1866; *Portage County Democrat*, Aug. 8, 15, 1866; *Cincinnati Daily Commercial*, Aug. 7, 1866; *Scioto Gazette*, Aug. 7, 1866; *Morgan County Herald*, Sept. 14, 1866. Congressman Samuel Shellabarger later concluded that evidence presented at congressional hearings on the New Orleans riot "showed overwhelmingly a deliberately arranged plan for a massacre." Shellabarger to James Comly, Dec. 29, 1866, Comly Papers.

23. McKitrick, *Johnson and Reconstruction*, 428-38; *Cincinnati Daily Commercial*, Aug. 28, 1866.

24. *Cleveland Leader*, Sept. 4, 1866; Trefousse, *Impeachment of a President*, 39; Cashdollar, "Andrew Johnson and the Philadelphia Election of 1866," 365-83.

25. Oder, "Andrew Johnson and the 1866 Illinois Election," 189-200; Kilar, "Andrew Johnson 'Swings' through Michigan: Community Response to a Presidential Crusade," 251-73.

26. John W. Andrews to Thomas Ewing, Sr., Sept. 5, 1866, Ewing Family Papers; W.C. Howells to James A. Garfield, Sept. 19, 1866, JAGP; Charles Cox to Jacob Cox, Sept. 24, 1866, Jacob Cox to James Monroe, Nov. 11, 1866, JDCP; *Ohio Repository*, Sept. 12, 1866; *Summit County Beacon*, Sept. 6, 13, 1866; *Daily Zanesville Courier*, Sept. 4, 1866; *Cadiz Republican*, Sept. 12, 1866; *Portage County Democrat*, Sept. 5, 12, 1866.

27. *Portage County Democrat*, Sept. 12, 19, 1866; *Dayton Daily Journal*, Sept. 5, 1866; *Summit County Beacon*, Sept. 6, 1866; *Ohio Repository*, Sept. 6, 1866; *Cincinnati Daily Commercial*, Sept. 1, 10, 11, 1866; Kleinpell, "Comly," 53; Van Offenbacher to John Russell, Sept. 18, 1866, John Russell Papers.

28. James Garfield to James Comly, Feb. 21, 1866; JAGP; Jacob D. Cox to James

Monroe, Nov. 11, 1866, JDCP; Benjamin Wade to My dear Cal, Sept. 30, 1866, BFWP. See also *Western Reserve Chronicle*, Aug. 29, 1866; *Morgan County Herald*, Oct. 5, 1866; *Summit County Beacon*, Oct. 4, 1866.

29. "Speech of Governor Cox at Columbus, August 21, 1866," *Cincinnati Commercial*, ed., *Speeches of the Campaign of 1866, in the States of Ohio, Indiana, and Kentucky*, 17; "Speech of John A. Bingham at Bowerston, Ohio, August 24, 1866," ibid., 19; "Speech of Senator John Sherman," ibid., 39.

30. "Speech of Sherman," ibid., 39. See also "Speech of General R.B. Hayes," ibid., 28; "Speech of Bingham," ibid., 19.

31. "Speech of Cox," ibid., 17; "Speech of Bingham," ibid., 19.

32. "Speech of the Honorable Samuel Shellabarger, August 16, 1866," ibid., 11. See also "Speech of Hayes," ibid., 28; "Speech of Hon. Benjamin F. Wade, September 11, 1866," ibid., 31; "Speech of Bingham," ibid., 19.

33. *Dayton Daily Journal*, Oct. 9, 1866. See also *Ohio Repository*, Aug. 29, 1866; *Miami Union*, Oct. 6, 1866; *Cincinnati Daily Commercial*, June 12, 21, Oct. 5, 1866; *Scioto Gazette*, Oct. 9, 1866; *Summit County Beacon*, Oct. 4, 1866; *Toledo Blade*, Oct. 2, 1866; *Dayton Daily Journal*, July 28, Aug. 25, Sept. 13, 1866; *Cadiz Republican*, Sept. 23, Oct. 23, 1866; *Springfield Daily News and Republican*, Oct. 4, 1866; Robert Schenck to W.D. Bickham, April 4, 1866, Bickham Papers; E.B. Sadler to Warner Bateman, May 29, 1866, W.H. Smith to Bateman, Sept. 25, 1866, Bateman Papers; Clark, "Radicals and Moderates on the Joint Committee on Reconstruction," 93; Kleinpell, "Comly," 52.

34. *Toledo Blade*, July 18, 1866; *Dayton Daily Journal*, Sept. 15, 1866, and Sept. 13, 14, 17, 1866. One example of a Western Reserve paper that agreed, at least during this campaign, that control over suffrage requirements was a state prerogative was the *Portage County Democrat*. See Aug. 15, 1866.

35. *Clinton Republican*, Nov. 15, 1866; *Cincinnati Daily Commercial*, Aug. 31, 1866; Rutherford B. Hayes to Guy Bryan, Oct. 1, 1866, in Williams, ed., *Diary and Letters* 3:32; John Sherman to William T. Sherman, July 2, 1866, in Thorndike, ed., *Sherman Letters*, 271-72; E.B. Sadler to John Sherman, May 9, 1866, JSP; Coggeshall Diary, June 26, 1866; "Speech of Jacob Cox," in *Commercial*, ed., *Speeches of 1866*, 17; Horowitz, *Great Impeacher*, 120-21.

36. *Dayton Daily Journal*, July 28, Oct. 9, 1866; *Springfield Daily News and Republic*, Oct. 2, 1866; *Scioto Gazette*, July 3, 1866.

37. *Scioto Gazette*, June 26, 1866.

38. *Morgan County Herald*, Oct. 5, 1866. For other examples of the fear of more war, see J.V. Offenbacher to J.J. Janney, Aug. 3, 17, 1866, Janney Papers; Jacob Cox to James Monroe, Nov. 21, 1866, JDCP; *Cincinnati Daily Commercial*, Aug. 20, 1866; *Clinton Republican*, Sept. 27, 1866; *Ohio Repository*, Sept. 12, 1866; *Dayton Daily Journal*, Sept. 13, 1866; *Portage County Democrat*, Sept. 12, Oct. 3, 1866; *Scioto Gazette*, Sept. 25, Oct. 9, 1866.

39. *Springfield Daily News and Republic*, Sept. 6, Oct. 2, 1866; *Clinton Republican*, Sept. 27, 1866; *Ohio Repository*, Aug. 29, 1866. See also James Oldham to Benjamin Wade, Aug. 30, 1866, BFWP; *Toledo Blade*, Oct. 2, 1866; *Springfield Daily News and Republic*, Sept. 6, 1866; *Cincinnati Daily Commercial*, Aug. 23, 1866.

40. "Speech of Sherman," in *Commercial*, ed., *Speeches of 1866*, 39.

41. "Address of the Democratic Members of the Ohio Legislature to the People of Ohio," *Portsmouth Times*, March 17, 1866.

42. *Portsmouth Times*, Sept. 1, 1866. See also *Circleville Democrat*, Sept. 28, 1866; *Cadiz Sentinel*, Aug. 15, Sept. 26, 1866.

43. "Speech of General George Morgan at Coshocton, August 21, 1866," in *Commercial*, ed., *Speeches of 1866*, 15; *Portsmouth Times*, May 18, Sept. 1, 1866; *Cincinnati Daily Enquirer*, Sept. 4, Oct. 3, 1866; *Circleville Democrat*, Sept. 28, 1866; (Delaware) *Weekly Herald*, Aug. 23, 1866; *Cleveland Plain Dealer*, March 14, 1866; Lewis Campbell to Isaac Strohm, Sept. 7, 1866, William Baker to Isaac Strohm, Sept. 28, 1866, Strohm Papers. For examples of Democratic conventions that pledged to support the president, see "Resolutions of Montgomery County Democrats," in *Dayton Daily Journal*, May 21, 1866; "Resolutions of Eighth Congressional District Democrats, July 31, 1866," in (Delaware) *Weekly Herald*, Aug. 23, 1866; "Resolutions of Pickaway County Democrats, August 4, 1866," in *Circleville Democrat*, Aug. 10, 1866; "Resolutions of Twelfth Congressional District Democrats, August 7, 1866," in *Putnam County Sentinel*, Aug. 9, 1866; "Resolutions of Third Congressional District Democrats, August 28, 1866," in *Cincinnati Daily Commercial*, Aug. 29, 1866; "Resolutions of Lawrence County Democrats," *Portsmouth Times*, Aug. 4, 1866.

44. *Portsmouth Times*, Sept. 1, 29, 1866; *Cincinnati Daily Enquirer*, Sept. 21, Oct. 1, 9, 1866; *Crisis*, Sept. 19, 1866; *Cleveland Plain Dealer*, July 3, 1866; *Marietta Times*, Oct. 4, 1866.

45. *Cleveland Plain Dealer*, July 3, 1866. See also *Cincinnati Daily Enquirer*, April 24, Oct. 1, 6, 1866.

46. *Portsmouth Times*, June 9, Sept. 1, 29, 1866; *Marietta Times*, Oct. 4, 1866; *Cleveland Plain Dealer*, March 20, July 3, 1866; *Cincinnati Daily Enquirer*, Sept. 21, 1866. Several Democratic conventions endorsed the call of the National Union Convention for immediate restoration of the South. For example, see the resolutions passed by the Democrats of the Second Congressional District in *Cincinnati Daily Commercial*, Sept. 5, 1866; Third Congressional District, ibid., Aug. 29, 1866; Fifteenth Congressional District in *Marietta Times*, Aug. 30, 1866.

47. *Cleveland Plain Dealer*, Sept. 13, 1866; *Portsmouth Times*, June 9, Aug. 4, Sept. 1, 1866; *Cincinnati Daily Enquirer*, Oct. 6, 1866; "Resolutions of the Democrats of the Third Congressional District," *Cincinnati Daily Commercial*, Aug. 29, 1866; "Speech of General George Morgan at Coshocton, August 21, 1866," in *Commercial*, ed., *Speeches of 1866*, 15.

48. *Cincinnati Daily Enquirer*, Oct. 6, 1866, and see Sept. 16, 20, 28, 1866; See also *Cleveland Plain Dealer*, July 10, 1866; *Portsmouth Times*, Feb. 17, Sept. 22, 1866; *Crisis*, Jan. 24, Sept. 5, 1866.

49. *Commercial*, ed., *Speeches of 1866*, 16. See also "Resolutions of Franklin County Soldiers, September 12, 1866," *Cleveland Plain Dealer*, Sept. 13, 1866.

50. *Cincinnati Daily Enquirer*, Oct. 3, 1866.

51. *Clinton Republican*, Aug. 30, 1866; *Ironton Register*, Sept. 6, 27, 1866; *Bucyrus Journal*, Sept. 8, 1866.

52. Benedict, *Compromise of Principle*, 169. See speeches of Representatives Tobias Plants, Feb. 24, 1866, and Martin Welker, Feb. 7, 1866, *Congressional Globe*, 39th Cong., 1st sess., 728, 1010-15.

53. Williams, ed., *Diary and Letters* 3:25; "Speech of R.B. Hayes in Cincinnati, September 7, 1866," in *Commercial*, ed., *Speeches of 1866*, 28.

54. *Congressional Globe*, 39th Cong., 1st sess., 2881; James Ashley to A.C. Gibbs, July 6, 1866, Gibbs Papers; Horowitz, *The Great Impeacher*, 121.

55. *Congressional Globe*, 39th Cong., 1st sess., 3146.

56. Ibid., 2462.

57. Quoted in *Cincinnati Daily Commercial*, Aug. 25, 1866.

58. Trefousse, *Benjamin Wade*, 311-12.

59. *Dayton Daily Journal*, Sept. 11, 1866.

60. Ibid., Sept. 15, 17, Oct. 6, 1866; *Cincinnati Daily Commercial*, June 29, Aug. 18, 26, 1866; *Cincinnati Daily Gazette*, Sept. 18, 1866; Kleinpell, "Comly," 38-39.

61. *Sandusky Daily Commercial Register*, Jan. 27, Feb. 10, 1866; Charles Cox to Jacob Cox, Sept. 24, 1866, A.F. Perry to Jacob Cox, June 9, 1866, JDCP; Rutherford B. Hayes to Warner Bateman, May 15, 1866, Bateman Papers; *Elyria Democrat*, May 16, 1866.

62. In the midst of depressing war news in the spring 1863, Ohio Democrats nominated for governor the peace advocate Clement Vallandigham, after he had been forced by a military court to leave the country for his antiwar activities. By the fall election, which attracted national attention, the Union armies had made stunning gains, and the Union party in Ohio succeeded in arousing a record number voters to the polls, where Vallandigham was overwhelmed, receiving just under 40 percent of the votes.

63. For election statistics, see *Annual Report, 1866*, 34-38; *Annual Report, 1868*, 108.

64. *Circleville Union*, Oct. 12, 1866; *Western Reserve Chronicle*, Oct. 17, 1866; *Ironton Register*, Oct. 18, 1866; *Norwalk Reflector*, Oct. 23, Nov. 27, 1866; *Cincinnati Daily Commercial*, Nov. 8, 28, 1866; Benedict, *Compromise of Principle*, 211, 257.

65. For examples of other northern electorates that endorsed the amendment, see Richard N. Current, "Wisconsin: Shifting Strategies to Stay on Top," in Mohr, ed., *Radical Republicans in the North: State Politics during Reconstruction*, 152-53; Nelson, "The North, the South, and the Republican Ideology," 133-34; Dilla, *The Politics of Michigan, 1865-1878*, 54, 57, 65-66n; Stebbins, *A Political History of the State of New York, 1865-1869*, 133. See also Brock, *American Crisis*, 168-69.

5. Reining in the Republicans

1. Benedict, "The Rout of Radicalism: Republicans and the Elections of 1867," 342-44.

2. *Western Reserve Chronicle*, Oct. 17, 1866; *Cincinnati Daily Commercial*, Oct. 10, 1866; *Portage County Democrat*, Oct. 10, 1866; *Circleville Union*, Oct. 12, 1866; *Ohio Repository*, Nov. 14, 1866; *Norwalk Reflector*, Nov. 27, 1866; A. Denny to John Sherman, Oct. 14, 1866, A. Stone to Sherman, Oct. 23, 1866, JSP.

3. *Cincinnati Daily Commercial*, Nov. 8, 1866. See also *Norwalk Reflector*, Oct. 23, 1866; *Portage County Democrat*, Nov. 14, 1866; T.E. Brincefield to John Sherman, Nov. 30, 1866, JSP; Benedict, *Compromise of Principle*, 210.

4. *Miami Union*, Oct. 13, 1866, and Nov. 24, 1866; *Circleville Union*, Jan. 18, 1867; *Cincinnati Daily Commercial*, Nov. 8, Dec. 15, 1866; Donald C. Swift, "John A. Bingham and Reconstruction: The Dilemma of a Moderate," 84-85. For an expression of concern that southerners might misinterpret the elections as victories for Radical Republicans, see John Hopley to John Sherman, Nov. 1, 1866, JSP.

5. McPherson, *Political History of the United States*, 194.

6. Anne Nelson's study of the northeastern Republican press indicates that although most moderate and conservative journalists in her sample were dismayed by southern rejection, some Radical editors were thrilled because it allowed stronger measures that would go farther toward recasting southern society in the northern image. See "The North, the South, and the Republican Ideology," 138.

7. Perman, *Reunion without Compromise*, 234-37.

8. Ibid., 238-65.

9. Nelson, "The North, the South, and the Republican Ideology," 112-15.

10. Benedict, *Compromise of Principle*, 212-16.

11. Garfield to Burke Hinsdale, Jan. 1, 1867, in Hinsdale, ed., *Garfield-Hinsdale Letters*, 88; Trefousse, *Benjamin Wade*, 278-81; Horowitz, *The Great Impeacher*, 144; *Congressional Globe*, 39th Cong., 2nd sess., 124-25; James M. Ashley to Governor A.C. Gibbs, July 6, 1866, A.C. Gibbs Papers.

12. *Congressional Globe*, 39th Cong., 2nd sess., 48, 224, 288-90.

13. Ibid., 598-600.

14. *Congressional Globe*, 39th Cong., 2nd sess., 128; John Sherman to Jacob Cox, Jan. 17, 1867, JDCP. In his analysis Larry Kincaid has ranked Sherman the fifth most conservative of the thirty-two Republicans in the Thirty-ninth Congress. Benedict placed Sherman in a category called Consistent (Republican) Centrists, though he singled Sherman out as "leaning towards conservatives." See Kincaid, "The Legislative Origins of the Military Reconstruction Act, 1865-1867," 63; Benedict, *Compromise of Principle*, 28, 352, 356.

15. *Portage County Democrat*, Oct. 3, 1866. For Sherman's role in drafting the Military Reconstruction Act, see Sherman, *Recollections of Forty Years*, 370-73; McKitrick, *Johnson and Reconstruction*, 481-85; Benedict, *Compromise of Principle*, 235-43.

16. *Congressional Globe*, 39th Cong., 2nd sess., 500-504; Swift, "Bingham," 85-86; Benedict, *Compromise of Principle*, 218-20, 223-31.

17. Jacob Cox to W.T. Coggeshall, Dec. 5, 1866, Cox to A.F. Perry, Jan. 14, 1867, JDCP; Cox to John Sherman, Jan. 11, 1867, Feb. 15, 1867, JSP.

18. William Dennison to Rutherford B. Hayes, Jan. 28, 1867, RBHP.

19. Kincaid, "Legislative Origins," 81-287.

20. Sherman, *Recollections of Forty Years*, 370-73; McKitrick, *Johnson and Reconstruction*, 473-85.

21. See for example Eric McKitrick, "Reconstruction: Ultraconservative Revolution," in C. Vann Woodward, ed., *The Comparative Approach to American History* (New York: Basic Books, 1968), 146-59, esp. 153; Benedict, *Compromise of Principle*, 223-43; Kincaid, "Legislative Origins," 248-64.

22. The votes on final passage and the override of Johnson's veto are in *Congressional Globe*, 39th Cong., 2nd sess., 1400, 1645, 1733, 1976. Kincaid has rated Hubbell the most conservative Ohio Republican in the Thirty-ninth Congress. See "Legislative Origins," 57. Republicans Ephraim Eckley and James Garfield did not vote on the bill but did vote to override the president's veto. Garfield's public statements indicate that he would have supported the bill had he been present. Peskin, *Garfield*, 278.

23. *Cincinnati Daily Commercial*, Jan. 23, 1867; *Circleville Union*, Jan. 18, 1867.

24. *Dayton Daily Journal*, Jan. 22, 1867; *Miami Union*, Feb. 2, 1867. In a letter that also denounced Johnson's use of patronage to thwart the will of the people, a Republican from Cleveland charged, "It is deemed the height of impudence in [Johnson] to set himself up against the Representatives of the people in that matter [ratification of the proposed amendment] and by his Executive influence and patronage seek to defeat their will." Earl Bill to John Sherman, Jan. 15, 1867, JSP.

25. *Dayton Daily Journal*, Feb. 13, 1867; *Summit County Beacon*, Feb. 28, 1867. See also *Ironton Register*, Feb. 28, 1867; *Dayton Daily Journal*, Feb. 15, 21, 1867; C.A. Trimble to John Sherman, Jan. 15, 1867, JSP; E.B. Sadler to John Sherman, Jan. 20, 1867, ibid.

26. *Cincinnati Daily Gazette*, Oct. 11, 16, Nov. 3, 22, Dec. 3, 7, 13, 17, 28, 31, 1866, Jan. 4, 1867.

27. *Cincinnati Daily Commercial*, Dec. 19, 1866, Jan. 31, Feb. 11, 14, 15, 18, 20, 27, March 4, 5, 9, 1867.

28. *Portage County Democrat*, Jan. 9, 1867; A.D. Kibbee to John Sherman, Jan. 17, 1867, JSP. See also *Ohio Repository*, Dec. 26, 1866; *Dayton Daily Journal*, Nov. 27, Dec. 8, 1866; *Miami Union*, Dec. 8, 1866; *Cincinnati Daily Commercial*, Feb. 14, 1867; *Summit County Beacon*, Feb. 28, 1867; Sherman Blocker to John Sherman, Jan. 15, 1867, JSP.

29. *Cincinnati Daily Gazette*, Feb. 1, 1867; Edgar Conklin to John Sherman, Feb. 21, 1867, JSP. See also Kincaid, "Legislative Origins," 134.

30. Anne Nelson has found that by Jan. 1867 all the northeastern Republican press in her sample, except the *New York Times*, advocated black suffrage in the South. See "The North, the South, and the Republican Ideology," 144. Larry Kincaid has argued that black suffrage in the South no longer divided congressional Republicans after January 1867 because of the "smashing victories of 1866, coupled with the atrocity stories coming out of the South." See "Legislative Origins," 135-37.

31. *Ohio Repository*, Dec. 9, 1866; *Summit County Beacon*, Dec. 20, 1866; *Dayton Daily Journal*, Jan. 16, 1867; *Cincinnati Daily Gazette*, Jan. 8, 1867; *Cincinnati Daily Commercial*, Feb. 27, March 5, 1867; J.J. Janney to John Sherman, Jan. 1, 1867, E.B. Sadler to Sherman, Jan. 20, 1867, JSP.

32. *Cincinnati Daily Commercial*, Nov. 19, 1866. For an example of sentiment in favor of universal adult male black suffrage in the South, see Sherman Blocker to John Sherman, Jan. 15, 1867, JSP. For support for impartial suffrage in the South, see *Summit County Beacon*, Nov. 22, 1867; *Portage County Democrat*, Nov. 28, 1867; R.M. Badeau to John Sherman, Feb. 8, 1867, JSP.

33. *Miami Union*, March 9, 1867; *Cincinnati Daily Gazette*, March 5, 1867; *Springfield Daily News and Republic*, March 5, 1867; *Ironton Register*, Feb. 28, 1867.

34. *Delaware Gazette*, March 8, 1867; John Sherman to William T. Sherman, March 7, 1867, in Thorndike, ed., *Sherman Letters*, 289. See also *Marietta Register*, March 7, 1867; *Ashtabula Sentinel*, Feb. 27, March 6, 1867; *Western Reserve Chronicle*, March 6, 1867; *Cadiz Republican*, March 13, 1867; *Summit County Beacon*, Feb. 28, March 7, 1867; *Bellefontaine Republican*, March 15, 1867; *Cincinnati Daily Commercial*, March 4, 9, 1867.

35. *Cleveland Plain Dealer*, March 4, 1867; (Delaware) *Weekly Herald*, March 6, 1867; *Cadiz Sentinel*, March 13, 1867. See also *Cincinnati Daily Enquirer*, Feb. 20, March 6, 1867; *Circleville Democrat*, March 8, 1867; *Holmes County Farmer*, Feb. 28, 1867.

36. T.E. Brincefield to John Sherman, Nov. 30, 1866, W.B. Gates to Sherman, Jan. 16, 1867, JSP; *Cincinnati Daily Commercial*, Feb. 27, 1867; A.F. Perry to Jacob Cox, Jan. 20, 1867, JDCP.

37. *Summit County Beacon*, Nov. 22, Dec. 27, 1866; *Sandusky Daily Commercial Register*, Jan. 29, 1867; *Miami Union*, Feb. 9. 1867.

38. *Ashtabula Sentinel*, Jan. 9, 1867; *Delaware Gazette*, Feb. 1, 1867.

39. Three Republican editors apparently believed the voters had endorsed enfranchising black males in the South. See *Morgan County Herald*, Oct. 12, 1866; *Geauga Democrat*, Oct. 17, 1866; *Portage County Democrat*, Nov. 28, 1866.

40. *Cincinnati Daily Commercial*, Nov. 15, 1866, Jan. 2, 22, 1867; *Ohio Repository*, Oct. 17, 1866; *Elyria Democrat*, Feb. 13, 1867.

41. The *Portage County Democrat*, Feb. 13, 1867, printed endorsements from Garfield, Dec. 21, 1866, E.C. Parsons, Dec. 26, 1866, and Robert A. Schenck, Jan. 14, 1867. Dennison's response, Dec. 31, 1866, is in *Summit County Beacon*, Feb. 12, 1867.

42. P.B. Cole to John Sherman, Jan. 16, 1867, A.D. Kibbee to Sherman, Jan. 17, 1867, JSP. Cole represented Union County in the Senate; Kibbee represented Trumbull County in the House.

43. *Journal of the House of Representatives of the State of Ohio* 63 (1867): 59, 132-33; Porter, *Ohio Politics*, 236; *Ohio State Journal*, Feb. 27, 1867.

44. *Journal of the House of Representatives*, 270-74; *Ohio State Journal*, Feb. 27, 1867; *Norwalk Reflector*, March 7, 1867. Rhodes's name has also been spelled Rhoades. See Smith, *History of the Republican Party*, 211.

45. *Ashtabula Sentinel*, Feb. 20, 1867. See also W.M. Dickson to Abner Kellogg, Feb. 27, 1867, in *Ohio State Journal*, March 6, 1867; *Dayton Daily Journal*, Feb. 28, 1867.

46. Alanson Davenport to Editor, *Ohio State Journal*, March 11, 1867.

47. John T. Clark to Editor, *Ohio State Journal*, March 20, 1867; Jacob Cox to William Coggeshall, April 8, 1867, JDCP. Murat Halstead was one of the Republican editors who responded angrily to the House action. See *Cincinnati Daily Commercial*, Feb. 27, 1867. The *Ohio State Journal*, March 5, 1867, printed editorials from three other irritated Republican editors.

48. "Speech of the Hon. E.B. Sadler of Erie County, In the Senate of Ohio, March, 21, 1867," *Sandusky Daily Commercial Register*, March 26, 1867.

49. *Ohio State Journal*, March 28, 1867; Porter, *Ohio Politics*, 227.

50. *Ohio State Journal*, April 4, 1867.

51. *Eaton Weekly Register*, April 11, 1867.

52. Ibid.; Porter, *Ohio Politics*, 238; *Ashtabula Sentinel*, April 10, 1867; *Cincinnati Daily Gazette*, April 5, 1867; Jacob Cox to William Coggeshall, April 8, 1867, JDCP.

53. *Ashtabula Sentinel*, April 10, 1867.

54. C.W. Moulton to Members of Ohio General Assembly, March 9, 1867, in *Ohio State Journal*, March 12, 1867, and March 11, April 4, 1867; *Cincinnati Daily Gazette*, April 4, 5, 1867.

55. Porter, *Ohio Politics*, 239, 243; Jacob Cox to William Coggeshall, April 8, 1867, JDCP.

56. *Cincinnati Daily Enquirer*, April 5, 1867; *Ohio Eagle*, April 18, 1867; *Cleveland Plain Dealer*, April 4, 8, 1867; *Weekly Herald*, April 11, 1867; *Crisis*, April 3, 1867.

57. Jacob Cox to Murat Halstead, April 19, 1867, JDCP. The *Cincinnati Daily Commercial* predicted the amendment would fail because of the disfranchisement clause. See April 4, 6, 8, 15, 22, 26, 1867.

58. *Cadiz Republican*, March 20, 1867; *Dayton Daily Journal*, April 5, 1867; *Ironton Register*, April 11, 1867; *Buckeye State*, April 11, 1867.

59. *Sandusky Daily Commercial Register*, April 5, 1867; *Cincinnati Daily Gazette*, March 28, April 4, 1867.

60. *Bellefontaine Republican*, April 12, May 10, Sept. 27, 1867. See also *Clinton Republican*, April 11, 1867.

61. *Cincinnati Daily Gazette*, April 5, 1867; *Summit County Beacon*, April 11, 1867; *Miami Union*, April 20, 1867. On April 15, 1867, the *Cincinnati Daily Gazette* printed portions of editorials from the *Summit County Beacon, Ohio Repository, Belmont Chronicle*, and *Madison County Union* that endorsed the amendment on the principle of justice to all men.

62. *Cincinnati Daily Gazette*, April 4, 1867; *Astabula Sentinel*, April 3, 10, 17, 1867; *Ohio State Journal*, April 8, 1867; *Eaton Weekly Register*, April 18, 1867; Edward D. Mansfield to William Henry Smith, April 4, 1867, Smith Papers.

63. Sharkey, *Money, Class, and Party: An Economic Study of Civil War and Reconstruction*, 82.

64. *Annual Report of the Secretary of the Treasury on the State of the Finances for the Year 1865* (Washington: Government Printing Office, 1865), 5, 14; Sharkey, *Money, Class, and Party*, 66-80; Unger, *The Greenback Era: A Social and Political History of American Finance, 1865-1879*, 43. See also Glenn M. Linden, "Congressmen, 'Radicalism,' and Economic Issues, 1861 to 1873" (Ph.D. diss., University of Washington, 1963), 80-81.

65. Sharkey, *Money, Class, and Party*, 99-101.

66. A. Denny to John Sherman, July 27, 1867, JSP.

67. *Cincinnati Daily Gazette*, Oct. 8, 1867; *Ohio State Journal*, Oct. 2, 1867; *Dayton Daily Journal*, Aug. 28, 30, 1867; *Toledo Blade*, Aug. 10, 1867.

68. *Portsmouth Times*, July 6, 13, 20, 27, Aug. 10, Sept. 21, 28, 1867; *Putnam County Sentinel*, Sept. 26, 1867.

69. *Portsmouth Times*, June 22, July 13, 1867; *Cadiz Sentinel*, June 26, 1867; *Crisis*, April 3, June 5, July 31, Aug. 14, 21, Sept. 4, 1867; *Mt. Vernon Democratic Banner*, July 6, Sept. 7, 21, 28, Oct. 5, 1867.

70. *Mt. Vernon Democratic Banner*, June 8, Sept. 21, 1867; *Crisis*, April 10, 17, July 31, 1867; *Cadiz Sentinel*, Oct. 9, 1867; *Portsmouth Times*, Aug. 17, 1867. The *Cincinnati Daily Enquirer* printed approximately forty-five antiblack and antisuffrage editorials, an average of nearly one every other day, from July 1, 1867, through election day in early October.

71. *Mt. Vernon Democratic Banner*, June 8, 1867; *Crisis*, Sept. 4, 11, 18, 25, Oct. 2, 9, 1867; *Cadiz Sentinel*, June 26, Oct. 9, 1867.

72. Smith, *Republican Party in Ohio* 1:233-34.

73. Porter, *Ohio Politics*, 241-43. Murat Halstead assailed the disfranchisement clause on several occasions, arguing that it endangered the party and would produce no meaningful positive result. See *Cincinnati Daily Commercial*, April 4, 15, 22, 26, 1867.

74. Despite, or perhaps because of, its hedging on major issues, Republican editors uniformly praised the platform. *Dayton Daily Journal*, June 20, 1867; *Bellefontaine Republican*, June 28, 1867; *Cadiz Republican*, June 26, 1867; *Bucyrus Journal*, June 21, 1867; *Ironton Register*, June 27, 1867; *Ashtabula Sentinel*, June 26, 1867; *Ohio State Journal*, June 20, 1867; *Cincinnati Daily Commercial*, June 20, 1867.

75. Jacob Cox to Benjamin R. Cowen, Jan. 25, 1867, John W. Andrews to Cox, Jan. 26, 1867, JDCP. Cox said that he would run if the party demanded his renomination. Cox to Aaron F. Perry, June 3, 1867, ibid.

76. *Dayton Daily Journal*, April 9, 1867; *Circleville Union*, April 19, 1867; *Bellefontaine Republican*, Feb. 15, 1867; *Cincinnati Daily Commercial*, May 31, 1867; Aaron F. Perry to Jacob Cox, Jan. 20, 1867, JDCP.

77. Jos. W. Dwyer to Columbus Delano, March 25, 1867, William Dennison to Delano, March 25, 1867, W.R. Hooker to Delano, April 16, 1867, Columbus Delano Papers, Library of Congress.

78. Hayes seems to have benefited from sentiment that opposed the nomination of anyone who might want Salmon Chase to win the 1868 Republican presidential nomination. See Jacob Cox to Aaron F. Perry, June 3, 1867, JDCP; Bonadio, *North of Reconstruction*, 102-3. Some Republicans, including Hayes, expressed concern over his congressional seat if he resigned to run for governor. The worry proved well founded when Samuel Cary, a coalition candidate, defeated Republican Richard Smith, the editor of the *Cincinnati Daily Gazette*, in the election to replace Hayes. See Hayes to William Henry Smith, Jan. 29, May 23, 1867, in Williams, ed., *Diary and Letters*

3:39-42; *Cincinnati Daily Commercial*, June 20, 1867. On the internal Republican bickering that probably resulted in Cary's victory, see Bonadio, *North of Reconstruction*, 12-14. For discussions of the prenomination politicking, see Ranson, "The Great Unknown: Governor Rutherford B. Hayes of Ohio," 56-68; Peskin, *Garfield*, 247-48, 278-79.

79. *Ashtabula Sentinel*, Sept. 18, 25, Oct. 2, 1867; *Circleville Union*, June 28, Sept. 27, 1867; *Dayton Daily Journal*, July 30, 1867; *Summit County Beacon*, Oct. 10, 1867; *Morgan County Herald*, Oct. 4, 1867; Jacob Cox to Colonel Jonathan Lynch, Aug. 12, 1867, JDCP; Ranson, "The Great Unknown," 79-80.

80. *Springfield Daily Republic*, Oct. 7, 1867.

81. *Cincinnati Daily Gazette*, Oct. 7, 1867; "Equal Rights" to editor of *Xenia Torchlight*, in *Miami Union*, Oct. 5, 1867.

82. *Cincinnati Daily Gazette*, Oct. 4, 7, 1867. "Wool" referred to the texture of the blacks' hair.

83. *Cincinnati Daily Gazette*, Oct. 4, 1867.

84. *Bellefontaine Republican*, Sept. 7, 1867; *Cincinnati Daily Commercial*, May 10, 1867; *Toledo Blade*, Aug. 5, 1867.

85. *Miami Union*, Oct. 5, 1867; *Cincinnati Daily Gazette*, Oct. 4, 1867; Levi Lough to William Lough, Sept. 29, 1867, Lough Papers.

86. *Cincinnati Daily Commercial*, Oct. 3, 1867; *Marietta Register*, Oct. 3, 1867; *Ohio State Journal*, Oct. 5, 1867; Kleinpell, "Comly," 60.

87. *Summit County Beacon*, Aug. 15, 1867; *Dayton Daily Journal*, Aug. 31, 1867; *Ohio State Journal*, Sept. 28, Oct. 4, 1867; *Marietta Register*, Oct. 3, 1867; *Toledo Blade*, Sept. 2, Oct. 5, 1867; *Cincinnati Daily Commercial*, Sept. 29, 1867; *Bellefontaine Republican*, Oct. 4, 1867; "Speech of Rutherford B. Hayes at Hamilton," in *Toledo Blade*, Aug. 16, 1867; Kleinpell, "Comly," 63; Joseph M. Nash to James Comly, Sept. 16, 1867, Comly Papers.

88. *Cincinnati Daily Commercial*, Aug. 21, 1867; *Toledo Blade*, Sept. 2, Oct. 5, 1867; *Dayton Daily Journal*, Sept. 20, 21, 26, 1867; *Buckeye State*, Sept. 12, 1867; *Summit County Beacon*, May 9, 1867; *Bucyrus Journal*, Aug. 16, 1867.

89. *Toledo Blade*, Oct. 5, 1867; *Morgan County Herald*, Oct. 4, 1867; *Cincinnati Daily Commercial*, Aug. 21, 1867; Burke Hinsdale to James Garfield, Sept. 30, 1867, in Hinsdale, ed., *Garfield-Hinsdale Letters*, 108.

90. *Ohio State Journal*, Oct. 7, 1867. Secretary of State William H. Smith, usually a shrewd political analyst, predicted a Republican sweep of the state legislature, the governorship, and the suffrage amendment. See Smith to Whitelaw Reid, October 3, 1867, Smith Papers.

91. Smith, *History of Republican Party* 1:239-40; Porter, *Ohio Politics*, 248.

92. *Annual Report of the Secretary of State of Ohio, 1868*, 107-8; Porter, *Ohio Politics*, 248.

93. *Annual Report, 1867*, 43.

94. Benedict, "The Rout of Radicalism," 342-44. Mantell, *Johnson, Grant, and the Politics of Reconstruction*, 5-70.

95. *Western Reserve Chronicle*, Oct. 16, 23, 1867; *Geauga Democrat*, Oct. 16, 1867; *Dayton Daily Journal*, Oct. 11, 14, 1867; *Bellefontaine Republican*, Oct. 11, 1867; *Ironton Register*, Oct. 10, 17, 1867; John Sherman to Schuyler Colfax, Oct. 20, 1867, Schuyler Colfax Papers, Indiana University Library, quoted in Benedict, *Compromise of Principle*, 273; James Garfield to Jacob Cox, Dec. 16, 1867, JDCP.

96. *Circleville Union*, Oct. 11, 1867; *Bucyrus Journal*, Oct. 11, 1867; *Lancaster Gazette*, Oct. 10, 1867; *Marietta Register*, Oct. 17, 1867; Kleinpell, "Comly," 63.

97. *Ohio State Journal*, Oct. 10, 14, 1867; *Dayton Daily Journal*, Oct. 11, 14, 1867; *Circleville Union*, Oct. 18, 1867; *Cincinnati Daily Gazette*, Oct. 16, 1867; *Elyria Democrat*, Oct. 16, 1867, *Cleveland Leader*, Oct. 9, 1867; *Toledo Blade*, Oct. 10, 1867; *Ironton Register*, Oct. 10, 1867; *Bucyrus Journal*, Oct. 11, 1867; Benjamin Wade to Zachariah Chandler, Oct. 10, 1867, Zachariah Chandler Papers, Library of Congress, quoted in Benedict, *Compromise of Principle*, 273; Ira T. Davis Diary, Oct. 8, 1867, Ira T. Davis Papers, Rutherford B. Hayes Memorial Library; Samuel Shellabarger to Schuyler Colfax, Oct. 17, 1867, Schuyler Colfax Papers, Hayes Library.

98. Grant's political views, see Mantell, *Johnson, Grant, and Reconstruction*, 3, 27-30, 67-70.

99. Burke Hinsdale to James Garfield, Oct. 22, 1867, in Hinsdale, ed., *Garfield-Hinsdale Letters*, 112; Garfield to W.C. Howells, Dec. 16, 1867, in *Ashtabula Sentinel*, Dec. 25, 1867; *Norwalk Reflector*, Oct. 22, 1867; *Toledo Blade*, Oct. 11, 1867; John Sherman to William T. Sherman, Nov. 1, 1867, in Thorndike, ed., *Sherman Letters*, 299; Friedrich Hassaurek to John Sherman, Jan. 27, 1868, JSP. Quite understandably, Radical Republicans attempted to burst the Grant bubble. One urged that Republicans not commit themselves too rapidly to any candidate "you do not know to be unquestionably committed, ingrained and dyed in a fast color to radical Republican principles." *Western Reserve Chronicle*, Oct. 30, 1867. See also *Ashtabula Sentinel*, Nov. 13, 1867; *Cincinnati Daily Gazette*, Oct. 25, 1867.

100. Samuel Shellabarger to Schuyler Colfax, Oct. 17, 1867, Colfax Papers; *Circleville Union*, Oct. 18, 1867; *Ohio State Journal*, Oct. 14, 1867; *Toledo Blade*, Oct. 10, 1867; Sharkey, *Money, Class, and Party*, 94-97; Benedict, *Compromise of Principle*, 273.

101. William Henry Smith to R.D. Mussey, Oct. 21, 1867, William Henry Smith Papers; H.P.B. Jewett to William Henry Smith, Nov. 4, 1867, ibid.; *Miami Union*, Oct. 12, 1867; *Springfield Daily News and Republic*, Oct. 14, 1867; Mantell, *Johnson, Grant, and the Politics of Reconstruction*, 64-65.

6. Success in Sight?

1. One central Ohio Republican expressed the growing sentiment in favor of more emphasis on economic questions, when he asserted that "the real principles of the Republican party are found in the currency, taxes, the tariff, the national Debt, and the Congressional plan of reconstruction." *Bucyrus Journal*, Oct. 25, 1867.

2. *Cleveland Leader*, Nov. 21, 1867; *Ohio State Journal*, Nov. 18, 23, 1867.

3. Garfield had decided to tie his political future to financial questions and gave decreasing attention to Reconstruction. For example, in July 1867 he embarked on a seventeen-week tour of Europe that kept him out of the country throughout the 1867 campaign. Upon his return he remarked that "the men who rise to the demands of the time on money matters will be the men who will make a name for the future." Peskin, *Garfield*, 280-83; Garfield to Hinsdale, Nov. 21, 1867, in Hinsdale, ed., *Garfield-Hinsdale Letters*, 113.

4. Burke Hinsdale to James Garfield, Jan. 20, 1868, in Hinsdale, ed., *Garfield-Hinsdale Letters*, 128; Hassaurek to Sherman, Jan. 27, 1868, JSP; H.A. Lane to the Editor, *Summit County Beacon*, Nov. 14, 1867. See also Simeon Nash to Benjamin Wade, March 10[?], 1868, BFWP.

5. *Morning Journal*, Feb. 8, 10, 1868; *Toledo Blade*, Oct. 11, 1867; *Cadiz Repub-*

lican, Nov. 6, 1867, Jan. 10, 1868; *Summit County Beacon*, Oct. 3, 1867; *Marietta Register*, Oct. 10, 1867.

6. Lyman Hall to James A. Garfield, Dec. 28, 1867, JAGP; Garfield to W.C. Howells, Dec. 16, 1867, in *Ashtabula Sentinel*, Dec. 25, 1867. See also Burke Hinsdale to Garfield, Oct. 22, 1867, in Hinsdale, ed., *Garfield-Hinsdale Letters*, 112. For examples of Republican indifference or hostility to the Grant nomination, see *Cleveland Leader*, Nov. 2, 13, 1867, May 5, 1868; *Miami Union*, Oct. 26, 1867; *Bucyrus Journal*, Oct. 25, 1867.

7. *Toledo Blade*, Aug. 31, 1867; Burke Hinsdale to James Garfield, Aug. 19, 29, 1867, in Hinsdale, ed., *Garfield-Hinsdale Letters*, 97, 99. For other examples of support for impeachment, see *Dayton Daily Journal*, July 20, 1867; *Miami Union*, July 27, Aug. 24, 31, 1867; *Ashtabula Sentinel*, Sept. 4, 1867, W.H.P. Denny to Benjamin Franklin Wade, July 2, 1867, BFWP.

8. T. Ewing, Sr., to My Dear Daughter [Ellen Sherman], Sept. 28, 1867, Ewing Family Papers.

9. Benedict, The *Impeachment and Trial of Andrew Johnson*, 72-76. In this "defiant" message Johnson denounced black suffrage as worse than military rule, again charged that Military Reconstruction was unconstitutional, and most ominously, raised the possibility of using force to defeat the will of Congress.

10. *Cleveland Leader*, Dec. 9, 1867. Smith definitely believed that Johnson could and should be removed for "usurpation and treachery" even in the absence of an unlawful act. *Cincinnati Daily Gazette*, Nov. 28, 1867.

11. *Ohio State Journal*, Nov. 18, 26, 27, 30, Dec. 2, 1867.

12. Burke Hinsdale to James Garfield, Dec. 9, 1867, in Hinsdale, ed., *Garfield-Hinsdale Letters*, 119; *Cleveland Leader*, Nov. 21, 28, 1867; *Ashtabula Sentinel*, Dec. 4, 1867.

13. *Bellefontaine Republican*, Dec. 13, 1867; *Summit County Beacon*, Dec. 12, 1867; James A. Garfield to Jacob Cox, Dec. 16, 1867, JDCP; Garfield to W.C. Howells, Dec. 16, 1867, in *Ashtabula Sentinel*, Dec. 25, 1867.

14. *Cleveland Leader*, Dec. 30, 1867. See also *Athens Messenger*, Feb. 6, 1868.

15. Benedict, *Impeachment*, 89-95; *Miami Union*, Jan. 4, 1868; *Ohio State Journal*, Dec. 31, 1867.

16. Benedict, *Impeachment*, 104-12.

17. *Cleveland Leader*, Feb. 22, 24, 27, March 2, 1868.

18. *Ohio State Journal*, Nov. 30, Dec. 21, 1867.

19. Ibid., Feb. 24, 1868, and see Feb. 25, 28, 29, March 2, 3, 9, 1868.

20. *Toledo Blade*, Feb. 25, 1868; Harry Rhodes to James A. Garfield, Feb. 28, 1868, T.J. McLain to Garfield, March 16, 1868, JAGP; S.A. Fitch to Benjamin F. Wade, Feb. 25, 1868, C.W. Neal, J.B. Rothchild, C.A. Crominger to Wade, March 4, 1868, BFWP.

21. *Cincinnati Daily Commercial*, Feb. 25, 1868. Senator Wade received two letters that contained conflicting reports on Republican attitudes toward impeachment and removal. Simeon Nash of Marietta, who endorsed impeachment, reported that "the noisy men are so [in favor of Johnson's conviction], but there are many others who wish the thing had not been done. These men say little but we cannot afford to loose [*sic*] them in Ohio" (March 10, 1868, BFWP). By contrast, D. Cadwell of Jefferson seems to have been closer to the statewide consensus when he told Wade, "I do not know nor have I heard of a single Republican, who does not most heartily wish to see impeachment successful" (March 7, 1868, ibid.).

22. *Dayton Daily Journal*, Feb. 24, 1868; *Belmont Chronicle*, Feb. 28, 1868; *Circleville Union*, Feb. 28, 1868; *Marietta Register*, Feb. 27, 1868; *Ohio Repository*,

Feb. 26, 1868; *Springfield Daily News and Republic*, Feb. 25, 1868; James A. Garfield to Burke Hinsdale, March 8, 1868, in Hinsdale, ed., *Garfield-Hinsdale Letters*, 132.

23. *Ohio Repository*, Feb. 26, March 4, May 13, 1868; *Athens Messenger*, Feb. 6, March 5, 19, 1868; *Ohio State Journal*, March 3, 1868; E. Jones to Benjamin F. Wade, March 9, 1868, BFWP; W.C. Howells to James A. Garfield, March 10, 1868, J.O. Converse to Garfield, March 19, 1868, JAGP; Bridges, "John Sherman and the Impeachment of Andrew Johnson," 180, 188.

24. *Toledo Blade*, April 29, 1868. See also *Ohio Repository*, Feb. 26, 1868.

25. Trefousse, *Wade*, 275, 284-87; *Cincinnati Daily Commercial*, Sept. 4, 1867.

26. *Bellefontaine Republican*, April 17, 1868; Geo. G. Washburn to Benjamin F. Wade, April 15, 1868, A. Denny to Wade, March 25, 1868, BFWP; F.E. Hutchins to James A. Garfield, May 16, 1868, JAGP.

27. Roswell Marsh to Benjamin F. Wade, May 13, 1868, W.R. Allison to Wade, May 13, 1868, N.A. Gray to Wade, March15, 1868, BFWP.

28. Both Hans Trefousse and Michael Les Benedict discuss the Wade issue, and both suggest it had some, but not a clear, influence on the Senate vote. See Trefousse, *Impeachment of a President*, 148-49; Benedict, *Impeachment*, 133-36.

29. James A. Garfield to Burke Hinsdale, May 3, 1868, in Hinsdale, ed., *Garfield-Hinsdale Letters*, 135; *Cleveland Leader*, April 24, May 2, 1868; *Ohio State Journal*, Feb. 26, 1868.

30. Burke Hinsdale to James A. Garfield, May 16, 1868, in Hinsdale, ed., *Garfield-Hinsdale Letters*, 137-39.

31. *Ohio State Journal*, Feb. 24, 1868; *Toledo Blade*, Feb. 25, 1868; O. Follett to Benjamin F. Wade, March 9, 1868, BFWP; John W. Andrews to Thomas Ewing, Sr., Feb. 25, 1868, Ewing Family Papers; James Garfield to Harmon Austin, Feb. 29, 1868, in Smith, *The Life and Letters of James Abram Garfield* 1:424.

32. Irad Kelley to Thomas Ewing, Sr., March 27, 1868, Ewing Family Papers.

33. Thomas Ewing, Sr., to My Dear Daughter [Ellen Sherman], Feb. 24, 1868, ibid. See also J.W. Andrews to Ewing, Feb. 25, 1868, ibid. On March 24, several weeks before the Senate vote, Ewing revealed his astuteness as a political observer when, after attacking the impeachment trial as a "ridiculous farce," he predicted, "There are however some seven or eight Senators of the majority who I think will hold their judicial oaths paramount to party obligations, and by their votes save what is left of the constitution." Ewing to Ellen Sherman, March 24, 1868, ibid.

34. *Portsmouth Times*, March 28, 1868; (Ashland) *States and Union*, May 13, 1868; *Crisis*, Feb. 26, 1868; *Cincinnati Daily Enquirer*, Feb. 24, 1868. Johnson received letters from William McDaniel, March 10, 1868, John Shoub, Feb. 22, 1868, and R. Stanbery, Feb. 15, 1868, all in AJP.

35. *Dayton Daily Journal*, May 18, 1868; *Cadiz Republican*, May 22, 1868; *Springfield Daily News and Republic*, May 16, 1868; *Ironton Register*, May 21, 1868; *Bellefontaine Republican*, May 22, 1868; *Elyria Democrat*, May 20, 1868; *Zanesville Daily Courier*, May 16, 1868; *Summit County Beacon*, May 21, 1868; *Ohio State Journal*, May 18, 19, 1868; *Cincinnati Daily Gazette*, May 18, 1868; *Cleveland Leader*, May 15, 18, 19, 1868; *Toledo Blade*, May 18, 1868; *Ohio Repository*, May 20, 27, 1868.

36. James Garfield to J.H. Rhodes, May 20, 1868, in Smith, *Life and Letters* 1:426. See also *Marietta Register*, May 21, 1868; *Ohio Repository*, May 27, 1868; *Steubenville Daily Herald*, May 19, 27, 1868.

37. *Cincinnati Daily Commercial*, July 26, 1867, May 16, 1868; Trefousse, *Benjamin Franklin Wade*, 305; Joseph Bruff to James A. Garfield, June 12, 1868, Will Hudson to Garfield, May 23, 1868, JAGP. After many years of reflection and observation

of subsequent events, Senator John Sherman ultimately regretted his vote to remove Johnson and expressed himself "completely satisfied" with the result. John Sherman, *Recollections of Forty Years*, 432.

38. *Springfield Daily News and Republic*, May 16, 1868.

39. Smith, *History of the Republican Party* 1:244; *Ohio State Journal*, Jan. 28, 1868; *Athens Messenger*, Jan. 30, 1868.

40. Smith, *History of Republican Party* 1:253.

41. For examples of the reaction in the Northeast to the Republican platform, see Nelson, "The North, the South," 206.

42. *Eaton Weekly Register*, March 12, 1868. See also *Ironton Register*, March 12, 1868; *Cadiz Republican*, March 13, 1868; *Athens Messenger*, March 12, 1868; *Ohio State Journal*, March 5, 1868; *Cincinnati Daily Commercial*, March 5, 1868.

43. *Ohio Repository*, May 27, 1868; *Cleveland Leader*, May 12, 22, 1868; *Steubenville Daily Herald*, May 25, 1868; *Toledo Blade*, May 25, 1868; *Xenia Torchlight*, May 27, 1868; *Zanesville Daily Courier*, May 23, 1868; *Portage County Democrat*, May 27, 1868; *Gallipolis Journal*, May 28, 1868; J.H. Rhodes to James A. Garfield, May 22, 1868, JAGP; Jacob Cox to J. Stiles, Sept. 8, 1868, JDCP.

44. Perman, *Reunion without Compromise*, 341. For examples of attacks on what Democrats considered the blatant political motives behind restoration of southern states, see *Cincinnati Daily Enquirer*, June 12, 26, 1868.

45. *Marion Independent*, June 25, July 2, 1868; *Cleveland Leader*, June 24, July 1, 1868.

46. Simeon Nash to Benjamin Wade, March 10[?], 1868, BFWP. For other examples that Republicans considered Reconstruction nearly over, see *Cleveland Leader*, April 28, 1868; *Toledo Blade*, May 19, 1868; *Delaware Gazette*, July 3, 1868. Moderate and conservative Republicans in the Northeast reacted very much like their counterparts in Ohio to the return of the southern states. See Nelson, "The North, the South", 216-17.

47. Smith, *History of the Republican Party* 1:242-43; Coleman, *The Election of 1868: The Democratic Effort to Regain Control*, 60-61; *Cleveland Plain Dealer*, Jan. 9, 1868; *Cincinnati Daily Enquirer*, Jan. 9, 1868; *Crisis*, Jan. 8, 15, 1868; *Ohio Statesman*, Jan. 9, 1868.

48. *Cincinnati Daily Enquirer*, April 25, 1868, and every issue in June 1868; *Ohio Statesman*, July 10, 1868.

49. Mantell, *Johnson, Grant, and the Politics of Reconstruction*, 122-23; Coleman, *Election of 1868*, 200-203.

50. *Ohio Statesman*, Oct. 12, 1868; *Crisis*, Feb. 19. 1868; *States and Union*, July 29, Sept. 30, 1868, *Cincinnati Daily Enquirer*, Aug. 21, Sept. 18, 26, Oct. 10, 12, 16, 1868; *Democratic Press*, Sept. 3, 10, 1868; *Zanesville Weekly Signal*, Sept. 24, 1868; *Portsmouth Times*, Aug. 1, 1868; *Cadiz Sentinel*, Oct. 7, 1868; *Marietta Times*, Oct. 8, 1868.

51. *Cincinnati Daily Enquirer*, July 11, Aug. 25, Sept. 2, 3, 10, 12, 16, 19, 22, 25, 28, 30, Oct. 3, 5, 7, 12, 24, 28, 29, 30, 1868; *Weekly Herald*, Sept. 24, Oct. 1, 1868; *Cadiz Sentinel*, Sept. 30, 1868; Coleman, *Election of 1868*, 287-88; Mantell, *Johnson, Grant*, 136-37. For a discussion of how and why the Democrats' monetary views differed from established Jacksonian doctrine, see Sharkey, *Money, Class, and Party*, 104-7.

52. Smith, *History of the Republican Party* 1:248- 49; Sharkey, *Money, Class, and Party*, 107-15.

53. James Garfield to Burke A. Hinsdale, March 8, 1868, in Hinsdale, ed., *Garfield-Hinsdale Letters*, 132-33; Peskin, *Garfield*, 282-83.

54. *Portage County Democrat*, July 1, 1868. See also *Gallipolis Journal*, March 12, 1868; *Ironton Register*, March 12, 1868; *Cincinnati Daily Commercial*, March 5, 1868.

55. Smith, *History of the Republican Party*, 1:253-54; *Gallipolis Journal*, May 28, 1868.

56. Republican conventions inn Huron, Trumbull, Muskingum, and Morgan counties and the seventh, ninth, tenth, and twelfth congressional districts specifically approved the national platform. See, respectively, *Norwalk Reflector*, Aug. 4, 1868; *Western Reserve Chronicle*, Aug. 12, 1868; *Zanesville Daily Courier*, June 22, 1868; *Morgan County Herald*, June 9, 1868; *Springfield Daily News and Republic*, July 16, 1868; *Norwalk Reflector*, Aug. 4, 1868; *Toledo Blade*, Aug. 20, 1868; *Circleville Union*, July 10, 1868. Republican conventions in the sixth, eighth, ninth, fifteenth, and sixteenth congressional districts and Montgomery and Crawford counties endorsed both the state and national platforms. See respectively *Clinton Repository*, June 11, 1868; *Delaware Gazette*, Aug. 7, 1868; *Bucyrus Journal*, July 31, 1868; *Marietta Register*, July 23, 1868; *Cadiz Republican*, July 10, 1868; *Dayton Daily Journal*, Aug. 3, 1868; *Bucyrus Journal*, July 31, 1868.

57. Peskin, *Garfield*, 289-91; *Ohio State Journal*, Jan. 7, 15, 16, 1868; *Western Reserve Chronicle*, Jan. 22, 1868. The Democrats of course argued that in attempting to rescind they were only following the desires the voters had expressed in October 1867. See *Cleveland Plain Dealer*, Jan. 16, 1868.

58. Sharkey, *Money, Class, and Party*, 103-4.

59. Ibid., 107-15; *Ohio Repository*, Jan. 22, 1868.

60. *Cleveland Leader*, July 22, Aug. 1, 14, 15, Sept. 4, 1868; *Ashland Times*, Aug. 27, Sept. 3, 10, 17, Oct. 1, 8, 1868; *Ohio State Journal*, Jan. 25, Feb. 21, 1868; *Marion Independent*, July 9, 1868.

61. *Ohio Repository*, July 22, Sept. 30, Oct. 7, 1868; *Ohio State Journal*, July 22, 1868; *Cleveland Leader*, Aug. 6, 1868; *Ironton Register*, Oct. 29, 1868; *Toledo Blade*, July 29, 1868; *Western Reserve Chronicle*, Sept. 9, Oct. 7, 1868; *Marion Independent*, June 4, Oct. 22, 1868; *Ashland Times*, July 23, Oct. 22, 1868.

62. U.S. Grant to General Joseph R. Hawley, President of National Union Republican Convention, May 29, 1868, in *Portage County Democrat*, June 10, 1868.

63. B.R. Cowen, Chairman, Union Republican State Party, to the Union Republican Voters of Ohio, March 4, 1868, BFWP.

64. *Western Reserve Chronicle*, Sept. 9, 1868; *Xenia Torchlight*, Sept. 9, 1868; *Ironton Register*, Sept. 24, 1868; *Delaware Gazette*, Oct. 9, 1868. See also *Dayton Daily Journal*, July 13, 18, 1868; *Cleveland Leader*, Oct. 8, 1868; *Portage County Democrat*, Oct. 7, 1868. Such reliance on the bloody shirt was hardly confined to Ohio. See Nelson, "The North, the South," 211-15.

65. *Cleveland Leader*, July 13, 1868; *Ohio Repository*, July 29, 1868; Silbey, *A Respectable Minority*, 229; Coleman, *Election of 1868*, 265. For more responses in Ohio, see M. Halstead to Thomas Ewing, Sr., Sept. 15, 1868; Ewing Family Papers; *Elyria Democrat*, Sept. 23, 1868; *Cincinnati Daily Commercial*, Oct. 10, 1868; *Xenia Torchlight*, Sept. 9, 1868; *Portage County Democrat*, July 29, 1868; *Cadiz Republican*, July 17, 1868; *Dayton Daily Journal* July 23, 28, Aug. 5, 6, Oct. 13, 1868.

66. *Cleveland Leader*, July 10, 21, 25, 1868; *Ashland Times*, Oct. 22, 1868.

67. *Gallipolis Journal*, Oct. 15, Nov. 12, 1868; *Highland Weekly News*, Oct. 15, Nov. 5, 1868; *Portage County Democrat*, Oct. 14, Nov. 4, 1868; *Cincinnati Daily Commercial*, Nov. 4, 1868; *Delaware Gazette*, Nov. 6, 1868; *Cleveland Leader*, Nov. 3, 1868; *Western Reserve Chronicle*, Oct. 21, Nov. 4, 1868; *Cadiz Republican*, Oct. 16,

1868; *Ashland Times*, Nov. 5, 1868. Michael Les Benedict and Marvin Mantell also concluded that with Grant's election Republicans considered the Reconstruction crisis ended. Benedict, *Compromise of Principle*, 324; Mantell, *Johnson, Grant*, 148- 49. See also Kleinpell, "Comly," 93.

Epilogue

1. Porter, *Ohio Politics*, 253-54; Smith, *History of Republican Party* 1:239.

2. *Western Reserve Chronicle*, Sept. 8, 1869; *Elyria Democrat*, Sept. 8, 1869; *Dayton Daily Journal*, Sept. 29, 1869; *Norwalk Reflector*, Aug. 3, 1869; *Ironton Register*, June 27, 1869. For examples of Republican papers that denied that suffrage was an issue or just refused to discuss it, see *Clinton Republican*, Sept. 23, 30, Oct. 7, 1869; *Circleville Union*, Oct. 1, 1869; *Bellefontaine Republican*, July 23, 1869.

3. *Xenia Torchlight*, Oct. 6, 1869; *Bellefontaine Republican*, July 2, 1869; *Eaton Weekly Register*, Sept. 23, 30, Oct. 7, 1869; *Belmont Chronicle*, Sept. 16, 23, 30, Oct. 7, 1869; *Hocking County Sentinel*, Oct. 7, 1869.

4. *Portsmouth Times*, July 31, Aug. 28, 1869; *Crawford County Forum*, Sept. 3, Oct. 1, 1869; (Ravenna) *Democratic Press*, Sept. 9, 30, Oct. 7, 1869; *Cadiz Sentinel*, Oct. 6, 1869; *Union Register*, Aug. 8, Sept. 3, 1869.

5. Despite his own lukewarm efforts on behalf of the amendment during the campaign, William Bickham of the *Dayton Daily Journal* trumpeted, "The voters of Ohio have fairly and squarely endorsed the XVth Amendment by a popular majority of 10, 050 votes. The issue was boldly made in the Ohio Republican platform" (Oct. 15, 1869). For similar conclusions about the significance of the results, see *Bellefontaine Republican*, Oct. 22, 1869; *Cadiz Republican*, Oct. 22, 1869; *Belmont Chronicle*, Oct. 14, 1869; *Elyria Democrat*, Oct. 20, 1869; *Eaton Weekly Register*, Oct. 21, 1869. In their election analyses at least two Republican editors saw no reason to suggest that the voters had endorsed the amendment. See *Ashland Times*, Oct. 21, 28, 1869; *Clinton Republican*, Oct. 21, 1869.

6. Gillette, *The Right to Vote: Politics and the Passage of the Fifteenth Amendment*, 140-45; Porter, *Ohio Politics*, 254.

7. Porter, *Ohio Politics*, 254.

8. Gillette, *Right to Vote*, 42-45, 164-65.

9. Cox and Cox, "Negro Suffrage and Republican Politics: The Problem of Motivation in Reconstruction Historiography," 303-30; Glenn M. Linden, "A Note on Negro Suffrage and Republican Politics," *Journal of Southern History* 36 (Aug. 1970): 411-20; Benedict, *Compromise of Principle*, 325-36; Foner, *Reconstruction*, 444-49.

10. Foner, *Reconstruction*, 449.

11. *Dayton Daily Journal*, Sept. 29, 1869; *Ironton Register*, Oct. 21, 1869; *Eaton Weekly Register*, Oct, 7, 1869; Bonadio, *North of Reconstruction*, 105; Jacob Cox to A.J. Ricks, Oct. 11, 1869, JDCP.

SELECTED BIBLIOGRAPHY

Manuscript Collections

Allen, William. Papers. Ohio Historical Society.
Anderson, Charles. Papers. Ohio Historical Society.
Bateman, Warner. Papers. Western Reserve Historical Society, Cleveland, Ohio.
Beatty, John. Papers. Ohio Historical Society.
Bickham, William D. Papers. Dayton Public Library, Dayton, Ohio.
Bingham, John A. Papers. Ohio Historical Society.
Birchard, Sardis. Papers. Rutherford B. Hayes Presidential Center Library, Fremont, Ohio.
Boys, Alexander. Papers. Ohio Historical Society.
Brasee, John T. Papers. Ohio Historical Society.
Bunts, William C. Papers. Rutherford B. Hayes Presidential Center Library.
Burchard, Matthew. Papers. Rutherford B. Hayes Presidential Center Library.
Burgoon, Isadore H. Papers. Rutherford B. Hayes Presidential Center Library.
Campbell, Lewis. Papers. Ohio Historical Society.
Chase, Salmon P. Papers. Cincinnati Historical Society.
Coggeshall, William T. Papers. Ohio Historical Society.
Colfax, Schuyler. Papers. Rutherford B. Hayes Presidential Center Library.
Comly, James. Papers. Ohio Historical Society.
Cox, Jacob Dolson. Papers. Oberlin College Library.
Curry, William. Papers. Ohio Historical Society.
Curtis, Henry. Papers. Ohio Historical Society.
Davis, Ira T. Papers. Rutherford B. Hayes Presidential Center Library.
Delano, Columbus. Papers. Library of Congress.
Doolittle, James R. Papers. State Historical Society of Wisconsin.
Ewing, Thomas. Papers. Ohio Historical Society.
Ewing, Thomas, Family. Papers. Library of Congress.
Fairchild, D.H. Papers. Oberlin College Library.
Finney, Charles H. Papers. Oberlin College Library.
Fitch, Edward H. Papers. Ohio Historical Society.
Galloway, Samuel. Papers. Ohio Historical Society.

Garfield, James A. Papers. Library of Congress.
Gibbs, A.C. Papers. Oregon Historical Society.
Gibson, William. Papers. Rutherford B. Hayes Presidential Center Library.
Giddings, Joshua. Papers. Ohio Historical Society.
Greene, William. Papers. Cincinnati Historical Society.
Halstead, Murat. Papers. Cincinnati Historical Society.
Hassaurek, Friedrich. Papers. Ohio Historical Society.
Hayes, Rutherford B. Papers. Rutherford B. Hayes Presidential Center Library.
Hickenlooper, Andrew. Papers. Cincinnati Historical Society.
Janney, J.J. Papers. Ohio Historical Society.
Johnson, Andrew. Papers. Library of Congress.
Klippart, John H. Papers. Ohio Historical Society.
Lanman, Charles. Papers. Rutherford B. Hayes Presidential Center Library.
Locke, Robinson. Papers. Rutherford B. Hayes Presidential Center Library.
Long, Alexander. Papers. Cincinnati Historical Society.
Lough, William. Papers. Cincinnati Historical Society.
Lowe, Thomas. Papers. Dayton Public Library.
Monroe, James. Papers. Oberlin College Library.
Pendleton, George H. Papers. Rutherford B. Hayes Presidential Center Library.
Russell, John. Papers. Ohio Historical Society.
Schenck, Robert. Papers. Miami University Library, Oxford, Ohio.
Scott, Robert K. Papers. Ohio Historical Society.
Sherman, John. Papers. Library of Congress.
Sherman, William T. Papers. Ohio Historical Society.
Siebert, William H. Papers. Ohio Historical Society.
Smith, William Henry. Papers. Ohio Historical Society.
Strohm, Isaac. Papers. Ohio Historical Society.
Summers, Benjamin. Papers. Western Reserve Historical Society.
Thurman, Allen G. Papers. Ohio Historical Society.
Trimble, John A. Papers. Ohio Historical Society.
Vallandigham, Clement L. Papers. Western Reserve Historical Society.
Wade, Benjamin F. Papers. Library of Congress.
Wilson, James W. Papers. Rutherford B. Hayes Presidential Center Library.

Published Primary Sources

American Annual Cyclopaedia and Register of Important Events for the Year 1865. New York: D. Appleton, 1866.
American Annual Cyclopaedia and Register of Important Events for the Year 1866. New York: D. Appleton, 1867.
Annual Report of the Secretary of State of Ohio, including the Statistical Report to the General Assembly for the Year 1864. Columbus: Columbus Printing, 1865.
Annual Report of the Secretary of State of Ohio, including the Statistical

Report to the General Assembly for the Year 1866. Columbus: Columbus Printing, 1867.

Annual Report of the Secretary of State of Ohio, including the Statistical Report to the General Assembly for the Year 1868. Columbus: Columbus Printing, 1869.

Brown, Harry James, and Frederick D. Williams, eds. *The Diary of James A. Garfield*. Vol. 1. East Lansing, Mich.: Michigan State Univ. Press, 1967.

Cincinnati Commercial, ed. *Speeches of the Campaign of 1866, in the States of Ohio, Indiana, and Kentucky*. Cincinnati: *Cincinnati Commercial*, 1866.

Cutler, William P. *The Duty of Citizens in the Work of Reconstruction*. Marietta, Ohio: n.p. 1865.

Dickson, William M. *The Absolute Equality of All Men before the Law, the Only True Basis of Reconstruction: An Address by William M. Dickson Delivered at Oberlin, Ohio, October 3, 1865*. Cincinnati: n.p. 1865.

Hinsdale, Burke A., ed. *The Works of James Abram Garfield*. Boston: James R. Osgood, 1882.

Hinsdale, Mary L., ed. *Garfield-Hinsdale Letters: Correspondence Between James Abram Garfield and Burke Aaron Hinsdale*. Ann Arbor: Univ. of Michigan Press, 1949.

Julian, George W. *Political Recollections, 1840-1872*. Chicago: Jansen, McClurg, 1884.

Kennedy, Joseph C.G., comp. *Agriculture of the United States in 1860; Compiled from the Original Returns of the Eighth Census under the Direction of the Secretary of the Interior*. Washington: GPO, 1864.

Manufactures of the United States in 1860; Compiled from the Original Returns of the Eighth Census under the Direction of the Secretary of the Interior. Washington: GPO, 1865.

Richardson, James D., comp. *A Compilation of the Messages and Papers of the Presidents, 1789-1902*. Vol. 8. Washington: Bureau of National Literature and Art, 1897.

Sherman, John. *Recollections of Forty Years in the House, Senate, and Cabinet*. 2 vols. Chicago: Werner, 1985.

Thorndike, Rachel Sherman, ed. *The Sherman Letters: Correspondence between General and Senator Sherman, 1837-1891*. New York: Scribner's, 1894.

The War of the Rebellion: A Compilation of the Official Records of the Union and Confederate Armies. Washington: GPO, 1895.

Williams, Charles R., ed. *Diary and Letters of Rutherford B. Hayes*. 5 vols. Columbus: Ohio State Archaeological and Historical Society, 1924.

Secondary Sources

Ahern, Wilbert, H. "The Cox Plan of Reconstruction: A Case Study in Ideology and Race Relations." *Civil War History* 16 (1970): 293-308.

———. "Laissez Faire vs. Equal Rights: Liberal Republicans and Limits to Reconstruction." *Phylon* 40 (1979): 52-65.

Appleby, Joyce. "Reconciliation and the Northern Novelist, 1865-1880." *Civil War History* 10 (1964): 117-29.

Baer, Elizabeth. "Groesbeck of Ohio: Lawyer of the Nineteenth Century." M.A. thesis, Miami Univ., 1958.

Baum, Dale. *The Civil War Party System: The Case of Massachusetts, 1848-1876*. Chapel Hill: Univ. of North Carolina Press, 1984.

Beale, Howard K. *The Critical Year, 1866: A Study of Andrew Johnson and Reconstruction*. New York: Harcourt Brace, 1930.

Belz, Herman. *A New Birth of Freedom: The Republican Party and Freedmen's Rights, 1861-1866*. Westport, Conn.: Greenwood Press, 1976.

———. "Origins of Negro Suffrage during the Civil War." *Southern Studies* 17 (1978): 115-30.

Benedict, Michael Les. *A Compromise of Principle: Congressional Republicans and Reconstruction, 1863-1869*. New York: W.W. Norton, 1974.

———. "Equality and Expediency in the Reconstruction Era: A Review Essay." *Civil War History* 23 (1977): 322-35.

———. *The Impeachment and Trial of Andrew Johnson*. New York: W.W. Norton, 1973.

———. "A New Look at the Impeachment of Andrew Johnson." *Political Science Quarterly* 88 (1973): 349-67.

———. "The Rout of Radicalism: Republicans and the Elections of 1867." *Civil War History* 18 (1972): 334-44.

Berwanger, Eugene H. "Reconstruction on the Frontier: The Equal Rights Struggle in Colorado, 1865-1867." *Pacific History Review* 44 (1975): 313-30.

Biographical Directory of the United States Congress, 1774-1989. Bicentennial Edition. Washington, D.C., 1989.

Blackburn, George M. "Radical Republican Motivation: A Case Study." *Journal of Negro History* 54 (1969): 109-26.

Bonadio, Felice A. *North of Reconstruction: Ohio Politics, 1865-1870*. New York: New York Univ. Press, 1970.

Bowen, David Warren, *Andrew Johnson and the Negro*. Knoxville: Univ. of Tennessee Press, 1989.

Bridges, Roger D. "Equality Deferred: Civil Rights for Illinois Blacks, 1865-1885." *Journal of the Illinois State Historical Society* 74 (1981): 83-108.

———. "John Sherman and the Impeachment of Andrew Johnson." *Ohio History* 82 (1973): 176-91.

Brock, W.R. *An American Crisis: Congress and Reconstruction, 1865-1867*. New York: Harper and Row, 1966.

———. "Reconstruction and the American Party System." In George M. Fredrickson, ed., *A Nation Divided: Problems and Issues of the Civil War and Reconstruction*. Minneapolis: Univ. of Minnesota Press, 81-112.

Brodie, Fawn. *Thaddeus Stevens, Scourge of the South*. New York: W.W. Norton, 1959.

Brown, Harry James. "Garfield's Congress." *Hayes Historical Journal* 3 (1981): 57-77.

Brown, Ira V. "Pennsylvania and the Rights of the Negro, 1865-1887." *Pennsylvania History* 28 (1961): 45-57.

Brownlow, Paul C. "The Northern Protestant Pulpit and Andrew Johnson." *Southern Speech Communication Journal* 39 (1974): 248-59.

———. "The Pulpit and Black America, 1865-1877." *Quarterly Journal of Speech* 58 (1972): 431-40.

Cashdollar, Charles D. "Andrew Johnson and the Philadelphia Election of 1866." *Pennsylvania Magazine of History and Biography* 92 (1968): 365-83.

Clark, John G. "Radicals and Moderates on the Joint Committee on Reconstruction." *Mid-America* 45 (1963): 79-98.

Cochrane, William Ghormley, "Freedom without Equality: A Study of Northern Opinion and the Negro Issue, 1861-1870." Ph.D. diss., Univ. of Minnesota, 1957.

Coleman, Charles H. *The Election of 1868: The Democratic Effort to Regain Control*. New York: Columbia Univ. Press, 1933.

Cottom, Robert I. "To Be among the First: The Early Career of James A. Garfield, 1831-1868." Ph.D. diss., Johns Hopkins Univ., 1975.

Cox, LaWanda, and John Cox. "Negro Suffrage and Republican Politics: The Problem of Motivation in Reconstruction Historiography." *Journal of Southern History* 33 (1967): 303-30.

———. *Politics, Principle, and Prejudice, 1865-1866; Dilemma of Reconstruction America*. New York: Free Press of Glencoe, 1963.

Cummings, Charles M. "The Scott Papers: An Inside View of Reconstruction." *Ohio History* 79 (1970): 112-18.

Current, Richard N. "The Politics of Reconstruction in Wisconsin, 1865-1873." *Wisconsin Magazine of History* 60 (1976/1977): 83-106.

Degler, Carl N. *Out of Our Past: The Forces That Shaped Modern America*. New York: Harper and Row, 1959.

Destler, Chester McArthur. "The Origin and Character of the Pendleton Plan." *Mississippi Valley Historical Review* 24 (1937): 171-84.

Dilla, Harriette M. *The Politics of Michigan, 1865-1878*. Columbia Univ. Studies in History, Economics, and Public Law, 118. New York: Columbia Univ., 1912; rpt. New York: Columbia Univ. Press, 1970.

Donald, David. *The Politics of Reconstruction, 1863-1867*. Baton Rouge: Louisiana State Univ. Press, 1965.

Downes, Randolph C. "The Vulgar Newspaper World of Cross-roads Ohio, 1865-1884." *Northwest Ohio Quarterly* 37 (1965): 61-73.

Edwards, John Carver. "Radical Reconstruction and the New Orleans Riot of 1866." *International Review of History and Political Science* 11 (Aug. 1973): 48-64.

Farley, Ena L. "Methodists and Baptists on the Issue of Black Equality in New York, 1865 to 1868." *Journal of Negro History* 61 (1976): 374-92.

Field, Phyllis F. *The Politics of Race in New York: The Struggle for Black Suffrage in the Civil War Era*. Ithaca: Cornell Univ. Press, 1982.

Filler, Louis, ed. "Waiting for the War's End: The Letter of an Ohio Soldier in

Alabama after Learning of Lincoln's Death." *Ohio History* 74 (1965): 55-62.

Fishel, Leslie H., Jr. "Repercussions of Reconstruction: The Northern Negro, 1870-1883." *Civil War History* 14 (1968): 325-45.

Foner, Eric. *Free Soil, Free Labor, Free Men: The Ideology of the Republican Party before the Civil War*. New York: Oxford Univ. Press, 1970.

———. *Reconstruction: America's Unfinished Revolution, 1863-1877*. New York: Harper and Row, 1988.

———. "Reconstruction Revisited." *Reviews in American History* 10 (1982): 82-100.

Franklin, John Hope. *Reconstruction after the Civil War*. Chicago: Univ. of Chicago Press, 1961.

Gambill, Edward L. *Conservative Ordeal: Northern Democrats and Reconstruction, 1865-1868*. Ames, Iowa: Iowa State Univ. Press, 1981.

Gara, Larry. "Slavery and the Slave Power: A Crucial Distinction." In Robert P. Swierenga, ed., *Beyond the Civil War Synthesis: Political Essays of the Civil War Era*. Westport, Conn.: Greenwood Press, 1975.

Gerber, David A. *Black Ohio and the Color Line, 1860-1915*. Urbana: Univ. of Illinois Press, 1976.

Gillette, William. *The Right to Vote: Politics and the Passage of the Fifteenth Amendment*. Baltimore: Johns Hopkins Univ. Press, 1965.

Harrison, John M. *The Man Who Made Nasby, David Ross Locke*. Chapel Hill: Univ. of North Carolina Press, 1969.

Heidish, Louise Oridge Schwallie. "Alexander Long—Ultra Conservative Democrat." M.A. thesis, Miami Univ., 1962.

Holt, Michael F. *The Political Crisis of the 1850s*. New York: John Wiley and Sons, 1978.

Horowitz, Robert F. *The Great Impeacher: A Political Biography of James M. Ashley*. New York: Brooklyn College Press, 1979.

Hyman, Harold M. *The Era of the Oath: Northern Loyalty Tests during the Civil War and Reconstruction*. Philadelphia: Univ. of Pennsylvania Press, 1954.

Jackson, Willie Sherman. "Ohio and Amendment Thirteen: A State Biography of the First National Reform Amendment, 1861-1865." Ph.D. diss., Ohio State Univ., 1969.

James, Joseph B. *The Framing of the Fourteenth Amendment*. Urbana, Ill.: Univ. of Illinois Press, 1956.

———. "Southern Reaction to the Proposal of the Fourteenth Amendment." *Journal of Southern History* 22 (1956): 477-97.

Joering, Margaret. "Jacob Dolson Cox, His Political Career, 1865-1872." M.A. thesis, Univ. of Cincinnati, 1962.

Joyner, Fred B. "Robert Cumming Schenck, First Citizen and Statesman of the Miami Valley." *Ohio State Archaeological and Historical Quarterly* 58 (1949): 286-97.

Kahn, Maxine Baker. "Congressman Ashley in the Post-Civil War Years." *Northwest Ohio Quarterly* 36 (1964): 116-33.

Kilar, Jeremy W. "Andrew Johnson 'Swings' through Michigan: Community Response to a Presidential Crusade." *Old Northwest* 3 (1977): 251-73.

———. "'The Blood-Rugged Issue Is Impeachment or Anarchy': Michigan and the Impeachment and Trial of Andrew Johnson." *Old Northwest* 6 (1980): 245-69.

Kincaid, Larry George. "The Legislative Origins of the Military Reconstruction Act, 1865-1867." Ph.D. diss., Johns Hopkins Univ., 1968.

Kleinpell, Eugene H. "James M. Comly, Journalist-Politician." Ph.D. diss., Ohio State University, 1936.

Levstik, Frank R. "A View from Within: Reuben D. Massey on Andrew Johnson and Reconstruction." *Historical New Hampshire* 27 (1972): 167-71.

Linden, Glenn M. "Congressmen, 'Radicalism,' and Economic Issues, 1861 to 1873." Ph.D. diss., Univ. of Washington, 1963.

———. "A Note on Negro Suffrage and Republican Politics." *Journal of Southern History* 36 (1970): 411-20.

Loewenberg, Ted. "The *Blade* and the Black Man, 1867." *Northwest Ohio Quarterly* 44 (1972): 40-50.

McGrane, Reginald. *William Allen: A Study in Western Democracy*. Columbus: Ohio State Archaeological and Historical Society, 1925.

McKitrick, Eric L. *Andrew Johnson and Reconstruction*. Chicago: Univ. of Chicago Press, 1960.

———. "Reconstruction: Ultraconservative Revolution." In C. Vann Woodward, ed. *The Comparative Approach to American History*. New York: Basic Books, 1968: 146-59.

McLaughlin, Tom L. "Grass-Roots Attitudes toward Black Rights in Twelve Nonslaveholding States, 1846-1869." *Mid-America* 56 (1974): 175-181.

McPherson, Edward. *The Political History of the United States during the Period of Reconstruction, April 15, 1865-July 15, 1870*. Washington, D.C.: Philp and Solomons, 1871.

McPherson, James M. *The Struggle for Equality: Abolitionists and the Negro in the Civil War and Reconstruction*. Princeton: Princeton Univ. Press, 1964.

Maizlish, Stephen E. *The Triumph of Sectionalism: The Transformation of Ohio Politics, 1844-1856*. Kent, Ohio: Kent State Univ. Press, 1983.

Mantell, Martin E. *Johnson, Grant, and the Politics of Reconstruction*. London: Cambridge Univ. Press, 1973.

Mayer, George H. *The Republican Party, 1854-1966*. 2nd ed. New York: Oxford Univ. Press, 1967.

Merrill, Horace Samuel. *Bourbon Democracy of the Middle West, 1865-1896*. Baton Rouge: Louisiana State Univ. Press, 1953.

Milton, George F. *The Age of Hate: Andrew Johnson and the Radicals*. New York: Coward-McCann, 1930.

Mohr, James C. *The Radical Republicans and Reform in New York during Reconstruction*. Ithaca: Cornell Univ. Press, 1973.

———. ed. *Radical Republicans in the North: State Politics during Reconstruction*. Baltimore: Johns Hopkins Univ. Press, 1976.

Montgomery, David. "Radical Republicanism in Pennsylvania, 1866-1873." *Pennsylvania Magazine of History and Biography* 85 (1961): 439-57.

Nelson, Anne Kusener. "The North, the South, and the Republican Ideology:

The Northeastern Republican Press, 1865-1869." Ph.D. diss., Vanderbilt Univ., 1977.

Nugent, Walter T.K. *The Money Question during Reconstruction*. New York: W.W. Norton, 1967.

Oder, Broeck N. "Andrew Johnson and the 1866 Illinois Election." *Journal of the Illinois State Historical Society* 73 (1980): 189-200.

Perman, Michael. *Reunion without Compromise: The South and Reconstruction, 1865-1868*. Cambridge: Cambridge Univ. Press, 1973.

Peskin, Allan. *Garfield*. Kent, Ohio: Kent State Univ. Press, 1978.

Porter, Daniel R. "Governor Rutherford B. Hayes." *Ohio History* 77 (1968): 58-75.

Porter, George H. *Ohio Politics during the Civil War Period*. Columbia Univ. Studies in History, Economics, and Public Law, 40.2. New York: Columbia Univ., 1911.

Powell, Lawrence N. "Rejected Republican Incumbents in the 1866 Congressional Nominating Conventions: A Study in Reconstruction Politics." *Civil War History* 19 (1973): 219-37.

Quill, J. Michael. *Prelude to the Radicals: The North and Reconstruction during 1865*. Washington: Univ. Press of America, 1980.

Quillin, Frank U. *The Color Line in Ohio*. Ann Arbor: G. Wahr, 1911.

Ranson, Frederick Duane. "The Great Unknown: Governor Rutherford B. Hayes of Ohio." Ph.D. diss., West Virginia Univ., 1978.

Roseboom, Eugene H. *The Civil War Era, 1850-1873*. Vol. 4 of Carl Wittke, ed., *The History of the State of Ohio*. 6 vols. Columbus: Ohio State Archaeological and Historical Society, 1944.

Schmiel, Eugene D. "The Career of Jacob Dolson Cox, 1828-1900: Soldier, Scholar, Statesman." Ph.D. diss., Ohio State Univ., 1969.

———. "The Oberlin Letter, the Post-Civil War Northern Voter, and the Freedman." *Northwest Quarterly* 43 (1971): 75-86.

Sharkey, Robert P. *Money, Class, and Party: An Economic Study of Civil War and Reconstruction*. Baltimore: Johns Hopkins Univ. Press, 1959.

Shipley, Max L. "The Background and Legal Aspects of the Pendleton Plan." *Mississippi Valley Historical Review* 24 (1937): 329-39.

Silbey, Joel H. *A Respectable Minority: The Democratic Party in the Civil War Era, 1860-1868*. New York: W.W. Norton, 1977.

Smith, Joseph P., ed. *History of the Republican Party in Ohio*. Vol. 1. Chicago: Lewis, 1898.

Smith, Theodore C. *The Life and Letters of James Abram Garfield*. 2 vols. New Haven: Yale Univ. Press, 1925.

Smith, Thomas H. "Ohio Quakers and the Mississippi Freedmen—'Field to Labor.'" *Ohio History* 78 (1969): 159-171, 221.

Stampp, Kenneth M. *The Era of Reconstruction, 1865-1877*. New York: Vintage, 1965.

Stebbins, Homer A. *A Political History of the State of New York, 1865-1869*. Columbia Univ. Studies in History, Economics and Public Law, 55. New York: Columbia Univ., 1913.

Swenson, Philip David. "The Midwest and the Abandonment of Radical Reconstruction, 1864-1877." Ph.D. diss., Univ. of Washington, 1971.

Swift, Donald C. "John A. Bingham and Reconstruction: The Dilemma of a Moderate." *Ohio History* 77 (1968): 76-94.

Taylor, John M. *Garfield of Ohio: The Available Man*. New York: W.W. Norton, 1970.

Therry, James R. "The Life of General Robert Cumming Schenck." Ph.D. diss., Georgetown Univ., 1968.

Toppin, Edgar A. "Negro Emancipation in Historic Retrospect: Ohio, the Negro Suffrage Issue in Postbellum Ohio Politics." *Journal of Human Relations* 11 (1963): 232-46.

Trefousse, Hans L. *Andrew Johnson: A Biography*. New York: W.W. Norton, 1989.

———. *Benjamin Franklin Wade: Radical Republican from Ohio*. New York: Twayne Publishers, 1963.

———. *Impeachment of a President: Andrew Johnson, the Blacks, and Reconstruction*. Knoxville: Univ. of Tennessee Press, 1975.

Unger, Irwin. *The Greenback Era: A Social and Political History of American Finance, 1865-1879*. Princeton: Princeton Univ. Press, 1964.

Voegeli, V. Jacque. *Free but Not Equal, The Midwest, and the Negro during the Civil War*. Chicago: Univ. of Chicago Press, 1967.

Wagstaff, Thomas. "The Arm-in-Arm Convention." *Civil War History* 14 (1968): 101-19.

Ware, Edith Ellen. *Political Opinion in Massachusetts during Civil War and Reconstruction*. Columbia Univ. Studies in History, Economics, and Public Law, 64.2. New York: Columbia Univ., 1916.

Wood, Forrest G. *Black Scare: The Racist Response to Emancipation and Reconstruction*. Berkeley: Univ. of California Press, 1970.

Woodward, C. Vann, ed. *The Comparative Approach to American History*. New York: Basic Books, 1968.

———. "Seeds of Failure in Radical Race Policy." *Proceedings of the American Philosophical Society* 110 (1966): 1-9.

Ziegler, Paul George, II. "The Politics and Philosophy of the Republican Right, 1861-1866." Ph.D. diss., Univ. of Virginia, 1973.

INDEX